Modern Critical Interpretations

E. L. Doctorow's
Ragtime

Edited and with an introduction by
Harold Bloom
Sterling Professor of the Humanities
Yale University

CHELSEA HOUSE PUBLISHERS
Philadelphia

Printed and bound in the United States of America

10 9 8 7 6 5 4 3 2 1

∞ The paper used in this publication meets the minimum
requirements of the American National Standard for
Permanence of Paper for Printed Library Materials,
Z39.48-1984

Library of Congress Cataloging-in-Publication Data
applied for

ISBN 0-7910-6343-7

Chelsea House Publishers
1974 Sproul Road, Suite 400
Broomall, PA 19008-0914

The Chelsea House World Wide Web address is
http://www.chelseahouse.com

Series Editor: Matt Uhler

Contributing Editor: Pamela Loos

Produced by: Publisher's Services, Santa Barbara, California

Modern Critical Interpretations

Contents

Editor's Note

My Introduction admires E. L. Doctorow's skill in evading an involuntary "period piece" by deliberately constructing *Ragtime* as the best kind of voluntary period piece, one that may become permanent.

Barbara L. Estrin contrasts *Ragtime* with Saul Bellow's *Humboldt's Gift*, finding in Doctorow's romance the elegance of "historical distance and personal indifference," and in Bellow's novel more of a personal "willingness to face . . . extremities." In a retrospect of *Ragtime's* initial success in 1975, Charles Berryman praises the book's narrative dexterity, while Paul Levine sees Doctorow's achievement as a revision of our sense of American history.

Marshall Bruce Gentry charmingly meditates upon the fate of Coalhouse Walker's Model T automobile as being an emblem of individuality despite Henry Ford's vision of uniformity, after which Cushing Strout surprisingly brings together Mark Twain's Connecticut Yankee and Doctorow's Coalhouse, arms mechanic and jazz pianist.

The problematic narrator of *Ragtime* is considered by Christopher D. Morris as contributing to the novel's implicit conclusion that history is repetitive and illusory, while Berndt Ostendorf, a superb authority upon American jazz, chronicles ragtime's progress as dominant popular music from 1906–1916, the decade covered by Doctorow's novel, and finds in Coalhouse Walker's story an image of Scott Joplin's frustration.

John G. Parks sees *Ragtime* as balancing judgments that America is a mistake by a joyous relativism, after which Douglas Fowler champions the book against Jonathan Raban's formidable judgment that it is at once cunning and fragile.

To John Williams, *Ragtime* saves itself as a historical novel by seeing history as a motion picture, while Michelle M. Tokarczyk concludes this volume with a meditation upon Doctorow's ambivalence towards the American Dream.

Introduction

Ragtime, while a charming romance to reread twenty-five years after publication, is far from being Doctorow's most eminent work. That seems to me the recent, highly experimental and poignant *City of God*, a superb phantasmagoria whose inmost concern is the Holocaust. Of Doctorow's earlier fictions, *The Book of Daniel* and *The Waterworks* linger on in my consciousness, as *Ragtime* will not. And yet *Ragtime* is not only Doctorow's greatly deserved popular success: it is a subtle inversion of the formulas that help engender all those period pieces we keep mistaking for permanent achievements, from *The Old Man and the Sea* through *Beloved*. By deliberately composing *Ragtime* as a period piece of 1916, covering the decade previous, Doctorow armors his entertainment against time's revenges. Jonathan Raban, in a formidable critique, found *Ragtime* to be more fragile than cunning, and yet the fragility is itself slyly deliberate.

Ragtime, like much of Doctorow, is a romance rather than a novel. I mean by this an authentic genre difference, since "romance" is now a debased term in our usage, meaning little more than a bodice-ripper. The romance, perfected in English by Sir Walter Scott, Hawthorne, the Brontës, and William Morris, is a narrative fiction in which psychological characterization is replaced by a concern with figurative types, states-of-being, visionary places, and fantastic transformations. Doctorow's *City of God* is his romance culmination, but only *The Book of Daniel* seems to me more novel than romance.

Coalhouse Walker, of the invented personalities in *Ragtime*, is at once the most interesting and the most derivative, since he is a version of Kleist's great story of injustice and violence, "Michael Kohlhaas." As a realistic representation, Walker would be absurd, but the huge irony and stylistic indirection of Doctorow's narrative make the jazz pianist-turned-rebel persuasive: Coalhouse Walker was never harsh or autocratic. He treated his

1

followers with courtesy and only asked if they thought something ought to be done. He dealt with them out of his constant sorrow. His controlled rage affected them like the force of a magnet. He wanted no music in the basement quarters. No instrument of any kind. They embraced every discipline. They had brought in several cots and laid out a barracks. They shared kitchen chores and housecleaning chores. They believed they were going to die in a spectacular manner. This belief produced in them a dramatic, exalted self-awareness.

The repetitions and reductive simplicity are cultic and ideological, and as such a little disquieting, since I could imagine substituting "Timothy McVeigh" for "Coalhouse Walker" in this passage, with each of the followers a Terry Nichols. Critics who complained that *Ragtime* was a Leftist allegory missed the point: Doctorow is not Jack London, and the comic-strip elements in *Ragtime* imply throughout that any political allegory is easily reversible.

You can say against *Ragtime*, when you stand back from it, that it is already the book of the epic musical it became. There is also the inevitable peculiarity that the historical personages are more exuberant and successful representations than Doctorow's invented figures: Emma Goldman has some force and substance, the revolutionary Younger Brother remains an abstraction. Yet Doctorow, well aware of this, takes every advantage of it. Coalhouse Walker and Younger Brother are not invested with any pathos or resonance; Harry Houdini is, and yet the investment is itself another controlled irony.

When I read *Ragtime* in 1975, its deliberate thinness or fragility bothered me; in 2001, rather less so. With George W. Bush as President, we are back in 1906 again, or at least we will get there if the current government is able to pass and implement its program. The age of J. P. Morgan has come again, but this time to an on-line America. Our current farce is prophesied by *Ragtime*, and Doctorow's insights into our country's nature and history are all-too-likely to be sustained in the years ahead.

BARBARA L. ESTRIN

Recomposing Time: Humboldt's Gift *and* Ragtime

Like the reader who scans the end of a novel first so he can relax and enjoy the plot, the historian knows the outcome of the events he studies; this knowledge affords him the luxury of retrospect and the pleasure of back-door premonition. As a historian, writing about the false nostalgia in the current craze for the early modernist period, Alfred Kazin argues, "All that Romantic jazz! It belongs to another world. But it was a world in which a few with better eyes than most saw that one day the whole gorgeous machine would go smash." *Better eyes than most* are what the visionary and the historian have in common. They recognize the seeds of disaster sown in even the most innocent of places.

The narrator of Delmore Schwartz's story "In Dreams Begin Responsibilities" possesses this keener view—a combination of foresight and hindsight. Watching, in a dream, a movie of his parents' courtship, the narrator stands up in the theater of his mind, shouting:

> Don't do it! It's not too late to change your minds, both of you.
> Nothing good will come of it, only remorse, hatred, scandal and
> two children whose characters are monstrous.

He wants to stop, before it is too late, the marriage which will culminate in the nightmare he now has. Such an act is logically impossible but morally

From *Denver Quarterly* 17, no. 1 (Spring 1982): 16–31. © 1982 by the University of Denver.

3

somehow right. If one knows that an ending is certain to be doomed, why not prevent it from happening instead of standing idly by? To rewrite history is a social act in the same sense as, say, protesting nuclear proliferation is one. If we know that the world will be blown up by the spread of bombs, if history teaches us that violence only begets violence, why not stand up in our darkening arena and say "No! Don't do it. It's not too late." Delmore Schwartz's narrator is booted out of the theater by an usher who tells him, "Don't you know you can't do things like this, you can't do whatever you want to do." In the usher's eyes and perhaps even in his own, the narrator emerges as a hysteric. To complain about the inevitable, to attempt to do what one wants, is to live at an inflated level of intensity. Schwartz's title has a degree of self-irony; it is only in dreams that individual men are responsible for the future. It is only an illusion that they matter. Why should the narrator believe that his life is of such consequence that he need eliminate its monstrosity?

Schwartz's narrator wakes up on the morning of his twenty-first birthday with an entrance into a manhood which he wished never to have come about. To contemplate twentieth-century America, after having experienced its maturation, is to look back over the ruins of time into a kind of green land where, nevertheless, the roots for subsequent destruction have taken hold. Schwartz's story begins in 1900. *Ragtime* begins in 1902 and *Humboldt's Gift*, a novel based in part on Schwartz's fictionalized life, surveys that era through the evocation of a historical character tying the two works together: Harry Houdini. With Houdini, both novels escape the present and return to the past. But they do so by seemingly contrary methods. *Humboldt's Gift* inherits from the fictionalized Schwartz that sense of hysteria present in such novels as *Portnoy's Complaint* and *Fear of Flying*. In *Humboldt's Gift*, the narrator, Charles Citrine, makes his entrance on the opening page so that we know that the history of the country, as it will be related in this novel, happens to him. When he describes the state of mind of his former wife, he seems also to be speaking of himself: "It was all one indivisible crisis."

High on the scaffold towers of a new Chicago skyscraper where he has been led by one of his underworld associates, Citrine acknowledges his psychological state at the beginning of the novel in terms of his physical position:

> My chief worry now was how to get down. Though the papers underplay it people are always falling off. But however scared and harassed, my sensation-loving soul also was gratified. I knew that it took too much to gratify me. The gratification-threshold of my soul had risen too high. I must bring it down again. It was excessive. I must, I knew, change everything. (*Humboldt's Gift*)

The gratification threshold for Citrine involves grandiose sensationalism. He loves having known the gifted Humbolt Fleischer (Bellow's Delmore Schwartz) in the flush of the poet's fame; he enjoys his Mafia connections; he likes (despite his disclaimers) being a literary sensation; he is thrilled by the big-breasted Renata, the mistress who encourages him to buy the big Mercedes which shows that he makes big money. Sexually and psychologically the continuing crises and climaxes of his life leave him as gratified as he is on top of the scaffold from which he might fall. To live life at the brink of destruction is to pretend that there is something inimitable worth destroying. Humboldt's gift, the legacy which the poet bequeaths to the narrator, is, finally, humbling, a pin puncturing the balloon of the inflated self.

The process of writing the novel enables the narrator to circumvent the tension dominating his life, to divest himself of his past by telling it, and to accept the gift of his friend. Citrine evokes the memory of Humboldt, the poet, whom he emulated at the height of his power and whom he avoided at the depths of his failure, forcing himself to think:

> As deep as the huge cap of December blue behind me entering the window with thermal distortions from the sun, I lay on my Chicago sofa and saw again everything that happened. One's heart hurt from this sort of thing. One thought, How sad, about all this human nonsense which keeps us from the large truth. But perhaps I can get through it once and for all by doing what I am doing now. (*Humboldt's Gift*)

To approach the large truth Citrine has to get through the human nonsense; the way to move forward is to return to the source of suffering, to the place where "one's heart hurts." The question which *Humboldt's Gift* raises is: how does one attain the detached perspective of the large truth—that knowledge which comes philosophically and which enables one to deal with (perhaps to do away with) the pain in the heart?

Ragtime begins with the answer for which Citrine is searching (and which he finds in the course of the novel): the truth lies in the movement away from panic, in the calm acceptance of calamity which will come no matter what one does to avoid it. *Ragtime* opens with an acknowledgment that the individual is subsumed by events, that history is not unilaterally linear, but eternally repetitious. At the end of the first chapter, where the great Houdini spent a sunny summer afternoon, while his car was being repaired, at the home of the WASP protagonists (the unnamed Family) of the novel, there is a moment of flash-forward which does not become significant until the end when Houdini remembers it. The narrator describes Houdini's leavetaking:

> The little boy had followed the magician to the street and now stood at the front of the macrocephalic image of himself in the shiny brass fitting of the headlight. Houdini . . . leaned over the side door. Goodbye, Sonny, he said holding out his hand. Warn the Duke, the little boy said. Then he ran off.

The child issues his warning in 1906, long before the assassination that set off World War I. On the next to the last page of the novel we learn for certain that the little boy is the narrator who has been telling us this story all along. The narrator describes the Father's death aboard the Lusitania which was carrying to England a shipment of explosives he himself had manufactured:

> Poor Father, I see his final exploration. He arrives at the new place, his hair risen in astonishment, his mouth and eyes dumb. His toe scuffs a soft storm of sand, he kneels and his arms spread in pantomimic celebration, the immigrant, as in every moment of his life, arriving eternally on the shore of the Self. (*Ragtime*)

We realize in the intrusion of the "I" that the parent we had known all along as an archetype was a father to the writer. Surreptitiously entering in the guise of the child, and in the way that Hitchcock makes an appearance in his films, the narrator shows that a fictional recreation is at once demonic and detached. With the insight he gains from subsequent experience, the little boy, prefiguring the storyteller he later becomes, informs the magician. We live our lives in the illusion that we can change things, in the hope that we amount to more than insignificant parts of a vast machine moving inexorably toward doom. The child anticipates, simultaneously as the narrator reconstructs, history, dallying with what Schwartz would call the dream of responsibility as if he were playing with toy soldiers. "Warn the Duke," he says, sounding a command that might alter the course of the novel we are about to read.

But Doctorow's narrator never assumes Schwartz's hysteria. His tone is casual, mischievous and, finally, self-effacing. What Charles Citrine knows at the beginning of the novel he writes is that life seems to be a series of headaches all of which lead him to the brink of crisis. *Humboldt's Gift* is an effort to arrive at the state of mind with which *Ragtime* begins, a state in which crises are reduced by the mainstream—by the instinctual lunge toward survival of the many at the expense of the few. Such a lunge turns life into the gambol and gamble of sport. *Ragtime* possesses an elegance that stems from historical distance and personal indifference. Its relaxed tone derives from the dismissal of individualized agony; that in *Humboldt's Gift* is arrived at finally by a willingness to face its extremities. The story in *Humboldt's Gift* proceeds through a series of dramatic situations which drive the hero to a point of financial and emotional bankruptcy. The story in *Ragtime* reaches a climax in an episode (the Coalhouse Walker siege) which is undermined by the pervading feeling that its outcome was so predictable, its conclusion so forecast by the forces of a society bent on the preservation of the industrial system, that the action comes to nothing. Thus, though they seem to be novels involving methods of tension, *Ragtime* and *Humboldt's Gift* emerge (because their protracted plots were predetermined to fizzle out) as novels of extension. The rubber bands of the stories are stretched so far out that when the break occurs instead of causing a complete and irreversible shock, the release seems hardly noticeable; it is acquired lightly, easily, calmly.

Ragtime and *Humboldt's Gift* come together philosophically in the larger truths which they affirm in their endings. They do so through three mutually present occurrences: the first is the destruction of a car which sets into action the most dramatic sequences of both novels; the second is the presence of Harry Houdini who, in both novels, tries desperately, by risking it theatrically, to avoid individual death; and the third is the recognition of the movies as an art form which becomes a means, in both novels, for the casual survival embodied in a relaxed tone.

I

The car stories demonstrate that even though Detroit survives by built-in obsolescence, the industry equips its products with built-in reparation. The havoc inflicted in the two works emerges as gratuitous. In *Ragtime*, the Model T of Coalhouse Walker (the Negro who wishes to marry the mother of the child found in the garden by the WASP Mother of the central Family) is vandalized out of racial prejudice by a local Yonkers fire chief. The destruction sets in motion a series of explosions culminating in the death of Walker's beloved and the subsequent siege by Walker and his friends of the house of J. P. Morgan. Walker initially demanded only the repair of his car as it originally was. The fire chief refused until Walker, enraged, almost started a five-man revolution threatening to blow up Morgan's house and its treasures. But in the final countdown, at Morgan's telegraphed request to GIVE HIM HIS AUTOMOBILE AND HANG HIM, the car was readied in a day:

> Several calls to the Ford motorcar people had brought forth by eight in the morning a truck carrying all the interchangeable parts for a Model T. The Pantasote Company delivered a top.

> Aides of Morgan had agreed that he would be billed for every-
> thing. As the crowd watched from the corner, Fire Chief
> Conklin, under the direction of two mechanics, piece by piece
> dismantled the Ford and made a new Ford from the chassis up.
> . . . New tires replaced old, new doors, running boards, wind-
> shield, headlamps, and upholstered seats. By five in the after-
> noon, with the sun still blazing in the sky over New York, a
> shining black Model T Ford with a custom pantasote roof stood
> at the curb. (*Ragtime*)

Thanks to Henry Ford and his system of interchangeable parts, the car is
replaced with ease. Walker is killed unnecessarily, his death, like his revolution, a meaningless sacrifice. Nothing was changed by it.

In *Humboldt's Gift*, after a morning of bumbling, Citrine takes his
battered car (it had been ravaged by an underworld figure, Rinaldo Cantibile,
who acted in revenge for Citrine having stopped payment on a check he
wrote for a poker debt) to the Mercedes shop. The destruction was devas-
tating; but the repair is painless:

> At the Mercedes Shop the distinguished official in the white
> smock was naturally curious but I refused to answer questions. "I
> don't know how this happened, Fritz, I found it this way. Fix it. I
> don't want to see the bill, either. Just send it to the Continental
> Illinois. They'll pay for it." (*Humboldt's Gift*)

The mechanic in the Mercedes shop has the audacity to wear a white smock.
Citrine benefits from an industrial system which wipes the patch-up job so
clean that he can remove himself completely from it. The expansive replacement set-up, evolving out of the period of *Ragtime*, functions without his
ever even having to see the bill.

Ragtime examines the philosophy of interchangeable parts as an
economic and psychological construct. The book's central thesis turns
human beings into cogs on the wheel of time. Henry Ford's theory allows for
metaphor: music is a flower; a flower is like music. At its worst, it admits that
we are all expendable. One thing simply substitutes for another:

> Ford established the final proposition of the theory of industrial
> manufacture—not only that the parts of the finished product be
> interchangeable but that the men who build the products be
> themselves interchangeable parts. (*Ragtime*)

As interchangeable parts, famous, near-famous, and infamous personalities of the period cross paths. Evelyn Nesbit, Harry K. Thaw, Sigmund Freud, J. P. Morgan, Emma Goldman appear as characters no more extraordinary than Doctorow's fictional inventions. And, as interchangeable parts, the three central and separate families of the novel not only meet but merge, become (either through adoption or intermarriage) proof positive that America is a melting pot. The WASP Westchester Family consisting of the nameless Mother, Father, and Little Boy adopts the orphaned child of Coalhouse Walker. By the end of the novel, Tateh, the widower-father of an immigrant Jewish family who has pulled himself up from poverty, marries the widowed Mother of the WASP Westchester clan. The new family thus formed has three children, one black, one brown-eyed Jewess, and one blue-eyed blonde.

This melting represents the great American idea as the narrator views it. The genius of the twentieth century is, by industrialization and by assimilation, to produce more of the same. "The value of the duplicable event was everywhere perceived. Every town had its ice-cream soda fountain of Belgian marble. Painless Parker the Dentist offered everywhere to remove your toothache." Doctorow manufactures his own "duplicating events" creating a series of parallel occurrences. Early in the novel Evelyn Nesbit falls in love with Tateh's daughter and longs to make the girl her own "urchin." The WASP Mother adopts the black baby she finds buried in her backyard, taking the place of the child's real mother. Emma Goldman, in turn, mothers Evelyn Nesbit.

History becomes a cycle of waxing and waning, of "interchangeable parts," as read by the characters in *Ragtime* themselves. Mass production, then, isn't new; it emerges simply as a different form of what existed long ago. J. P. Morgan sees in Henry Ford an extraordinary resemblance to Seti I, the father of the great Rameses of Egypt and he tells Ford about Hermetic theory. Ford, in his blunt way, answers that he, too, had the same idea only he called it simply reincarnation. "I explain my genius this way—some of us have just lived more lives than others."

The notion of the volatility of things reaches even the Little Boy who is to become the narrator. He treasures "anything discarded," waiting to make use of what, in time, will become his inheritance. He listens attentively to his grandfather's "stories out of Ovid which proposed to him . . . that everything in the world could as easily be something else." Further, "it was evident to him that the world composed and recomposed itself constantly in an endless process of dissatisfaction." This acceptance of the interchangeability of things gives the narrator the sense of relaxation he transmits to the book. Explaining the pleasure of repetition in terms of baseball, the great

American pastime, the Little Boy underlines his ease of heart. His father asks him:

> What is it you like about this game? . . . The Boy did not remove his gaze from the diamond. The same thing happens over and over, he said. The pitcher throws the ball so as to fool the batter into thinking he can hit it. But sometimes the batter does hit it, the father said. Then the pitcher is the one who is fooled, the boy said. (*Ragtime*)

Once we are assured that nothing changes, that nothing fundamental can be destroyed, baseball, like life, is likeable. Either the batter is a fool or the pitcher is. They simply change places. Because events are relative, time appears circular.

Early in *Humboldt's Gift*, Citrine espouses a system of philosophical beliefs which he claims to hold. These beliefs are very similar to the ones forming the central thesis of *Ragtime:*

> What a human being is—I always had my own odd sense of this. For I did not have to live in the land of horses, like Dr. Gulliver, my sense of mankind was strange enough without travel. In fact, I traveled not to seek foreign oddities, but to get away from them. I was drawn also to philosophical idealists because I was perfectly sure that *this* could not be *it*. Plato in the myth of Er confirmed my sense that this was not my first time around. We had all been here before and would presently be here again. (*Humboldt's Gift*)

In his philosophy—in his casual tone and assurance that this life isn't all there is (isn't the great *it*), Citrine sounds just like the Little Boy describing the baseball game. We may be here today and gone tomorrow—but the next time we'll be back.

As a philosopher, he would like to believe that "everything could as easily be everything else," but as a human being, he has trouble accepting the possibility. What if *he* were the part exchanged? With that question, and contemplating his beloved Renata, Citrine becomes again hysterical, the victim of what he calls his "complicated subjectivity." Worrying that he might be late for a dinner appointment with Renata, he imagines that she will simply invite his rival, Flonzaley:

> I was expected at seven o'clock for dinner. Renata would be upset. It vexed her to be stood up. She had a temper, her temper

always worked in a certain way; and also, if my suspicions were correct, Flonzaley was never far off. Substitutes are forever haunting people's minds. Even the most stable and balanced individuals have a secretly chosen replacement in reserve somewhere, and Renata was not one of the stablest. As she often fell spontaneously into rhymes, she had surprised me once by coming out with this:

> When the dear
> Disappear
> There are others
> Waiting near.

Thus, the Platonist who accepts his "disappearance" philosophically, in the assurance that it is only temporary, is replaced by the lover who fears his replacement waiting in the wings. Citrine's quest in the novel is to arrive at the point where he can live out his theoretical beliefs and so do away with the terror of the immediate. The narrator in *Ragtime* delights in the idea of the volatility of things partly because he himself is never in the physical or psychological position of the *replacee*. As the child, he merely observes the action; as the narrator he whimsically controls the plot. Through this uniquely invulnerable vantage point (too young then for the events to hurt him, too old now for them to touch him), he lends to the situation he invents an indisputable verifiability and to the connections he draws a retrospective impartiality. Citrine can arrive at that point of distance only when he has, in fact, nothing to lose. At the end of the novel he has nothing *left* to lose. He has been dispossessed of everything: his friends, his fortune, his wife, his children, his job, his woman.

II

Alone, in Spain, in ruins, having sacrificed Renata to his rival and his fortune to his wife, Citrine begins to act out his beliefs. In his room, he talks to the dead: "It seemed after all that there are no non-peculiar people. This was why I looked forward to acquaintance with the souls of the dead; they *should* be a little more stable." The way to achieve composure—the tone necessary for his new life—is to return for sustenance to those who have already lived: the stable dead. It is at this juncture that Citrine remembers Harry Houdini, who was, like him, born in Appleton, Wisconsin, and who seemed, as Citrine would likewise wish, to be able to escape the present and predict the future. In *Humboldt's Gift*, Houdini squirms out of everything "including the grave":

Yes this Houdini defied all forms of restraint and confinement, including the grave. He broke out of everything. They buried him and he escaped. They sank him in boxes and he escaped. They put him in a strait jacket and manacles and hung him upside down by one ankle from the flagpole of the Flatiron Building in New York. . . . He could do anything! In Czarist Russia the Okhrana stripped him naked and locked him in the steel van it used for Siberian deportations. He freed himself from that too. He escaped from the most secure prisons in the world. And whenever he came home from a triumphal tour he went straight to the cemetery. He lay down on his mother's grave and on his belly through the grass he told her in whispers about his trips, where he had been, and what he had done. Later he spent years debunking spiritualists. He exposed all the tricks of the medium-racket. In an article I once speculated whether he hadn't had an intimation of the holocaust and was working out ways to escape from the death camps. Ah! If only European Jewry had learned what he knew. But then Houdini was punched experimentally by a medical student and died of peritonitis. So you see, nobody can overcome the final fact of the material world. Dazzling rationality, blazing of consciousness, the most ingenious skill—nothing can be done about death. Houdini worked out one line of inquiry completely. (*Humboldt's Gift*)

Houdini freed himself from the confines of his place in time, talked to his dead mother who preceded him and prepared (by his example) for the holocaust which was to follow. Citrine muses, "Ah! If only European Jewry had learned what he knew."

In *Ragtime* too, the one place from which the magician does not escape is from the grave; early in the novel, the narrator describes the failure, echoing nevertheless Citrine's attraction to Houdini and anticipating the pleasure of the novel he is writing. He steps in here, again, reminding us of his unique vantage point by talking about the large audience for escapes *today*, watching his readers now as they view Houdini through the lens he focuses:

He was buried alive in a grave and could not escape, and had to be rescued. Hurriedly, they dug him out. The earth is too heavy, he said gasping. His nails bled. Soil fell from his eyes. He was drained of color and couldn't stand. His assistant threw up. Houdini wheezed and sputtered. He coughed blood. They cleaned him off and took him back to the hotel. Today, nearly fifty years since his death, the audience for escapes is even larger. (*Ragtime*)

In both novels, Houdini is a figure who exposes the quackery of phony mediums, performs daring feats, is obsessed with his dead mother, and grovels on her grave. In both novels, his effort is to come to grips with the past, to move out of the limitations and hysteria of the present. By so maneuvering, Houdini comes finally to understand that war (in *Ragtime:* World War I, and in *Humboldt's Gift:* World War II) is always in the cards. Houdini learns, through the process of his escapes, that there is no way of avoiding the catastrophes—the holocausts—of the century. His appeal (what Doctorow calls his "audience today") is "larger" because he presents still the grand hope that we can dig out from a present rooted in a ravaged past and leading to a cataclysmic future.

Doctorow's Houdini high above the *Times* tower in New York has an epiphany:

> He was upside down over Broadway, the year was 1914, and the Archduke Franz Ferdinand was reported to have been assassinated. It was at this moment that an image composed itself in Houdini's mind. The image was of a small boy looking at himself in the shiny brass headlamp of an automobile. (*Ragtime*)

That image is of the narrator warning Houdini about the assassination leading to the war. It is, of course, too late, and that is also what Houdini sees; but he understands what he could have done had he been granted the power of vision for which he has been searching all the while. Houdini tries to call on the family again to tell the Little Boy something of what he has learned:

> We have the account of this odd event from the magician's private unpublished papers. Harry Houdini's career in show business gave him to overstatement, so we must not relinquish our own judgment in considering his claim that it was the one genuine mystical experience of his life. Be that as it may, the family archives show a calling card from Mr. Houdini dated just a week later. Nobody was home to receive him. The family had by this time entered its period of dissolution. (*Ragtime*)

Like the era of *Ragtime* itself, the family had "run out," dissolved in the way a movie scene fades into the next one. Because there was no one to share it with, Houdini's mystical experience became not an exciting climax of fate but an accident of missed connections. The effect of *Ragtime* is to render casual the grand events and by so doing to achieve the elegance of style that makes nostalgia possible. To revive history is to duplicate it and anything that can come back twice cannot be terribly intense. "The war was fought and won," he says in the last paragraph, fitting the bloody event into its proper niche in the grand scheme of things where all men die but life continues regardless of individual displacement.

III

In both books, however, there is one twentieth-century invention which can record dispassionately, in order to make permanent and irrefutable, all missed connections: the film. Tateh describes the trade which has transformed him from desperate immigrant to successful mogul:

> In the movie film, he said, we only look at what is already there. Life shines on the shadow screen, as from the darkness of one's mind. It is a big business. People want to know what is happening to them. For a few pennies they sit and see their selves in movement, running, racing in motor cars, fighting and, forgive me, embracing one another. This is most important today, in this country where everybody is so new. There is such a need to understand. (*Ragtime*)

With his knowledge of the people's "need to understand," Tateh has found a means to make himself rich. The need to understand, as he sees it, however, is the need to be reassured that we exist. To know what is happening is to see it happening, to see life "shining," reflected, and finally repeated. The movies are the "duplicable event"; they only show what has already been there. To be reproduced on the screen has a soothing effect; it takes away the fear of having only one time to live. To sit and see oneself in movement running, racing, fighting, embracing is to live vicariously, to remain still while the world turns and thereby to eliminate the pain of its motion. In the movies the actors take us away from the present by living it for us.

At the end of the novel, Tateh, looking out of the window at the three children who are now his, decides to make a film of them:

> He saw the three children sitting on the lawn. Behind them on the sidewalk was a tricycle. They were talking and sunning them-

selves. His daughter, with dark hair, his tow-headed stepson and
his legal responsibility, the schwartze child. He suddenly had an
idea for a film. A bunch of children who were pals, white black,
fat thin, rich poor, all kinds, mischievous little urchins who would
have funny adventures in their own neighborhood, a society of
ragamuffins, like all of us, a gang, getting into trouble and
getting out again. Actually not one movie but several were made
of this vision. (*Ragtime*)

In the catalogue of three groups, "white black, fat thin, rich poor," are
contained the now-merged separate entities that dominate the novel. The
drama among them—the great course of action—is reduced by Tateh's focus
into the endearing adventures of a society of ragamuffins whose troubles are
easily surmounted and whose problems become those of picaresque adventures. They are "like all of us": survivors. The interchangeable parts now
appear as roles in a series sounding like the popular *Our Gang*. With its
moving silhouettes, the film captures the spirit of the machine age, fusing
history into something no more than a tune on a player piano. For Tateh, the
series becomes a means for entering the new era, the one after that of
Ragtime had "run out."

For Citrine, too, the movies become quite by accident the way to make
a "basic change in [his] life" and to enter his new era. *Humboldt's Gift* was two
film scripts; the story line of one became the plot for a pirated movie already
produced and successful. This plagiarism endows Citrine with the power to
sue the company and cash in. The second script offers another version of the
duplicable event. It involves a writer who takes the same trip twice—once
with his mistress and the second time with his wife. He, like Citrine, loses
them both in the end, but the book he writes about the experience becomes
an enormous success. With the money he makes from the suit and from the
sale of the second script, Citrine can give Humboldt a proper burial and
honor Humboldt's surviving uncle, Waldemar, splitting the profits from both
deals evenly with him.

The novel ends with the reburial of Humboldt, attended by Waldemar,
Menasha (an old friend of the Citrine family and presently Waldemar's
companion), and Citrine. At the grave, on the day of the interment, the late
start of spring seemed to corroborate the finality of the event:

It was a low moment. There was a massive check threatened, as
if a general strike against nature might occur. What if blood
should not circulate, if food should not digest, breath fail to
breathe, if the sap should not overcome the heaviness of the

trees? And death, death, death, death, like so many stabs, like murder—the belly, the back, the breast and heart. This was a moment I could scarcely bear. Humboldt's coffin was ready to move. 'Pallbearers?' said one of the funeral directors. He looked the three of us over. Not much manpower here. Two old fuddy-duddies and a distracted creature not far behind them in age. We took honorific positions along the casket. I held a handle—my first contact with Humboldt. There was very little weight within. Of course I no longer believed that any human fate could be associated with such remains and superfluities. The bones were very possibly the signature of spiritual powers, the projection of the cosmos in certain calcium formations. But perhaps even such elegant white shapes, thigh bones, ribs, knuckles, skull, were gone. Exhuming, the grave diggers might have shoveled together certain tatters and sooty lumps of human origin, not much of the charm, the verve, and feverish invention, the calamity-making craziness of Humboldt. Humboldt, our pal, our nephew and brother, who loved the Good and the Beautiful, and one of whose slighter inventions was entertaining the public on Third Avenue and the Champs-Elysées and earning, at this moment, piles of dollars for everyone. (*Humboldt's Gift*)

Citrine moves, in this passage, from the "low moment" of the beginning to the elan of "this moment" at the end. He makes the move by way of what he calls the "unbearable" moment: the facing of death as something which will happen to him. At first, the time of year becomes an expression for the disjunction Citrine feels. It was that "low" moment occurring every year before spring, when we doubt its return; psychological time and natural time appeared synchronized in a mutual expression of mourning. "There was a massive check threatened, as if a general strike against nature might occur." Citrine fears, then, that, in sympathizing with Humboldt, nature joined in a conspiracy against him, refusing to allow him the escape valve of imperception. The four-times-repeated "death" becomes not something happening to some other body in the grave but to his own at its edge, coming "like so many stabs, like murder," to all the parts Citrine (in his efforts to remain physically and mentally fit) had fought so long to sustain. There was, at the graveside, no place to hide. The "low moment" becomes the bottom toward which Citrine had been plummeting throughout the novel; it marks the final deflation of his gratification-threshold; changing everything meant facing this "unbearable" moment, experiencing the descent of the "lowering movement"—the drop-ping of the casket into its terminal point—where space and time converged.

With the funeral director's question "pallbearers?" the focus shifts. We see the mourners through the funeral director's eyes and the sight becomes similar to the one presented on the lawn at the end of *Ragtime*. "He looked the three of us over. Not much manpower here. Two old fuddyduddies and a distracted creature not far behind them in age." The three men are simply "our gang" grown old and tired. They become the geriatric equivalent of Doctorow's "society of ragamuffins": fuddyduddies. A lightness of tone steps in as Citrine takes hold of the casket and discovers there was "very little weight within." From this point on, Citrine is able to remember Humboldt without high seriousness and without great pain. Humboldt emerges as a member of the gang grouped at the grave; he becomes "our pal." He is revered because he loved the good and the beautiful and was a poet. But he is remembered, too, because, with elegance, he escaped the hysteria of his final days with that "slighter invention" now earning, in the great American way, "piles of dollars for everyone." Humboldt becomes the Tateh of this novel, providing for his friends the "duplicable event" by which they might overcome the "unbearable moment" at the grave.

In *Ragtime*, the children of our gang grow up believing—as we all do—in the "possibility of getting into trouble and getting out again"—in the carefree ideal of the melting pot which remains cool by assimilating everything. It provides a survival based on the displacement of passion and the loss of identity symbolized by the Armistice Day Parade which becomes the final scene of the novel. Parades begin and end wars and in the excitement of the musical moment the impending and preceding event is forgotten. *Ragtime* is full of deliberate repetitions. Eventually, all the ends turn on themselves and return to their beginnings, the way Houdini migrates back to the narrator's house. Doctorow takes a piece of time from history, 1902–1914, and stitches it back into place, leaving no ragged edges.

Humboldt's Gift, likewise, ends with an annual recurrence. In Bellow's novel the fusion occurs not by overstepping individual death but by acknowledging it. Citrine observes the descent of Humboldt's casket and has another moment of panic:

> But then, how did one get out? One didn't, didn't, didn't! You stayed, you stayed! There was a dry light grating as of crockery when contact was made, a sort of sugar bowl sound. Thus, the condensation of collective intelligences and combined ingenuities, its cables silently spinning, dealt with the individual poet. (*Humboldt's Gift*)

In the end, having honored him, Citrine understands that the individual poet is silenced by the grating of the collective intelligence, the combined ingenuity against which he fought and with which he could, in the film scripts (his final personal concession to the general), deal. By honoring Humboldt—by getting "through it" once and for all—Citrine is ready to inherit the gift and to accept both the finality of the individual and the survival of the general. Stumbling through the dead leaves, Menasha finds what he thinks is a flower and Citrine realizes that the spring which he thought earlier might go on strike is coming anyway. The flower represents a reprieve.

But Menasha and Citrine try to downplay the significance of what they see:

> "So it's a little flower," Menasha said. "They used to tell one about a kid asking his grumpy old man when they were walking in the park, 'What's the name of this flower, Papa?' and the old guy is peevish and he yells 'How should I know? Am I in the millinery business?' Here's another, but what do you suppose they're called, Charlie?" "Search me," I said, "I'm a city boy myself. They must be crocusses." (*Humboldt's Gift*)

Despite the disclaimer reducing the wonder of spring to a matter of pecuniary interest and the pretended indifference of the shrugging "search me," the men are reawakened to the surprise of creation. Citrine's response, spoken with the defensive innocence of an urchin and in the temporary hedging of his "I'm a city boy," only adds a note of poignancy to the cycle he observes. Like the spectators of *Ragtime*'s concluding parade, Citrine and Menasha are reassured by a happening which will occur "annually." The distance of their tone indicates that they can now take the cosmic casually. Life becomes a sporting event which Citrine and his pals can joke about and in which they might occasionally still take a turn at bat. In both novels the sense of calm is achieved through a conscious recognition that the individual self is always decomposing even as the larger world (that of nature in *Humboldt's Gift* and that of society in *Ragtime*) is always recomposing itself, and recovering from the pain of private loss.

CHARLES BERRYMAN

Ragtime *in Retrospect*

A chorus of praise greeted the publication of E. L. Doctorow's *Ragtime* in the summer of 1975:

> "No recent novelist has brought such possibilities together in a big popular book." (*Newsweek*, 14 July 1975)

> "A unique and beautiful work of art . . . Doctorow has added a grace to our history." (*Saturday Review*, 26 July 1975)

> "Will be the most read, the most critically applauded, and yes, perhaps the most accoladed novel of the year." (*New Republic*, 5 July 1975)

With so much attention the novel climbed quickly to the top of the best-seller lists and stayed there for many weeks. More than three million copies of *Ragtime* were soon in print. The publicity campaign had been prepared with unusual care by Random House. A special edition of the novel had been printed early and distributed to Doctorow's friends and selected media representatives. Doctorow's years in publishing—senior editor for New American Library and editor-in-chief for Dial Press—no doubt added to the interest in the advertising campaign. The publishing industry after all was celebrating one of its own.

From *The South Atlantic Quarterly* 81, no. 1 (Winter 1982): 30–42. © 1982 by Duke University Press.

The successful wave of publicity led within six months to a riptide of criticism. Early in 1976 the reviews began to turn hostile:

> "A simple-minded, whimsical, socio-historical pageant . . . comes nearer to qualifying as a comic-book." (*Times Literary Supplement*, 23 January 1976)

> "Too much attention on the reader's part kills it stone-dead." (*Encounter*, February 1976)

> "*Ragtime* gets my vote as The Most Overrated Book of the Year." (*Atlantic Monthly*, January 1976)

Do these negative views represent a sober reconsideration of the value of the novel, or do they merely indicate annoyance with the excessive hoopla that accompanied the book's appearance? Seldom has a novel been so well received, then so violently attacked, and all the time so little understood. While celebrating the dynamic quality of the narrative, the reviewers did not begin to inquire about the identity of the narrator. While attacking the mixture of fiction and history, the critics failed to understand how the two fit together. Why should Henry Ford, J. P. Morgan, Emma Goldman, Commander Peary, Sigmund Freud, and Harry Houdini, not to mention two invented families with opposite backgrounds, all be in the same novel? Neither praising *Ragtime* as an "inventive mixture of history and fancy," nor dismissing it as a comic book, begins to explain its complex design.

"When critics disagree," as Wilde suggested, "the artist is in accord with himself." Doctorow has wisely accepted his new status as a literary celebrity without volunteering much comment on the subtlety of his own work. If he is asked to distinguish the fictional and historical characters, Doctorow replies, "I used to know but I've forgotten." When asked what liberties have been taken with history, Doctorow calls his book "a novelist's revenge on an age that celebrates nonfiction." Three million readers have been left to discover for themselves the enigmatic nature of the narrator, the significance of mixing fiction and history, and the double theme of disintegration and renewal.

Although the novel has been praised and condemned for many of the wrong reasons, *Ragtime* is a critical as well as a popular step forward in Doctorow's career. His first novel, *Welcome to Hard Times*, was published in 1960. Hardly a commercial success, this novel about fear, courage, and violence in the old Dakota Territory was at least made into a western film. After the publication of *The Book of Daniel* in 1971 the praise of a fellow novelist helped Doctorow to win a nomination for the National Book Award.

"A nearly perfect work of art, a cause for rejoicing," wrote Joyce Carol Oates, "I can think of no higher praise for a work of fiction." Although *The Book of Daniel* also escaped popular success, the very good reviews and the nomination for the National Book Award did set the stage for the commercial breakthrough Doctorow was able to achieve with *Ragtime*.

The complexity of Doctorow's earlier novels should have alerted reviewers to the potential subtlety of *Ragtime*. Doctorow is not an artist content with offering the mere illusion of history. The story of the rise and fall of a western town is told in *Welcome to Hard Times* by a narrator who is a survivor of the history he has suffered, promoted, and perhaps invented. The story of the trial and conviction of the Rosenbergs was transformed in *The Book of Daniel* into a novel with a double narrative structure and a subtle political spectrum. Doctorow ranks high among the recent authors—Barth, Pynchon, Vonnegut—willing to experiment with the form of the novel in order to reach an artful compromise with modern history. The wide popularity of *Ragtime* does not mean that Doctorow has abandoned his experimental approach to the form of the novel or departed from the quality of his earlier work. The structure of *Ragtime* is indeed complex, and the novel's political and psychological vision is also quite intricate. But the surface of the novel is so rich with events and personalities that its dynamic life may be quickly enjoyed without pausing to analyze its remarkable structure. Thus the great popularity of the book, and the equally great incomprehension.

The first problem is to locate the narrator. Almost all of the fictional characters belong to two families: one well established in New Rochelle with a father who manufactures flags and fireworks, and a poor immigrant family with a father who makes silhouettes. Before the novel is over the families will merge and their fortunes will reverse. The narrator of the novel refers to the parents of the New Rochelle family as Father and Mother. Their only child is a little boy in a sailor suit who is seen infrequently in the book and seldom appears to be a significant character. A casual reader of the novel might not identify the little boy as the narrator, but enough is gradually revealed about his personality to allow us to see how the novel has been put together from his recollections and his research.

Doctorow does let us know just a few pages into the book that the little boy "had reached that age of knowledge and wisdom in a child when it is not expected by the adults around him and consequently goes unrecognized." Is this the "wisdom and knowledge" necessary to tell the story of his family? If the child is the narrator why does he refer to his parents as Father and Mother but always to himself in the third person as "the little boy"? A similar narrative strategy was used by Doctorow in *The Book of Daniel*, where parts of the story are told by a small boy in the first person, and parts are told by the same character in later years when he looks back upon his childhood and often refers to himself in the third person. But in *Ragtime* the mature or present narrator is never directly introduced. Instead it is necessary to infer that the little boy has the ability at a later date to look back and assemble the various pieces of his history.

Doctorow waits until chapter fifteen to reveal the qualities of the boy's mind and personality which allow him to assemble and focus the events of the novel. Only then does Doctorow explain how the boy "treasured anything discarded. He took his education peculiarly and lived an entirely secret intellectual life." The novel is an extraordinary montage of bits and pieces from the past, and it is the secret intellectual life of the little boy that saves and assembles the many images. The journal of a trip to the North Pole recorded by his father and the artistic silhouettes cut by his stepfather both eventually come into the possession of the little boy. Thus he gains the evidence necessary to tell about the journey to the Arctic with Commander Peary and to imagine the frustration of the immigrant artist cutting silhouettes on a street corner in New York.

If gathering scraps from the past is the secret activity of the little boy, what sense of order will he be able to impose upon them? "He was alert not only to discarded materials," Doctorow says of his narrator, "but to unexpected events and coincidences." Few novels since Dickens have possessed so many unexpected events and coincidences. Freud and Jung sail through the Tunnel of Love together on their 1909 visit to Coney Island. J. P. Morgan emerges from the Great Pyramid at Giza just in time to see the New York Giants swarming over the Sphinx. Harry Houdini is hanging upside down over Times Square when he recalls, too late, how he might have saved the life of Archduke Ferdinand. *Ragtime* is a comic novel, and much of the comedy depends upon the coincidences of history and fiction that come together in the mind of the narrator.

What education does the narrator have to enable him to assemble the comic patterns? "He learned nothing at school," it is reported, "so it was left to Grandfather to cultivate what might be the boy's oddity or merely his independence of spirit." Grandfather is a retired professor of classics, and he tells the body stories from Ovid. "They were stories of people who become animals or trees or statues. They were stories of transformation." With this education it is not surprising that the little boy becomes the narrator of a novel about transformations. He will describe how his own father is transformed from a confident explorer into a frustrated and helpless man. When this parent is lost with the sinking of the *Lusitania*, the little boy will acquire a new father who has experienced an even more remarkable transformation—from an immigrant Latvian socialist to a successful Hollywood producer. While some of the historical figures in the book, J. P. Morgan and Henry Ford, discuss their belief in reincarnation, the fictional characters are shown in the stages of their metamorphoses. The narrator's uncle will change from a secret admirer of Evelyn Nesbit to a secret agent of protest and revolution. Coalhouse Walker will change from a ragtime piano player to a violent terrorist who threatens to destroy the Morgan Library with high explosives. The most accomplished performer of quick changes is Houdini who has long been the little boy's idol.

The narrator of *Ragtime* listens to his grandfather tell the stories from Ovid, and thereby comes to accept change as the basic condition of life: "Grandfather's stories proposed to him that the forms of life were volatile and that everything in the world could as easily be something else. . . . He found proof in his own experience of the instability of both things and people." If the world in *Ragtime* is drifting into war, the narrator dramatizes the tide of change by selecting the news events from the period which prove "that the forms of life were volatile." The common denominator of such events is violence: the murder of Stanford White, the assassination of Archduke Ferdinand, the vengeance and death of Coalhouse Walker, and the loss of the narrator's father on the *Lusitania*. The little boy will survive this decade of flux, and later assemble the shifting images in accord with the truth learned from his grandfather about "the instability of both things and people."

The dramatic change in America in the decade prior to World War I is symbolized in the novel by the change of fathers experienced by the little boy. The father who accompanies Commander Peary on his expedition to the North Pole believes at first that all the world exists for him to explore. The flags and fireworks made in his factory contribute to the display of national pride inspired by the administration of Teddy Roosevelt. But just as the blind patriotism of Roosevelt proves inadequate to control either his own political party or his country, the aggressive confidence of the narrator's original father will turn to frustration and defeat. When members of his own family become involved in murder and revolution, the father simply does not know why the world is drifting into violence. His inability to look ahead is dramatically symbolized by his passage on the *Lusitania*.

The narrator's stepfather will be the immigrant socialist who has risen from poverty as an artist in New York to affluence and power as a filmmaker in Hollywood. The success of the second father depends on the extraordinary development of the motion picture industry at the beginning of the century. After some bitter days as an artist in New York, and a troubled period in the textile mills of Massachusetts, the immigrant father follows in the footsteps of Benjamin Franklin arriving in Philadelphia. Like Franklin, who was also escaping from servitude in Massachusetts, the immigrant father arrives in Philadelphia with only a few coins, purchases a roll to eat, and spends his first day walking the streets of the city. Doctorow's narrator, who loves "unexpected events and coincidences," calls attention to the historical parallel by having the father come by accident to the Franklin Novelty Company where he is soon employed to draw picture books which create the illusion of motion. His work with silhouettes will thus lead to moving pictures.

Does the novel have a character who spends as much time as possible in moving picture theaters? The narrator is identified as one who "liked to go to the moving picture shows downtown," and he is especially fascinated by the metaphysical nature of the images and shadows recorded with the mind's eye. "He knew the principles of photography but saw also that moving pictures depended on the capacity of humans, animals or objects to forfeit portions of themselves, residues of shadow and light which they left behind." *Ragtime* is a montage of the shadows and lights accumulated by the little boy who watches all the pictures move and then becomes the narrator of the novel.

The little boy observes the changing of all things, but he is most observant when the image is his own reflection. At the end of the first chapter the boy has a chance to meet Harry Houdini. The magician unexpectedly pays a visit to the boy's family, and parks his touring car in front of their house. What does the little boy do? Characteristically he is preoccupied with "gazing at the distorted macrocephalic image of himself in the shiny brass fitting of the headlight." His world as narrator of *Ragtime* will be a series of comic mirrors.

Chapter fifteen includes a further analysis of the boy's fascination with reflected images. Doctorow moves beyond the obvious—"And then he took to studying himself in the mirror, perhaps expecting some change to take place before his eyes,"—to explore the metaphysics of mirror images: "He would gaze at himself until there were two selves facing one another, neither of which could claim to be the real one. The sensation was of being disembodied. He was no longer anything exact as a person. He had the dizzying feeling of separating from himself endlessly." It is the narrator's experience of separation from himself that explains why he refers to himself in the third person throughout the novel. If the narrator feels the "sensation of being disembodied," it is not surprising that the reader of the novel may forget how the narrator is related to the character of the little boy. Few novels have ever been told by a narrator who thinks of himself as gazing into a mirror and does not know which image is the real one. Doctorow is able to dramatize a world of shifting images precisely because his narrator feels that he is "no longer anything exact as a person." The spectrum of the novel is produced by the diffraction of the narrator's personality in the mirror of history.

The importance of mirrors in Doctorow's novel suggests how much *Ragtime* has in common with the legend of Narcissus. Does the narrator lose himself like the hero of the Greek myth in the vain pursuit of his own image? Is Doctorow's novel a reflection of Shakespeare's narcissistic Richard II who breaks the mirror in petulant despair because it shows him his own broken face? As the deposed Richard sees the glass cracked in a hundred slivers, he cannot avoid the thought of his coming destruction. "A brittle glory shineth in this face," he cries, "as brittle as the glory is the face." The narrator of *Ragtime* shows a variety of faces reflected in a decade of history, and he knows that the images will be shattered when the decade ends in war. It is not the vanity of the narcissistic quest that so much concerns Doctorow's narrator, but rather the diffraction of the image and the inevitable destruction. Mutability and death haunt the final movements of *Ragtime* on the eve of international violence. The narrator does not love what he sees in the mirror, but he is fascinated with the cycles of change. "It was evident to him that the world composed and recomposed itself constantly in an endless process of dissatisfaction."

Does the unrecognized "knowledge and wisdom" of the little boy include a foreknowledge of the impending cycle of destruction? If the narrator is telling his story in retrospect, then of course he enjoys the omniscient perspective gained from the experience which has been sifted through recollection and supported by research. The narrator, for example, has had time to read his father's North Pole journal, and he even claims to have gained access to Houdini's private, unpublished papers. But early in the novel there is a bizarre moment when the dialogue of the little boy, not the voice of the mature narrator, reveals an accurate and unexpected knowledge of the future. At the end of the first chapter, when Houdini visits the family of the narrator, the little boy tells the magician to "Warn the Duke." The remark does not make sense to anyone present, and the boy runs away. Readers of the novel will also be puzzled because thus far in the book there has not been any mention of a duke. Only at the end of chapter thirteen will Houdini unexpectedly meet the ill-fated heir to the Austro-Hungarian throne. At that time Houdini does not remember his message for the duke. It is only at the end of the novel when Houdini is hanging upside down eleven stories over Times Square that he remembers the warning of the little boy, and realizes, now that it is too late, that perhaps he had a chance to prevent the assassination and the cycle of destruction that will follow.

Houdini's unexpected vision of the little boy at the climax of the novel is a recollection of the first and only meeting of the magician and the future narrator. How could the boy at the beginning of the book have known enough about the future to be able to advise Houdini to warn the unfortunate archduke? More than one reviewer of the novel has been disturbed by the boy's foreknowledge of the duke's fate. "This," complains Martin Green in the *American Scholar*, "is merest whimsy. It cannot serve serious imaginative interests." Such criticism tends to ignore the credentials of the boy as the future narrator of the novel, and also to overlook the importance of the moment for Houdini. After the death of his mother, Houdini has followed a second career of exposing the fraud of spiritualists, soothsayers, and various charlatans with their claims of extrasensory perception and clairvoyance. But when he thinks about the warning of the little boy, Houdini decides that "it was the one genuine mystical experience of his life." His attempt to rediscover the boy, however, is frustrated. Houdini returns a week later to the home of the narrator in New Rochelle only to find that the little boy and his family have disappeared. The narrator is typically lost in the mirror of history, and Houdini is left with his inexplicable memory.

At least Houdini retains the memory of "one genuine mystical experience." The majority of the characters in the novel, whether the reflections of history or fiction, all follow adventures that are frustrating and inconclusive. The unsatisfactory nature of the heroic quest is illustrated in a variety of adventures: Commander Peary takes his expedition in search of the North Pole; J. P. Morgan attempts to contact the ancient gods of Egypt by spending a night in the Great Pyramid; Coalhouse Walker seeks justice through revolutionary violence; Houdini wishes to contact his dead mother; and Emma Goldman wants to break the tyranny of capitalism. What do all of these quests have in common? Why does Doctorow bring them all together in *Ragtime*? Doctorow's novel is a picture of Western society moving inevitably to the weapons and death of world conflict. Doctorow shows how the many adventures of human will are frustrated, and how the frustration leads to the violence of war.

At the beginning of the novel the father of the narrator believes in the heroic fulfillment of selfhood. He looks forward to the adventure of accompanying Commander Peary to the North Pole. His belief in life as a perpetual quest is attributed to the philosophy of William James which he received as a student at Harvard. "Exploration became his passion: he wanted to avoid what the great Dr. James had called the habit of inferiority to the full self." But his role in the expedition to the North Pole is far from successful. The father of the narrator cannot tolerate the extreme cold of the Arctic, and he is among the first to turn back. He returns home changed in appearance and spirit. The man who had gone away "burly and self-confident" came back "gaunt and hunched and bearded." He also returns to discover that his wife has become more independent and that his family has learned to do without him. Whatever the father does in the rest of the novel will leave him with the feeling that the world is slipping away from his control. When he takes his son to a baseball game in New York, all of the players turn out to be rude immigrants, and the father has to remind himself sadly how it was once a gentlemen's sport at Harvard. He cannot know, only dimly fear, that an immigrant socialist will eventually take his place at home. The father who began with the conviction of heroic adventure feels more and more frustrated and insignificant as violent events begin to intrude upon his life. The helplessness of this man who manufactures flags and fireworks is symptomatic of his country's drifting in the direction of war. When the father turns to the manufacture of weapons and munitions, he will become himself a victim of the international violence. Near the very end of the novel the narrator provides an extraordinary description of how one passenger from the *Lusitania* sinks to the ocean floor: "Poor Father, I see his final exploration. He arrives at the new place, his hair risen in astonishment, his mouth and eyes dumb. His toe scuffs a soft storm of sand, he kneels and his arms spread in pantomimic celebration, the immigrant, as in every moment of his life, arriving eternally on the shore of his Self." Thus the father of the narrator becomes an immigrant to the land of death, and the "full self" he had always hoped to reach becomes an image of the final desolation.

The failure of the confident explorer is predetermined by the vanity of his ambitions and the blindness of his conduct. At the beginning of the novel the father of the narrator takes his wealth and power for granted. He supports the proud gestures of Teddy Roosevelt without thinking about the poor immigrants in America who cannot share in the masculine vanity of hunting parties and polar expeditions. The man in the White House is a Republican and all seems right with the world. But not for long. The novel dramatizes life in the tenements of New York and labor conditions in the textile mills of Massachusetts. Everything that the narrator's father would rather not recognize will soon gather sufficient momentum to overwhelm him. His wife adopts a black child and will later marry a Jewish socialist. Weapons for the revolution are manufactured without the father knowing about it right in his own factory. His brother-in-law, who sides completely with the rights of the oppressed, makes the final judgment—"You have traveled everywhere and learned nothing." His last journey, vain and blind as usual, takes him to his reward on the ocean floor.

All of the quests in the novel, with the exception of the immigrant father's success in Hollywood, prove inconclusive and unsatisfactory. Commander Peary, for example, has spent most of his life planning for the moment of victory when he can be the first man to stand at the very top of the earth. But his triumph is uncertain: "No one observation satisfied him. He would walk a few steps due north and find himself going due south. On this watery planet the sliding sea refused to be fixed. He couldn't find the exact place to say this spot, here, is the North Pole." The anticlimactic nature of Peary's quest is typical of what happens to the many adventurers in Doctorow's novel. Morgan expects to receive signs from Osiris in the Great Pyramid of Egypt. Instead he finds himself covered with bedbugs. Coalhouse Walker would like to have his automobile restored in a symbolic gesture of civil and racial justice. Instead he is shot by the police when he steps from the Morgan Library. Houdini intends to prove his strength against the confinement of death by escaping from a buried coffin. Instead he discovers that the weight of the earth is too much, and he must be dug from the grave by his desperate assistants.

Why do all of the adventures prove inconclusive? It is the narrator of the novel who clearly perceives the mutability of all things. Skating on the pond near his home the young boy watches "only the tracks made by the skaters, traces quickly erased of moments past, journeys taken." The novel is a vision of the many journeys and moments traced on the melting ice. It is his sense of the world in flux that informs the narrator's description of Peary's attempt to locate the North Pole—"On this watery planet the sliding sea refused to be fixed." And just as Peary "shuffled back and forth over the ice" at the inconclusive height of his quest, J. P. Morgan is described as moving blindly about in the King's Chamber of the Great Pyramid—"He paced from the west to the east, from the north to the south, though he didn't know which was which."

While the narrator of the novel recognizes that history is a comic mirror, many of the characters in the book believe in the illusions of themselves cast back by the changing times. J. P. Morgan, for example, believes that Henry Ford and himself are reincarnations of the great pharaohs who commanded the building of the pyramids. The narrator of *Ragtime* explains how Morgan is trying to escape from a world of mutability: "His desperate studies settled, inevitably, on the civilizations of ancient Egypt, wherein it was taught that the universe is changeless and that death is followed by the resumption of life." But the novel at every turn reveals the vanity of Morgan's thesis. Nothing is permanent in a world that "refused to be fixed," and all of the adventurers are trapped by the illusions of self cast back by the turning mirror of history. The one successful character in the novel is therefore the immigrant father who can rise to power and fortune in Hollywood because he knows that history is a reel of illusions.

Even the master of illusion, Harry Houdini, also becomes its victim. All of his staged escapes are mere vaudeville tricks unless Houdini can escape from death itself. After his mother dies Houdini desperately wants to believe in the possibility of some form of supernatural life. But his visits to spiritualists and other conductors of seances all over America only convince him of their fraud and vanity. He wages a national campaign against their trickery with all of the outrage and hurt of a child who has just seen that the wizard is a humbug. Houdini may escape from jails and straitjackets and a Chinese torture machine; he may be among the first to climb into the air at the controls of his own plane; he may hang upside down eleven stories over Times Square; but the only time in his life when a true key to the future is placed in his hands Houdini does not recognize its value until it is too late. He remains just as locked in mortal time as Morgan and Peary. Only the little boy who told him years in advance to "Warn the Duke" will be able to separate from himself in order to put together the novel of illusions.

Houdini's attempt to break from the confinement of a buried coffin is described very early in the novel: "He was buried alive in a grave and could not escape, and had to be rescued. Hurriedly, they dug him out. The earth is too heavy, he said gasping. His nails bled. Soil fell from his eyes. He was drained of color and couldn't stand." Some characters in the novel, nevertheless, enjoy being buried alive. The little boy and his stepsister play on the beach by covering one another with sand. "The burial game," the narrator remembers, "was their most serious pleasure." They lie on the beach under sculptured images of their bodies, much like the mummy of the pharaoh in his sculptured coffin, until they escape from the mound of sand and run to wash themselves in the ocean. This ritual escape from burial is sought in vain by Houdini and Morgan. Only the children of the novel, especially the narrator as the little boy, can break free from the mold of self and then baptize a new life.

All of the inconclusive quests in the novel are symptoms of the frustration and suppressed violence that will explode at the end of the book with the advent of World War I. The decade of tension prior to the war is characterized by the very title of the novel, and also by the life of the great composer Scott Joplin, who led the way in the creation of ragtime music. His words are used for the epigraph to Doctorow's novel, and his career is echoed throughout *Ragtime*. Although critics have rightly pointed to Heinrich von Kleist's *Michael Kohlhaas* as a probable source for the character and predicament of Coalhouse Walker, there are also many similarities between Doctorow's jazz pianist and the career of Scott Joplin. In the narrator's home in New Rochelle it is Coalhouse Walker who plays some of the famous Joplin pieces such as "Wall Street Rag" and "The Maple Leaf Rag." After the fire station of New Rochelle is destroyed by the vengeance of Coalhouse Walker, and the newspapers of New York are competing with one another for news of the black terrorist, a picture of Scott Joplin is mistakenly printed by Hearst's *American*. Doctorow allows history and fiction to mirror one another until the reflections become interchangeable. Joplin and Walker are both reported to have come from St. Louis to New York at about the same time. Joplin's opera, *Treemonisha*, tells the story of a dark skinned infant discovered beneath a tree. The child in the opera matures through adversity to become a symbol of black pride and triumph. Coalhouse Walker's son in *Ragtime* is found buried alive near the maple trees in the garden of the narrator's boyhood home. Rescued by the narrator's mother, the black child will be adopted by the narrator's family, and eventually become the minority hero of a series of films created in Hollywood by his third father. The dark child's resurrection from a shallow grave relates him symbolically to the other two children in the novel who play their burial games. The future belongs to all three children, boy and girl, black and white, who will live together in Hollywood, and serve as models for a popular film series. Their lives are thus projected by the mirrors of count-less reruns into the unknown future.

Although the children in the opera and the novel live happily ever after, their fathers, with the exception of the immigrant socialist, come to violent ends. The tragic conclusion of Joplin's career is reflected in Doctorow's novel by the misfortune and death of Coalhouse Walker. More than five hundred pieces of music, including a ballet and two operas, were composed by Joplin, but his popularity rested largely upon a few pieces like "The Maple Leaf Rag." He sought in vain for a producer in New York to stage *Treemonisha*. Bitterness and disappointment convinced him that racial prejudice was the cause of his rejection as a serious composer. After years of extraordinary creativity and extreme frustration, he was committed to a mental hospital. While the tension of Doctorow's novel is released in the madness of a world plunged into war, Joplin dies offstage in the mental asylum. But his counter-part in the novel, Coalhouse Walker, directs a violent challenge to the bigotry and conceit of the white community. Walker's threat to blow up the Morgan Library is the occasion for Doctorow to create the novel's most dramatic scene of revolutionary theater. Coalhouse Walker does not survive his violent protest, but the revolution will be continued; and eventually, in 1972, a successful production of *Treemonisha* will be staged in New York. *The Collected Works of Scott Joplin* were published in the same year, and thus E. L. Doctorow was prepared to write *Ragtime*.

The rhythms of violence and rebirth are syncopated in Doctorow's novel like the rich interplay of recurring themes and melodies in ragtime music. The subtlety of its narrative strategy and the complex arrangement of its mirrored images are in harmony with the words of Scott Joplin which Doctorow uses as the epigraph for his novel: "Do not play this piece fast. It is never right to play Ragtime fast."

PAUL LEVINE

Fiction and History

But in retrospect, I suppose (speaking of Ragtime *and* The Book of Daniel) *there is some kind of disposition—and no more than that—to propose that all our radicals (and we've had an astonishing number of them) and our labor leaders and our Wobblies and our anarchists and so on, have really been intimate members of the family— black sheep, as it were, whom no one likes to talk about. And I suppose one could make a case for my disposition to suggest that they are indeed related, that they are part of the family, and that they've had an important effect on the rest of us.*
—E. L. Doctorow

The second climactic scene of *The Book of Daniel* takes place, appropriately enough, in Disneyland. The confrontation between Daniel and Mindish which involves an attempt to retrieve the past occurs in the place which has already abolished history. Under Daniel's analysis, Disneyland is revealed as a suitable symbol for the coming 'one-dimensional society' described by Herbert Marcuse. By a 'radical process of reduction' Disneyland eliminates the dialectical dimension of both literature and history in its 'cartoon' rendering of reality.

From *E. L. Doctorow*. © 1985 by Paul Levine.

The life and life-style of slave-trading America on the Mississippi
River in the 19th century is compressed into a technologically
faithful steamboat ride of five or ten minutes on an HO-scale
river. The intermediary between us and this actual historical
experience, the writer Mark Twain, author of *Life on the Mississippi*, is now no more than the name of the boat.

Furthermore, the one-dimensional nature of Disneyland is mirrored by
the homogeneous character of its clientele. Just as its version of American
history excludes minorities and deviant groups, so Daniel notices how few
blacks, Mexicans, hippies and long-haired young people are permitted in
Disneyland. Daniel is aware of the political implications in all this.

What Disneyland proposes is a technique of abbreviated short-
hand culture for the masses, a mindless thrill, like an electric
shock, that insists at the same time on the recipient's rich psychic
relation to his country's history and language and literature. In a
forthcoming time of highly governed masses in an overpopulated
world, this technique may be extremely useful both as a substitute for education and, eventually, as a substitute for experience.

This Disneyland view of American reality is the starting point of
Doctorow's next novel, *Ragtime*, which returns us to the beginning of this
century. As the narrator tells us on the first page:

Patriotism was a reliable sentiment in the early 1900's. Teddy
Roosevelt was President. The population customarily gathered
in great numbers either out of doors for parades, public
concerts, fish fries, political picnics, social outings, or indoors
in meeting halls, vaudeville theatres, operas, ballrooms. There
seemed to be no entertainment that did not involve great
swarms of people. Trains and steamers and trolleys moved them
from one place to another. That was the style, that was the way
people lived. Women were stouter then. They visited the fleet
carrying white parasols. Everyone wore white in the summer.
Tennis racquets were hefty and the racquet faces elliptical.
There was a lot of sexual fainting. There were no Negroes.
There were no immigrants.

'That was the style, that was the way people lived.' From the beginning, the cool, detached, slightly ironic narrative voice, so different from

Daniel's intense, involving, complex rhetoric, distances us from the events of *Ragtime* as it rewrites American history. *Ragtime* begins with the conventional view of the turn of the century as an age of innocence but then reveals the social and economic conflicts that remained barely suppressed beneath the surface. 'Apparently there *were* Negroes. There *were* immigrants.' If American history has traditionally been written from the vantage point of the dominant culture, then in *Ragtime* Doctorow rewrites it 'from the bottom up'.

Doctorow's revisioning of American history bears comparison with that of John Dos Passos and, indeed, several critics have drawn attention to the similarities between *Ragtime* and *U.S.A.* John Seelye has observed:

> What Doctorow has done is to take the materials of John Dos Passos' *U.S.A.*—a sequential series of fictional, biographical and historical episodes—and place them in a compactor, reducing the bulk and hopelessly blurring the edges of definition. And yet the result is an artifact which retains the specific gravity of Dos Passos' classic, being a massively cynical indictment of capitalist, racist, violent, crude, crass and impotently middle-class America.

But despite these striking resemblances, *Ragtime* is not modelled on *U.S.A.* In fact, as Barbara Foley has pointed out, their views of history are opposite. For Dos Passos, history has an objective order which provides the structure of his fiction. For Doctorow, on the other hand, objective history is a chimera. 'There is no history except as it is composed,' he has written. 'That is why history has to be written and rewritten from one generation to another. The act of composition never ends.' Similarly, in *Ragtime* it is evident to the little boy who will grow up to write the narrative that 'the world composed and recomposed itself in an endless process of dissatisfaction.'

In *U.S.A.* history and fiction are treated as distinct entities and separated into discrete compartments of narrative, newsreel, biography and autobiography. Dos Passos is scrupulous in his historical research to the point where he was actually accused of plagiarism in one of his biographies. History in *U.S.A.* is highly interpreted but it is never invented: indeed, Dos Passos's faith in an objective order of reality led him to portray his biographical figures as the agents of history and his fictional figures as its victims. On the other hand, *Ragtime* is shaped by the conflation of history and fiction where the boundary line between the two seems to disappear. Not only does Doctorow invent incidents in the lives of his historical personages but his 'real' and 'imagined' characters meet and mingle promiscuously on an equal footing, both victims and agents of their own projections of history. In Doctorow's view, 'history is a kind of fiction in which we live and hope to survive, and fiction is a kind of speculative history, perhaps a superhistory, by which the available data for the composition is seen to be greater and more various in its sources than the historian supposes.'

The freedom that Doctorow achieves by this strategy is quite dazzling. The fictional characters like Coalhouse Walker take on a certain gravity as they enter history while the representative figures of the age are both illuminated and demythologized, as in Freud's boat trip through the Tunnel of Love with Jung. Even the great villains of an era of rapacious capitalism are radically altered. Compare, for instance, Dos Passos's dour picture of the House of Morgan with Doctorow's witty portrait of J. P. Morgan. In *Ragtime*, the irresistible engine of monopoly capitalism is driven by a group of quite ordinary men who do not comprehend the forces they have unleashed. When Morgan invites the dozen most powerful men in America to a 'historic' dinner party he finds them to be less prepossessing than he had imagined.

> He was hoping the collected energy of their minds might buckle the walls of his home. Rockefeller startled him with the news that he was chronically constipated and did a lot of his thinking on his toilet. Carnegie dozed over his brandy. Harriman uttered inanities. Gathered in this one room the business elite could think of nothing to say.

Nevertheless, Morgan hands out laurel wreaths and has a photograph taken of the 'historic' occasion.

Here, as elsewhere in the novel, appearance belies reality. In Doctorow's hands, history demystified becomes a ragbag of accidents (the Archduke is assassinated when his chauffeur takes a wrong turn); coincidences (both Tateh and Henry Ford deal with the same Franklin Novelty Company); parallels (Coalhouse Walker meets Booker T. Washington in the same place that J. P. Morgan entertained Henry Ford); and misunderstandings (the Archduke congratulates Houdini on the invention of the aeroplane). To impose order on chaos requires an imaginative act. Like Daniel, the little boy must learn to make connections; like Doctorow, he is never surprised by contingency. Yet reality remains as elusive as the precise location of the North Pole. Admiral Peary 'couldn't find the exact place to say this spot, here, is the North Pole. Nevertheless there was no question that they were there.' The artist's perception remains a matter of shifting perspectives as Theodore Dreiser demonstrates when he tries to properly align his chair. 'Throughout the night Dreiser turned his chair in circles seeking the proper alignment.'

The kaleidoscopic quality of *Ragtime* underscores the protean nature of reality, like the stories from Ovid that the boy hears from his grandfather. Some critics have seen in this interplay of forces a pattern of repetition which suggests a cyclical view of history. 'Little has changed despite all that has occurred in *Ragtime*,' argued Arthur Saltzman; 'the novel opens with Father making a living from patriotism, and the market still exists when the novel's frame is completed years later.' True enough. But this fails to take into account the fundamental changes that occur in the course of the novel. On the personal level, *Ragtime* begins by chronicling the lives of three 'families'—WASP, immigrant and black—whose existences are entirely segregated. By the end of the book these three families have become one. On the public level, *Ragtime* describes the transformation of American society from small-town WASP homogeneity to big-city ethnic heterogeneity. The immigrants and Negroes who were excluded from American reality at the beginning of the novel have by the end become part of the family.

Furthermore, the generational conflicts in the novel suggest shifting political perspectives. Just as Younger Brother is more radical than Father, so Coalhouse Walker is less revolutionary than his younger followers. Thus Father comes to the conclusion that he and Coalhouse are true contemporaries who share similar beliefs in dignity, property and justice. 'But the people following him were not. They were another generation. They were not human. Father shuddered. They were monstrous! Their cause had recomposed their minds. They would kick at the world's supports. Start an army! They were nothing more than filthy revolutionaries.'

The view of history presented here is more dialectical than cyclical. At times, particularly in the story of Coalhouse Walker, Doctorow's treatment of history is deliberately anachronistic in the way it reshapes the past to parallel the present. Walker's meeting with Booker T. Washington, for instance, echoes the contemporary debate between integrationists and black separatists. Similarly, Henry Ford is described as the father of mass society and Evelyn Nesbit is depicted as the first sex goddess of mass culture. The revolutionary implications of Evelyn's image are recognized both by the businessmen who manufacture it and by the radicals who challenge it. 'I am often asked the question How can the masses permit themselves to be exploited by the few,' Emma Goldman explains to Evelyn. 'The answer is by being persuaded to identify with them. Carrying his newspaper with your picture the laborer goes home to his wife, an exhausted workhorse with the veins standing out in her legs, and he dreams not of justice but of being rich.'

In its mixture of fact and fiction, *Ragtime* is closer to romance than to the conventions of traditional history fiction. Though it is the witty historical inventions which have received the most attention, Doctorow was as concerned with the stylistic problems of his narrative.

> In *Ragtime* it was the historical imagery and the mock historical tone which most interested me. And the idea of composition at a fixed narrative distance to the subject, neither as remote as history writing—which is very, very distant from what is being described—nor as close as modern fiction, which is very intimate with the subject. I was aiming for the narrative distance of the historical chronicle that you find, for instance, in Kleist who, of course, was very important in the composition of that book.

Indeed, *Ragtime* owes more to Heinrich von Kleist's 'Michael Kohlhaas' than to Dos Passos's *U.S.A.* Kleist's tale, itself based on a historical chronicle, recounts the efforts of an honest and respected horse dealer to obtain justice from the corrupt feudal society he had accepted. 'I had always wanted to rework the circumstances of Kleist's story,' observed Doctorow. 'I felt the premise was obviously relevant, appropriate—the idea of a man who cannot find justice from a society that claims to be just.' Doctorow's translation into an American cultural idiom is both apt and inventive. Michael Kohlhaas becomes Coalhouse Walker and Kohlhaas's disputed horses are transformed into Coalhouse's ruined car. Even Kohlhaas's fateful interview with Martin Luther is repeated in Coalhouse's meeting with Booker T. Washington. Finally, there is a sly hint of acknowledgement when Coalhouse uses a silver tankard from J. P. Morgan's collection that had once belonged to Frederick, the elector of Saxony, to communicate with the police.

But the parallels which Doctorow wishes to exploit are more than merely formal. Both Kohlhaas and Coalhouse live in societies whose fragile surface order belies a fundamental instability. The protagonists' desperate actions, predicated upon their belief in the values their societies profess, reveal not simply the hypocrisy of the social order but its vulnerability in a time of profound social transformation. According to John Seelye, 'Michael Kohlhaas' describes the clash over the rights of property between the old landed and new monied classes which defined the transformation of Europe during the Renaissance. Similarly, *Ragtime* depicts the growing class conflict which characterized the era of the emerging modern American state where the belief in the sacredness of property took precedence over the commitment to the principle of equality before the law. Thus both Kohlhaas and Coalhouse become victims of their faith in a social system which is revealed to be based upon power and not justice. As Kleist describes Kohlhaas, 'the world would have had cause to revere his memory, had he not pursued one of his virtues to excess. But his sense of justice made him a robber and murderer.' Similarly, Doctorow describes how Coalhouse Walker's pursuit of justice is transformed into an implacable desire for vengeance. 'Or is injustice once suffered, a mirror universe, with laws of logic and principles of reason the opposite of civilization's?'

Yet Doctorow's adaptation has an added dimension. First, there is the intractable element of racism in American society which makes a normal life impossible for the protagonist despite all his efforts. Coalhouse Walker's problems begin with his refusal to accept his assigned social role. 'Walker didn't act or talk like a colored man. He seemed to be able to transform the customary deferences practised by his race so that they reflected to his own dignity rather than the recipient's.' Coalhouse's ignorance of his racial identity is more calculated than innocent. He knows that possession of a car will be a provocation for many white people, especially members of the working class who envy his achievement. But the racism he experiences is an integral part of a class system in which the lower orders identify with their oppressors and maintain their precarious position on the slippery ladder of success by oppressing those beneath them. 'By what other standard could the craven and miserable Willie Conklin, a bigot so ordinary as to be like all men, become Pierpont Morgan, the most important individual of his time?'

Second, Doctorow transforms Kleist's horse dealer into a modern artist: Coalhouse Walker's ragtime piano provides the central metaphor of the novel. 'The pianist sat stiffly at the keyboard, his long hands with their pink nails seemingly with no effort producing the clusters of syncopating chords and the thumping octaves.' The musical image of 'syncopating chords' playing against 'thumping octaves' suggests the dialectical relationship in *Ragtime* between fiction and fact, individual will and historical necessity, the organic vision of community expressed by Emma Goldman and the mechanical view of corporate society created by Henry Ford. But ragtime is an appropriate image for the creative act itself. As Coalhouse plays Scott Joplin's 'Wall Street Rag' the little boy is transported to a world elsewhere. 'Small clear chords hung in the air like flowers. The melodies were like bouquets. There seemed to be no other possibilities for life than those delineated by the music.'

But Coalhouse Walker is not the only proletarian artist in the novel. Both Houdini and Tateh also come from the working class and rise by creating new cultural forms. Houdini is a headliner in vaudeville, a forerunner of the superstars of the electronic media. But though he dedicates himself to the American ideal of self-perfection, he realizes that he can never escape his working-class origins. And though his escape acts become more sensational, he knows that they are merely escapist entertainments divorced from the real world where history is made. Houdini's problem is that he could never make the connection between art and life. Thus he 'never developed what we think of as a political consciousness. He could not reason from his own hurt feelings. To the end he would be almost totally unaware of the design of his career, the great map of revolution laid out by his life.' This is in contrast to Coalhouse Walker who is compelled by his colour to make the appropriate connections himself. When Emma Goldman is asked about her influence on the ragtime pianist-turned-terrorist, she responds: 'Wealth is the oppressor. Coalhouse Walker did not need Red Emma to learn that. He only needed to suffer.'

More problematical is the story of Tateh, the silhouette artist who becomes a pioneer movie-maker. He begins as a socialist but his bitter experience of poverty and class oppression destroys his faith in revolutionary change. 'From this moment, perhaps, Tateh began to conceive of his life as separate from the fate of the working class.' Whereas Coalhouse must give up the piano and become a terrorist, Tateh makes his escape by becoming a commercial artist and pointing 'his life along the lines of flow of American energy. Workers could strike and die but in the streets of cities an entrepreneur could cook sweet potatoes in a bucket of hot coals and sell them for a penny or two. A smiling hurdy-gurdy man could fill his cup.' Tateh compromises in ways that Coalhouse cannot. He not only embraces the American dream as a way of erasing the past but he exploits the myth of success in the popular entertainment he now creates. Like a figure out of Horatio Alger, he creates a new existence as Baron Ashkenazy, a truly self-made man. 'His whole personality had turned outward and he had become a voluble and energetic man full of the future. He felt he deserved his happiness. He'd constructed it without help.' Yet Tateh's success has its costs in his loss of personal identity and though he has consciously betrayed his convictions he has not completely surrendered his beliefs. His final vision of transforming his new interracial family experience into a series of *Our Gang* comedies is both a touching reminder of his lost idealism and an ironic example of his corrupted sensibility.

If ragtime and movies are the controlling images of art in the novel it is because both are formally appropriate and quintessentially American. Whereas in Europe high and popular culture are strictly segregated and the influences are legitimized from the top down, in America the two cultures are interwined and the distinctively American impulses move from the bottom up. *Ragtime* and motion pictures, vaudeville and baseball were all nourished by contributors from the lowly group of immigrants and blacks. For Doctorow, the genius of American culture lies in its popular roots which flourish in the rich soil of ordinary life. Thus architects like Stanford White and collectors like J. P. Morgan, with their custodial view of culture, are really the 'alien' figures since they simply wish to impose European cultural standards on the conditions of American life. But in describing the resistance to the wholesale appropriation of European high culture, Doctorow is aware of the difference between an organic and creative popular culture and a mechanical and manufactured mass culture. As he observes about Houdini: 'Today, nearly fifty years since his death, the audience for escapes is even larger.'

Interestingly enough, the publication of *Ragtime* illustrated some of Doctorow's ideas about the fluidity of American culture. Not only was the novel a critical success but it became a media event. *Ragtime* won the first National Book Critics Circle Award for fiction and was the best-selling novel of the year, even outstripping *Jaws*. In the first year of its publication, nearly a quarter of a million hardback copies were sold in the United States alone. Less than a year later, almost three million copies of the paperback edition had been printed. Rarely, if ever, had a serious novel entered the dizzying world of mass culture with such a splash. Kathy Piehl has chronicled the advertising campaigns launched by Random House and Bantam Books to make *Ragtime* a household word. But public relations alone cannot account for the tremendous popularity that the novel enjoyed. Rather its fusion of 'highbrow' and 'popular' elements and its blend of 'revisionist' history and wry cynicism about national myths caught the imagination of post-Watergate America in much the same way as Robert Altman's contemporaneous film, *Nashville*. Ironically, the warm reception in America led British reviewers to treat the novel with a greater degree of scepticism. Yet the extraordinary success of *Ragtime* established Doctorow as a major figure in contemporary American letters.

Like his first two novels, *Ragtime* explores elements of popular culture. Like *The Book of Daniel*, it revises our understanding of modern history. Just as he celebrates those disreputable cultural forms that are distinctly American, so he commemorates those despised ethnic groups that have hitherto been excluded from American history. In the climactic scene of *U.S.A.*, Dos Passos hailed the martyred anarchists Sacco and Vanzetti as the true heirs to the American pioneer spirit. In *Ragtime*, Doctorow goes a step further to suggest how the American character has been profoundly affected by its foreign and alienated elements. As in his earlier fiction, Doctorow uses the family as a symbol of our connectedness even in the midst of our great differences.

> But in retrospect, I suppose . . . there is some kind of disposition
> . . . to propose that all our radicals (and we've had an astonishing
> number of them) . . . have really been intimate members of the

family—black sheep, as it were, whom no one likes to talk about. And I suppose one could make a case for my disposition to suggest that they are indeed related, that they are part of the family, and that they've had an important effect on the rest of us.

Ragtime is not only proof of the proposition but a splendid example of how fiction can revise our understanding of history, of how imagination can reclaim the world of facts. 'If you ask me whether some things in the book "really" happened,' Doctorow affirms, 'I can only say, "They have now."'

MARSHALL BRUCE GENTRY

Ragtime *as Auto Biography*

The Model T automobile at the center of E. L. Doctorow's popular novel *Ragtime* may seem essentially sinister, the product of Henry Ford's assembly-line mentality and of an oppressive myth of American success. *Ragtime* might then seem the perfect example of a novelistic attack on automobile culture in America. One of Carol Yeh's drawings for the illustrated Bantam edition of *Ragtime* could be seen as expressing this view: Harry Houdini is bound and chained inside automobile tires from which he will presumably make one of his not-quite-satisfying escapes. The novel's statement that Houdini never damages or unlocks the enchaining materials from which he releases himself could be taken as confirmation that the societal forces embodied in an automobile are unchanged by our temporary escapes. That the society of the ragtime era appeared to value automobiles more highly than people may even make the auto a grotesque symbol of a culture's collective neurosis, especially since the automobiles have names like Pope–Toledo Runabout or Pierce Arrow Opera Coach while human beings are named simply: Mameh and Tateh, Mother and Father, Mother's Younger Brother, the Little Girl and Little Boy.

David Emblidge argues for what is perhaps the most pessimistic reading of *Ragtime* possible, saying that "Life in the present in *Ragtime* is a continuous recapitulation of the past." Emblidge sees the novel as presenting

From *Kansas Quarterly* 21, no. 4 (Fall 1989): 105–112. © 1990 by the *Kansas Quarterly*.

us with a fascinating set of illusory indications of change that fails to effect any genuine change in mankind's hopeless condition. In this reading, the automobile and Ford's system of mass production are part of a "double apotheosis" (along with J. P. Morgan's theories about order) of the duplicable event. Another critical view of the automobile in *Ragtime* could be expressed in the terms of one of Father's observations during the final negotiations with Coalhouse Walker Jr.: "The car has no real value." For some readers the multiple significances of the automobile effectively empty it of meaning; in other words, the automobile is merely part of a whirlpool of chaotic, noisy, violent images in which human meaning is lost. For Geoffrey Galt Harpham, Coalhouse Walker's "Model T on whose uniqueness he paradoxically insists is actually a case of duplication so utter that there cannot even be said to be an original," it seems to follow that *Ragtime* is "a book with no meaning." In this view the novelist Theodore Dreiser might seem like a human being pushed down to the status of a defective automobile, turning hopelessly "in circles seeking the proper alignment."

In contrast to these views, I would like to suggest that the automobile in *Ragtime* is crucial to Doctorow's vision of how human individuality and artistic value are created. Even as Doctorow's characters desperately use their autos as "getaway cars" or drive toward the chaos symbolized by water, we discover various ways in which the automobile is more than a toy that capitalism uses to distract and manipulate the masses. In Coalhouse Walker's receipt of a restored Model T, and in the Little Boy's visions of the car as a reflection of himself and of his society, we have definitions of how the self can do more than dissolve into a mass of humanity that makes America seem, as it does to J. P. Morgan at one point, merely part of "an empty universe" full of "horse's asses." Ultimately I think *Ragtime* says that we, like the Little Boy or Coalhouse, are like automobiles, that we are at least potentially individuals while paradoxically being all alike, and that this novel is itself an automobile. Like *Ragtime* as novel, we should be at once part of the mass (it was and is a popular novel) and in some sense unduplicable (although many novels mix historical "fact" and fiction fancifully, they also aspire to be original achievements). And when we become aware of how like an automobile we are and how like an automobile a novel is, we can discover more of the individuality of ourselves and of *Ragtime*.

Another way of stating my point is to say that *Ragtime* emphasizes the social origin of human individuality and of art. Just as the Model T is a product of a mass of working class laborers, all the characters in *Ragtime*, all the readers of the novel, and the novel itself, are presented as products of a mass of contributing forces. But this societal basis to reality does not destroy characters or readers or the novel; it simply shifts the rules by which we discover individualized significance. Even as we learn that Evelyn Nesbit's celebrity is an industrial construction, even as we realize that we readers have been trained to ignore many versions of American history, and even as we struggle with the multiple narrative points of view in the novel, we are given a new, more complex, more valid understanding of human personality, of the reader's role in the production of meaning, of authorship, and perhaps even of the American automobile. Martin Green has accused Doctorow of encouraging "nostalgia" for the early automobile, but I think Doctorow's treatment of the automobile demonstrates a fascinatingly complex understanding of the automobile's meaning.

Some historical background might make it easier to recognize the positive aspects of the automobile in *Ragtime*. In many ways American culture has associated the automobile with freedom, and the Model T would be an especially good symbol of human freedom since it was, as Reynold M. Wik points out, "especially designed to travel over difficult terrain." Warren Belasco has even described the period from 1900 to 1920 (roughly the time period covered by *Ragtime*) as the era of anarchic "gypsying," of the use of automobiles to travel freely around the country without planning and to camp each night without expenses. Belasco concludes that "the automobile industry became the backbone of modern industrial capitalism, yet it was born in a spirit of rebellion against that system." If we recall that only 8,000 automobiles were registered in America in 1900 and that 8,000,000 were registered in 1920, we might conclude reasonably that the automobile symbolizes an explosion of rebelliousness on the part of Americans.

One related, positive aspect of the automobile in *Ragtime* is that it almost always succeeds in its function as a getaway car. Evelyn Nesbit discovers Tateh and the Little Girl when she uses her chauffeured car to get away from her husband. Coalhouse Walker Jr.'s revolutionaries repeatedly use automobiles to escape the police. The New Rochelle family drives to Atlantic City and thereby escapes newspaper reporters. The interesting exception is the Archduke Ferdinand's assassination as he attempts to flee Sarajevo by automobile. It is interesting to note that the automobile often seems least helpful when a character does *not* use it for escape. Houdini's car wrecks when he is "thinking of buying some property" in Westchester, presumably to improve his social status. Evelyn Nesbit's trips in her auto to defend Harry K. Thaw (and thereby to protect her own social position) fail. Sigmund Freud has a miserable time on an automobile tour of New York. Perhaps the automobile itself is valuable in *Ragtime* whenever it is part, as it often is, of a character's struggle toward a valuable end—such as freedom as opposed to status. Even the implied description of Theodore Dreiser as an automobile at the end of Chapter 4, often discussed by critics as an image of futility, might be taken positively. Dreiser's turning "his chair in circles" in search of "the perfect alignment" becomes like the turning of a wheel that carries an automobile along, and we should remember that Dreiser's struggles described in the novel had, after all, just produced *Sister Carrie*. As Arthur Saltzman has suggested, Theodore Dreiser was to some extent right: his struggle reminds us, says Saltzman, that "no one version of the Ragtime era should satisfy the conscientious artist or reader."

The automobile in *Ragtime* often seems to be symbolically opposed to the sea, with the auto suggesting humanity's technological control and the sea suggesting chaos, irrationality, emotion. But in at least two significant instances, the symbols come together in ways that suggest positive qualities for the automobile—when Coalhouse Walker's car enters the Firehouse Pond, and when Mother drives herself, the Little Boy, and Coalhouse Walker III to Prout's Neck, Maine, home of Winslow Homer, who had once painted light associated with chaos:

> Homer painted the light. It gave the sea a heavy dull menace and shone coldly on the rocks and shoals of the New England coast. There were unexplained shipwrecks and brave towline rescues. Odd things went on in lighthouses and in shacks nestled in the wild beach plum. Across America sex and death were barely distinguishable.

The early reference to Homer is significant because, during the Atlantic City storm that seems to bring Mother and Tateh together once and for all, she resembles "in her wet form the ample woman in the Winslow Homer painting who is being rescued from the sea by towline." I would suggest that the movement of the car towards water in both the Coalhouse Walker story and the story of the New Rochelle family symbolizes a complex interaction of forces in which the automobile, *like* the ocean to which it may *seem* to be opposed, is associated with some of the positive aspects of chaos.

As we turn to the issue of how the automobile provides a model for the achievement of human individuality, it may seem difficult to decide how seriously we are to take Coalhouse Walker Jr. as a heroic figure in what is sometimes considered the one traditional plot line in *Ragtime*. According to Martin Green, Doctorow's attitude toward Coalhouse Walker and toward Sarah is "uncritically romantic" and therefore flawed. While it may be true that Coalhouse Walker "defends his personal dignity fanatically, refusing to bend at all in the face of money-power and racial prejudice," it is also true that he has accepted the dominant culture's belief that possessions like a Model T can add to his status and dignity, and when his car is desecrated and pushed into a pond by Willie Conklin and other volunteer firemen, who significantly have not yet made the switch from horses to motors, we may wonder how much Doctorow expects us to want Walker to regain the car. For Leonard and Barbara Quart, it is "a bit absurd" for Coalhouse Walker to be willing "to sacrifice and destroy lives with no larger political end than redeeming his car and gaining personal respect." Barbara L. Estrin makes this issue of Coalhouse Walker's heroism a major part of the novel's point. The story of Coalhouse Walker's occupation of the Morgan Museum "is undermined by the pervading feeling that its outcome was so predictable, its conclusion so forecast by the forces of a society bent on the preservation of the industrial system, that the action comes to nothing." Because of the "system of interchangeable parts" that allows the easy replacement of Coalhouse Walker's car, Walker's death is unnecessary, "his death, like his revolution, a meaningless sacrifice. Nothing was changed by it." All the characters of *Ragtime* are, according to Estrin, "cogs on the wheels of time," and thus the novel seems to say "that we are all expendable."

I would like to suggest that Coalhouse Walker grows into his individuality, that it is precisely when Mother's Younger Brother is astonished to see Walker equating a mere car with justice that Walker has achieved heroism. It is crucial to the novel that Coalhouse Walker Jr. receives a car that is indeed a duplicate of his original Model T with the PANTASOTE top and at the same time a different car. Surely the car is more significant in its replacement form because the whole of New York's political establishment is watching it. The remade car is also different from the original in the sense that it is *not* produced by assembly line: "Fire Chief Conklin . . . piece by piece dismantled the Ford and made a new Ford from the chassis up." One might wonder whether Doctorow is claiming that this car produced by an individual is in some sense morally superior, or whether Doctorow is arguing for a return to the individual craftsman, and my answer would be yes but also no—it is impossible (following a logic that the novel suggests) to have individual craftsmanship, because Willie Conklin becomes the mass of society, "so ordinary as to be like all men," and, at least while he is building the car, he "become[s] Pierpont Morgan, the most important individual of his time." Even as Coalhouse Walker's demand is met, another Model T comes out of mass production. At the same time, it is worth noting that if a Ford cannot be produced by only one individual, not even Henry Ford can make a Ford by himself. The view that presents the Model T as a product of the entire society frees the automobile from Ford's tyranny to some extent. And there is something of a victory for Coalhouse even as the police equate him with the replaced car, complete with what might be considered the symbolically crucial customizing PANTASOTE top. He exchanges his life for the car *and* for the lives of his band of revolutionaries, all in a sense duplicates of Walker who call themselves Coalhouse.

The issues of the establishment of selfhood in a world of mass production are spelled out even more complexly in the story of the narrator, the Little Boy. *Ragtime* claims, through the Little Boy as narrator, that it is essential that one perceive (and maintain) the differences within apparent duplicates, as well as the similarities in things that seem chaotically dissimilar. Chapter 15 is crucial to an understanding of the Little Boy's fondness both for change, as taught by his grandfather, and for pattern. Not enough has been said critically about the significance for the boy of minor changes within pattern, of the rare occasion when the hairbrush or window does not remain still, of the slight changes that prove "even statues did not remain the same." The Little Boy seems to understand that the slight difference within sameness is the metaphor for his own individuality. Much has been made of the Little Boy's fondness for baseball because, he says, "The same thing happens over and over." According to Barbara L. Estrin, among others, baseball is a prime example of the sameness that rather depressingly underlies the appearance of change. But even here we see some delight in novelty, for as soon as the Little Boy praises the pattern, he is excited by the unusual occurrence of a foul ball that ends up in his hands. The point surely is that the Little Boy can always see both sides, and therein lies his power. Much has been said about the boy's vision of a "macrocephalic image of himself" in Houdini's headlight as a sign that the Little Boy is overly subjective, and some readers have been troubled by such a possibility. Barbara Foley criticizes *Ragtime* for implying that historical meaning as produced by this narrator is "chimerical and at best highly subjective," based on the notion "that whatever coherence emerges from the represented historical world is attributable to the writer's power as teller of his story." The Little Boy's amazing and initially obscure advice for Houdini, that he warn the Archduke Ferdinand of his coming assassination and of WWI, may even seem significant primarily for its pointlessness. In Estrin's interesting reading, the Little Boy's warning in the first chapter is a sort of failed authorial intrusion demonstrating the power of the machine over us all:

> With the insight he gains from subsequent experience, the little boy, prefiguring the storyteller he later becomes, informs the magician. We live our lives in the illusion that we can change things, in the hope that we amount to more than insignificant parts of a vast machine moving inexorably toward doom. The child anticipates, simultaneously as the narrator reconstructs, history. . . . "Warn the Duke," he says, sounding a command that might alter the course of the novel we are about to read.

Although I do not agree with Barbara Cooper's description of the narrative persona of *Ragtime* as "anonymous," I agree with her idea that the narrator "transcends the limitations of a single human perspective." I would like to emphasize the idea that the narrator's ability to combine points of view is more nearly the ground of his selfhood than a dilution of it. The narrator is at once a product of his time and an individual exercising some effect upon his time. His visions are not all of the sort that ends the first chapter and that Houdini somewhat pathetically reproduces near the novel's end. More should be made of the fact that the Little Boy's eyes are compared to a "school globe" and of the line in the description of Sarah's funeral that insists emphatically that the boy sees not just himself but the rest of this society: Sarah's hearse "was so highly polished the boy could see in its rear doors a reflection of the entire street." This line suggests that the Little Boy's visions are at once internal and external. Even in the episode in which the Little Boy stares at Houdini's headlight and sees himself, we can find more than an indication that the boy is at once able to predict world events and to be obsessed with his own head. Before he realizes that Houdini's car is approaching, the Little Boy equates the car visually with a fly. He fixes "his gaze on a bluebottle fly traversing the screen in a way that made it appear to be coming up the hill from North Avenue. The fly flew off. An automobile was coming up the hill from North Avenue." Perhaps the fascination with the fly is the result of the fly's possession of multiple eyes, in which case the boy's fascination with the car seems to be related to the automobile's multiplicities. The automobile in this passage suggests the value of multiple perspectives, not just the Little Boy's perspective. The narrator's possession of mystical powers seems far-fetched to some readers, but it does function to combine the options of reading *Ragtime* as mass-produced and of reading it as the production of an individual author. Although Geoffrey Galt Harpham says that the novel has "no consistent or even possible narrative persona," surely the key to understanding the narrative voice is in noticing, as Harpham himself points out, that the narrator "materializes miraculously at the very end as an older narrator." The point, I believe, is not so much that the Little Boy "will grow up to write the narrative," as that he writes the narrative in order to grow up, that the construction of the novel is the construction of its creator as well, that the Little Boy achieves genuine individuality in duplicating—with a difference—the data produced by the assembly-line of ragtime America. Harpham claims that Mother and Tateh "most conspicuously" enjoy the "fate" of a "happy ending" as they "achieve individuation by mastering the processes of replication." While I accept the direction of Harpham's argument here, it also seems true that achievement and mastery are terms better applied to the Little Boy or Coalhouse than to

Mother and Tateh, and Harpham does label the Little Boy the novel's "most successful character."

Angela Hague has argued that the duplicated event is "a way of over-coming—and, paradoxically, exemplifying—the fluidity of reality" and that the Little Boy's "attempt" at "self-duplication . . . accomplishes the negation of his own distinct personality." When he gazes into a mirror, the Little Boy feels that

> there were two selves facing one another, neither of which could claim to be the real one. The sensation was of being disem-bodied. He was no longer anything exact as a person. He had the dizzying feeling of separating from himself endlessly.

We need not consider this vision of multiplicity any more valid than the opposing sense of selfhood, however. It may be true that for a youngster, a sense of a fluid self is closer to the truth than the understanding such a child might have about wholeness, but it still ought to be possible to believe that the Little Boy as an adult will be able to balance the fluid and static impres-sions of the self. I think that Hague is absolutely correct in pointing out that motion pictures "both contradict and reinforce" the Little Boy's beliefs about change, but I am inclined to consider Doctorow to be more pleased than displeased about such a state of affairs.

The socialization of authorship involved in seeing a novel as an auto operated by a narrative persona at once himself and everybody is not all that different from what Doctorow describes as the traditional novelistic device of "gaining authority for the narrative" through the dissociation of the indi-vidual author from it ("False Documents"). Just as we may have more faith in a car produced by collective effort, we may trust the novel that presents the views of everyone in society, at least by implication. Even Barbara L. Estrin admits that *Ragtime* presents mass production as nothing new, that "it emerges simply as a different form of what existed long ago." It would seem to follow that the automobile cannot represent a decline in civilization, even in Estrin's reading, that it represents the duplication with a modern wrinkle of the ways in which human beings have always achieved meaning. *Ragtime* uses the automobile to suggest how we can satisfy our desire for individuality in spite of the societal forces demanding uniformity.

CUSHING STROUT

Twain, Doctorow, and the Anachronistic Adventures of the Arms Mechanic and the Jazz Pianist

"THE LOCUS of fiction is the unruly jostling of all the objects of culture," as Avrom Fleishman has said, "—of the real with the illusory, the found with the imagined, the irreducible with the artificial." He notes that it is a paradox of our time, in which "the 'fictionality' of fiction has become a watchword of literary pundits, that many currently approved fictional works have incorporated pieces of the real world in an increasingly self-assured way." Indeed, one vivid literary sign of our times is the breaking down of *any* boundary between novelists and historians. On the theoretical level, it is reflected in the work of Hayden White, who has insisted that written histories presuppose certain narrative forms, derived from literature, and these are held to be built on a few basic figurative forms of language, or tropes. Among journalists, the same tendency is evident in Norman Mailer's strategy in *The Armies of the Night* (1968), his account of the March on the Pentagon in 1967, which is subtitled "History as a Novel/The Novel as History." Among novelists, John Barth in *The Sot-weed Factor* (1960) characteristically mixes real and invented documents, borrowing his title, hero, and diction from a real person, who in 1731 published a verse satire in Maryland. Barth's novel deliberately blurs the line so that "we cannot be sure when we are in touch with facts, as opposed to fictionalized versions of facts."

From *Making American Tradition: Visions and Revisions from Ben Franklin to Alice Walker*. © 1990 by Cushing Strout.

The novelist who captured the popular imagination by this tendency to collapse history and fiction together is E. L. Doctorow. The traditional historical novel tends to keep historical persons on the margin of the fictional scene, but *Ragtime* (1975), a best-seller made into a popular movie, freely intersects the lives of historical characters with each other as well as with fictional characters. Its intention is to suppress in the reader's mind any question about "what actually happened" as a matter of detail, but at the same time to suggest to the reader something pertinent in contemporary terms about the meaning of the past. The author himself told a reporter: "If you ask me whether some things in the book 'really' happened, I can only say, 'they have now.'"

Ragtime was advertised in its jacket copy as a sport: "You will never have read anything like *Ragtime* before. Nothing quite like it has ever been written before." But, in some important respects, it has at least one unnoticed classic American precursor as a speculative and satirical history: Mark Twain's *A Connecticut Yankee in King Arthur's Court* (1889). Like Twain's romance (three times made into a movie), *Ragtime* is also a time-travel story with a deliberate anachronism built into its structure; with a magician playing an important part in the plot, and with an ironic and violent climax involving military technology.

The analogy between these two comic historical romances may seem implausible. Twain's story, unlike Doctorow's, which is told by an imitation of an impersonal historian's narrating voice, is a vernacular, first-person narrative, and its material is legendary, the Arthurian Camelot, far removed from the author's own time and country, unlike Doctorow's prewar period of America. Moreover, the plot of *Ragtime* turns centrally on racial conflict, which is absent from Twain's sixth-century Britain. Yet, the more each text is read over the shoulder of the other, the more interesting correspondences do appear. Are they accidental or was Doctorow, at some level of his mind, aware of Twain's story, which he never mentions in connection with *Ragtime*? At any rate, the audience for *Ragtime* eagerly assimilated its deceptively simple declarative sentences without paying any attention to its epigraph, a warning by Scott Joplin: "It is never right to play Ragtime fast." A good way to play it slowly is to read the novel side by side with Twain's story. If *A Connecticut Yankee* is not a close relative of *Ragtime*, it is surely at least a first cousin once removed.

It is clear that Doctorow was self-consciously rewriting (though few of his readers know it) another precursor text; his hero Coalhouse Walker is an updating of the hero in Heinrich von Kleist's Michael Kohlhaas (1810) which is set in the time of Martin Luther but is based on an earlier medieval document. The American hero's first name, overlapping with the German hero's last name, is Doctorow's only offered clue (as he has confessed) to this "intertextual" aspect of the story. He has changed Kohlhaas's horses to an automobile, but the hero's retaliatory and escalating violent acts, done to avenge the unjust loss of his vehicle, is the pattern in both stories.

Twain's romance also has its self-conscious reference to a precursor—Sir Thomas Malory's fifteenth-century version in *Morte d'Arthur* of the sixth-century Arthurian legend, a text Twain read in 1884 when George Washington Cable gave it to him while they were on tour, doing public readings on stage. Another classic, *Don Quixote*, which Twain echoed earlier in his pairing of Huck Finn and Tom Sawyer, can also be heard as a presence in the Yankee's recreation of the Quixote project to laugh away the chivalric tradition, which he believed Sir Walter Scott's *Ivanhoe* had romantically restored in antebellum Southern imaginations as a prop for slavery. The usual Cervantes polarities are reversed by the Yankee's time travel: "The past is made vividly present and the present is relegated to a visionary future." It is possible that Twain knew of even another precursor for some of the ingredients of his story. Marcus Cunliffe has noted that Edward Bulwer Lytton's *The Last of the Barons* (1843), a book in Twain's library, involves three characters who are literary relatives of Twain's cast: the fifteenth-century Earl of Warwick, an inventor of a kind of steam engine, and a villain who is a friar. Twain's story opens in Warwick Castle and the Warwick Arms Hotel. The point of my method, however, is not to accumulate evidence for all the possible influences on the making of a book; it is rather to put texts side by side, or back to back, to see how they illuminate each other. From this point of view, a comparison of *Ragtime* with *A Connecticut Yankee in King Arthur's Court* will have to carry its own evidence of its value.

Twain's Hank Morgan, a superintendent of a Hartford arms factory in 1879, is obviously anachronistic in Arthurian England, and he can only get there by a kind of magical time travel. The hero speaks mysteriously about the transposition of epochs and bodies. (J. P. Morgan in *Ragtime* believes in reincarnation.) He claims to have been responsible for a bullet hole in a suit of armor, on display at Warwick Castle, the costume once worn by a knight of the Round Table. From reading Malory in the Warwick Arms, the narrator turns to reading Morgan's own bizarre story of his time travel (the result of a blow on the head) to Camelot. At the end of Morgan's account, called "The Tale of the Lost Land," we learn from a postscript that Merlin, disguised as an old woman, has magically put his rival to sleep for thirteen centuries. (In *Ragtime*, Houdini disguises himself as a veiled gray-haired widow while attending seances.)

Twain's narrative technique has not only licensed his extravagant departures from realistic historical standards, but also alienated his hero. In a second postscript, this time by "M. T.," we learn how he has finished reading Morgan's manuscript and finds him in a last delerium in his bed. Twain's additional spin to the time-travel idea is to have the dying man imagine that he is back in Camelot. He speaks, in fact, as if his real home were in ancient Britain, while his nightmare is that he has been set down thirteen centuries later in the England of 1879, which "M. T." inhabits. Morgan's time-travel experience has dislocated him from both time periods so that he is a stranger when he is in Camelot and a stranger when he is in the Warwick Arms.

This ending connects with a precedent in Twain's own work, his short account of his war experience in "A Campaign That Failed," written four years earlier. In it a stranger in civilian clothes, fatally shot by Twain's band of rangers, looks at him reproachfully and mumbles, "like a dreamer in his sleep," about his wife and child; and the situation is partly replicated when "M. T." bends over another stranger, Hank Morgan, and hears him make precisely the same kind of murmur. As Justin Kaplan has pointed out about the Civil War story, "the victim is related to all the other 'strangers' who populate Mark Twain's fiction," and the biographer could have cited Hank Morgan as a highly charged example.

Doctorow's narrative strategy is similar in its effect. His hero, the black jazz pianist, Coalhouse Walker, is anachronistic because he engages in confrontational violence against the establishment in a way that was characteristic of the 1960s and quite unthinkable for blacks in the ragtime era before the First World War. Moreover, *Ragtime*'s plot also begins with a magical element, a premonition that is fantastic rather than historical: a small boy mysteriously tells a magician, Harry Houdini, to "warn the Duke," and many years (and pages) later it will be the Archduke Ferdinand's assassination that triggers the First World War. Houdini is notoriously effective in exposing fraudulent mediums, and his own magic is entirely naturalistic. But *Ragtime* links him to the paranormal by portraying his love for his dead mother as a motive that drives him to visit seances in the hope of finding a genuine medium who can put him in touch with his mother.

Morgan's final homelessness is paralleled by Coalhouse Walker's displacement from the 1960s to the ragtime era. Doctorow subtly acknowledges his hero's unhistorical presence by telling us that there is no information about his parentage, no school records, no explanation for his vocabulary and manner of speaking—except perhaps "an act of will." (That act, of course, is the author's decision to put him into the ragtime era.) In the end, his wife having been fatally wounded by a militia man and a Secret

Service man at a public appearance of the Vice-President, the bereft Walker is suicidally prepared to be shot down when he leaves the Morgan Library, after successfully negotiating the rebuilding of his car and the escape of his terrorist band of supporters. No more than Hank Morgan does Walker have any secure place in the earlier era to which he too brings the outlook of a later one.

The climax of both stories shows an embattled hero, surrounded by a small band of youthful supporters, using modern firepower in a showdown with armed authorities. To carry the analogy even further, there is a final stroke of irony in the use of weaponry. Hank Morgan in the Battle of the Sand-belt, aided by a small band of fifty-two young boys, confronts the massed might of the Arthurian establishment and defeats the enemy by the effectiveness of his electric fence, Gatling guns, and an artificially created flood. Nevertheless, the poisonous air bred by the dead puts the victors in a trap of their own making. Similarly, one of Doctorow's major characters, Father, a flag manufacturer, goes to London on the *Lusitania* with a shipment of grenades, depth charges, and puttied nitro invented by his son, Younger Brother, and thus inadvertently contributes to the explosion that kills him when the ship is torpedoed by a German submarine.

Both Twain and Doctorow by their technique of deliberate anachronism put two eras into juxtaposition. In both books, the later one judges the earlier one. Twain's preface tips his hand, signaling his critique of the Arthurian era, by explaining that if he refers to any laws or customs that did not actually exist in the sixth century, "one is quite justified in inferring that whatever one of these laws or customs was lacking in that remote time, its place was competently filled by a worse one." Doctorow is moved by a similar political indignation to subvert any sentimental nostalgia for the earlier era. He begins with the mock-historical tone of a social historian: "Patriotism was a reliable sentiment in the early 1900's." Then he shifts gears: "There were no Negroes. There were no immigrants. . . . Across America sex and death were barely distinguishable." The mention of Emma Goldman, the revolutionary anarchist, an immigrant Jew, leads him to this second thought: "Apparently there *were* Negroes. There *were* immigrants." The end of chapter 6 coldly enumerates with cumulative force the oppressions suffered by miners, child workers, immigrants, and blacks, while trusts proliferate and the rich entertain themselves by playing at being poor.

Both authors underline the continuity as well as the differences in their comparison of earlier with later times. Twain's treatment of serfdom explicitly insists on its continuity with slavery in the Old South and the old regime in France. By dramatizing the racial conflict of the ragtime era through the takeover of the Morgan Library, a tactic characteristic of radical politics in the 1960s, Doctorow underlines the persistence of racial injustice. More subtly, when the conservative black leader Booker T. Washington encounters the militant Coalhouse Walker in the library, the narrator notes on the wall portraits of Martin Luther, and Washington prays that the Lord may lead his people to the promised land—a strong echo of Martin Luther King, Jr., with Walker playing the role of the radical Malcolm X. Walker's supporters speak in revolutionary terms of setting up a provisional American government. At the same time the story dramatizes another aspect of the 1960s, the reluctance of the authorities to enter into, or respect, negotiations with the rebels.

What saves both books from historical smugness is their refusal to follow a traditional Whig interpretation of history with its idea of progress that congratulates the past for having led to the present. Twain judges the British past by his endorsement of the American and French revolutions. But from this point of view, his present is also criticized. When the Round Table becomes a stock exchange, wildcat manipulations (with which Twain as a heavy investor in the market was familiar) lead to warfare among the knights and the end of the Boss's new deal. He may think that his anomalous position in the kingdom makes him "a giant among pygmies, a man among children, a master intelligence among intellectual moles; by all rational measurement the one and only actually great man in that whole British world." But the reader is made increasingly aware of the dark side of the Boss's project with its complacency about his own assumption of power and his addiction to a technocratic "progress" that depends heavily on weapons of destruction. His political and cultural imperialism is the other side of his role as the democratic reformer.

Similarly, Doctorow is aware of the comic absurdity in some of the radicals' 1960s-style gestures. The small isolated band of terrorist blacks speak ideologically about being "a nation," and neurotic Younger Brother, in his disgust with his father, his identification with the rebels, and his obsession with violence, corks his face black the better to be one of them in their occupation of the library. He ends up, as a *villista* in Mexico, wearing cartridge belts crossed over his chest, making bombs, and leading reckless guerrilla raids for the *zapatistas*. Emma Goldman sees that this "poor dangerous boy" is like the assassin of President McKinley, Leon Czolgosz. (He had heard her lecture on anarchy, and when she was falsely arrested as a coconspirator, she had insisted that he was a troubled homeless man who had acted alone. The reader of the novel in 1975 would probably think of Lee Harvey Oswald.)

Doctorow's hero is locked into an escalating confrontation with the bigoted firechief Willie Conklin, who trashed Walker's car, because each man is as intractable as the other, and their violent methods become virtually indistinguishable. Eventually, with eight people dead by his hand, Walker transforms Pierpont Morgan into his enemy, substituting for an ordinary bigot one of the most influential people of his era, and captures his library as a symbol of the white world. Struck by the arrogance of the avenger, the narrator's mock-historical voice speculates: "Or is injustice, once suffered, a mirror universe, with laws of logic and principles of reason the opposite of civilization's?"

The other Morgan—Hank, not Pierpont—in his own way mirrors his rival Merlin, who exploits the credulity of the public. When the Yankee is first captured by a knight on horseback, Morgan assumes that he is someone from the circus; and Morgan later virtuously contrasts his "new deal" program of education with a violent revolution that would appeal to "the circus side" of his own nature. It constantly erupts, nevertheless, with comic effect in his various stunts to impress the populace culminating in the liberation of the imprisoned king by five hundred knights on bicycles, "one of the gaudiest effects" Morgan ever instigated. In his duel with Sagramor on behalf of "common sense and reason" the Yankee incongruously appears in flesh-colored tights and uses a lasso like a cow-boy in a circus Wild West Show. It is quite in the Boss's style, foreshadowed in Dan Beard's sketch, introducing "The Tale of the Lost Land," that shows a check-suited man in a derby, looking like a carnival barker or pitchman, tickling the nose of the British lion with a straw.

Ragtime has its own strong link to show business. Evelyn Nesbit's testimony in the murder trial of Harry K. Thaw "created the first sex goddess in American history," an inspiration for "the concept of the movie star system." The Jewish immigrant Tateh's upward mobility carries him out of the labor movement into making drawings that move by flipping the pages and on to the new movie industry and a made-up identity as Baron Ashkenazy, who acquires a WASP wife and a new career as a director of popular comedies. Doctorow's impersonal historian's voice interprets this development: "Thus did the artist point his life along the lines of flow of American energy. . . . The value of the duplicatable event was everywhere perceived."

Its corollary in business is Henry Ford's Model T automobile, and Doctorow pictures Ford regarding his first car on the moving assembly line: "His derby was tilted back on his head. He chewed on a piece of straw." It is uncannily like the image, sketched by Dan Beard for Twain's book, of the Yankee mechanic tickling the British lion with a straw. Ford in *Ragtime* is an evil genius because he establishes not only that the parts be interchangeable, "but that the men who build the products be themselves interchangeable parts." It is the reverse of Twain's idea of the Yankee's "man-factories," where he is going "to turn groping and grubbing automata into *men*." Twain himself, however, is aware that the factory has its own automatism, and he burlesques the process of mass production in a scene where Simon Stylites, praying on his pillar, is hitched up to a sewing machine in order to use his energy to produce cheap shirts for the masses. The Yankee also shrewdly understands that the creation of wants by advertising is necessary to the economy of popular consumption, and he uses knights to advertise stove polish before there are any stoves.

Both writers are joined as well by an amusing, American talent for using vernacular culture to poke fun at more pretentious or foolish high-mindedness. They both use baseball for that purpose. The Yankee replaces the chivalric ritual of a tournament with a baseball game, in which all the players are kings, to preserve the spirit of emulation without the violence of jousting. Doctorow shows Father's disdainful surprise at finding out that ballplayers are not Yale boys, but immigrants; and he portrays J. P. Morgan's even greater disdain and surprise when, after spending a chilly, itchy night, fruitlessly awaiting revelation from Osiris, in service to his obsession with a religious belief in reincarnation, he emerges from Egypt's Great Pyramid and is stunned to see the New York Giants baseball team scrambling over the Great Sphinx. Both Twain and Doctorow see the comic possibilities in the American reversal of the profane and the sacred.

Both writers, for all their demystifying spirit, do not escape, however, some sentimentality. Twain's Yankee improbably describes his marriage with Alesande ("Sandy") in Camelot as "the dearest and perfectest comradeship that ever was," and when he is dying, he yearns for Arthurian England again because it contains "all that is dear" to him, "all that could make life worth the living!" Doctorow's story is more tough-minded and sexually explicit, in the modern manner, but it sentimentalizes Walker's beautiful wife Sarah, who is portrayed as a pure innocent "who understood nothing but good-ness." Nevertheless, she attempts to kill her newborn child.

The time-travel idea poses a problem for Hank Morgan's republi-canism as it does for Coalhouse Walker's insistence on equality of respect, because both are obviously utopian in eras totally unprepared for them. Even the Yankee realizes that his educational work is cut out for him, and he some-times doubts its value because "no people in the world ever did achieve their freedom by goody-goody talk and moral suasion: it being immutable law that all revolutions that will succeed must *begin* in blood, whatever may answer afterward. If history teaches anything, it teaches that." He believes that a reign of terror would be necessary, as in the French Revolution, but he thinks that he is "the wrong man" for that role.

If training is everything, how can it be reversed? In the end, he discovers that it cannot be done: "The mass of the nation had swung their caps and shouted for the republic for about one day, and there an end!"

When the church, the nobles, and the gentry frowned upon them, the masses like sheep had begun "to gather to the fold." The Boss can only use his technological superiority to tip the balance in his favor, but it is only snatching defeat from the jaws of victory because of the ironic result of his success in extermination. Doctorow's Houdini does not have Merlin's triumph, but *Ragtime* does return to the magician after Walker, doomed by the scale of his own resistance to injustice, has been shot. On the day that the Archduke Ferdinand is assassinated, the magician, hanging upside down in a straitjacket during one of his daring escapes, remembers the boy, who had warned him about the event.

If we raise the question about the meaning of history in these two historical romances, we are faced with problematic answers in both cases. In the chapter "The Beginnings of Civilization," the Yankee brags that he has with his hidden program conspired to have "the civilization of the nineteenth century booming" under the nose of the kingdom, but he also calls it "as substantial a fact as any serene volcano, standing innocent with its smokeless summit in the blue sky and giving no sign of the rising hell in its bowels." Morgan speaks here as if he has condemned his own project before he has accomplished it. He sounds as if he were both a character and the author's mouthpiece, though the two outlooks are not the same. Morgan's bragging is characteristic; his metaphor of the volcano is not; it registers the profound unstable ambivalence of Twain's own relation to the nineteenth-century civilization that is the Boss's goal. Twain's uneasiness was accentuated by his frustrating investment in the Paige typesetting machine that was too fiendishly complicated ever to function properly, "a sublime magician" that bankrupted him soon after he finished his novel.

Twain does not entirely explode the idea of progress—at least not yet for himself, whatever the modern reader may think. The American and French revolutions still make sense out of history for him in 1889, as his letters show, even after he finished the book. Dan Beard, Twain's illustrator, whose work much pleased the author, read the novel as a "great missionary work to bring Americans back to the safe honest and manly position, intended for them to occupy, by their ancestors when they signed the declaration of independence." Twain told Howells, who edited the novel and liked its references to the French Revolution, that "next to the 4th of July & its results, it was the noblest and the holiest thing and the most precious that ever happened in this earth. And its gracious work is not done yet—nor anywhere in the remote neighborhood of it." Twain shared Howell's lament that "an aristocracy-loving oligarchy" had replaced "the American Republic."

Yet, either Twain's hold on the Yankee as a republican slips badly at some points or else he is trying to trace a change that modifies the Yankee's outlook by Arthurian influences. Morgan falls into a didactic reformer's meditation about the power of training over originality and then incongruously adds that all he thinks about in "this plodding sad pilgrimage, this pathetic drift between the eternities, is to look out and humbly live a pure and high and blameless life." It is as if he were a monk, more influenced by the sixth century than by the nineteenth. At another point Morgan seems to lose his republican identity when he sees the crowd doing homage to the king and reflects that "really there is something peculiarly grand about the gait and bearing of a king, after all." When the Yankee learns of the king's death, he is surprised because he did not think "that any wound could be mortal to him"; he seems to have succumbed to the idea, which he has always scorned, of the divinity of kings. These changes would be appropriate if Twain were bent on doing an international novel, in the mode of Henry James, with the European milieu having its forbidden attractions for the New World American, as it certainly did for Morgan's creator, who eventually resided in Vienna as if he were the American literary ambassador to Europe. Twain's Yankee has some of the same charm and naiveté of James's Christopher Newman as a fellow innocent abroad. Yet the novel cannot consistently be read in this way, even though it would make its ending more appropriate. The ending is problematic for both republicanism and feudalism. With Hank Morgan's "redoubled homelessness," as Walter Reed has called it, he becomes "exiled from the past that had previously exiled him from the present, and neither time nor place retains its identity."

Morgan's showmanship is replicated in his creator's performance as a comic writer, and Morgan's conflict between Camelot and Hartford replicates his creator's life as an exile from the South, a deserter from the Confederacy, who became an admirer of General Grant, whose memoirs he published, and then an independent Republican Mugwump, who voted in 1884 for the Democrat Grover Cleveland. Dualism is built into Clemens's choice of a pen name. In a notebook entry for 1897, appropriately made while he was living in Freud's Vienna, Twain expressed his interest in Stevenson's *Dr. Jekyll and Mr. Hyde* as an attempt to account for "the presence in us of another *person*." Twain went on to argue that experiments with hypnotism show that the two persons are not known to each other. He elaborated the idea into "a dream self" who can make "immense excursions" in the role of one's "spiritualized person." He humorously called his other self "Watson," rather than Mr. Hyde, but surely one of those "immense excursions" of his dream self was Hank Morgan's journey to Camelot.

Doctorow ends his story with the historical facts of the First World War and the deportation of Emma Goldman. But he also suggests the circularity of history by his last line, which refers to the murderer Harry K. Thaw, marching in the annual Armistice Day Parade, after obtaining his release from an asylum. This last note brings the music of time back to its beginning, as if none of the author's changes in the mosaic of the past has changed time's repetitious tune. Doctorow makes it explicit: "The era of Ragtime had run out, with the heavy breath of the machine, as if history were no more than a tune on a player piano."

Doctorow's point of view is hard to elicit from *Ragtime* because at one point he devotes a chapter to the meditations of the boy in Father's family as a theme for the novel. The boy seems to be a mouthpiece for the author in expressing thoughts too metaphysical for a child. Listening to his grandfather, the boy learns that "the forms of life were volatile and that everything in the world could as easily be something else." The boy finds proof of this in his own experience of "the instability of both things and people," and his own self-duplication in the mirror gives him a sense of having two selves "neither of which could claim to be the real one." (Mark Twain would have no trouble understanding him.) His conclusion is simple: "It was evident to him that the world composed and recomposed itself constantly in an endless process of dissatisfaction."

From this point of view, the world is pure contingency; nothing is necessary; time has no meaningful direction, and there is no place to stand from which judgments can be made. Twain himself did move towards this nihilism. With Doctorow, however, the boy's strange meditation is perhaps a rationalization for Doctorow's own playful rearrangements of history— anything might be anything else in the historical past. He has elsewhere cited the structuralist critic Roland Barthes on behalf of the proposition that historical discourse is itself "a particular form of fiction," and Doctorow concluded that fiction itself is "a kind of speculative history, perhaps a super-history, by which the available data for the composition is seen to be greater and more various in its sources than the historian supposes."

This erosion of any difference between fiction and history is too facile. It is even contradictory. The idea of a "superhistory" itself suggests some kind of referentiality, not explained by "fiction," yet it is not at all clear what constraints would discipline this new kind of history. Doctorow's byplay with historical characters, however, is not as fancy-free as it might appear at first, for it is controlled by his own considerable historical knowledge. To take what seems to be a bizarre example: Emma Goldman's orgasm-inducing massage of Evelyn Nesbit. The event never took place, but Goldman's criticisms of Nesbit's life in that scene are entirely authentic ideologically, and the erotic aspect of the moment connects with an historical fact: Goldman admitted that her friendship with Margaret Anderson, editor of the *Little Review*, had stirred feelings expressive of a "previous theoretic interest in sex variation."

Doctorow himself is not prepared to question that "some facts, for instance the Nazi extermination of the Jews, are so monstrous as to seem to stand alone." His example is revealing. His earlier novel *The Book of Daniel*, the strongest expression of Doctorow's historical consciousness, fictionalizes the story of the electrocuted Rosenbergs, as seen from the point of view of their children, to dramatize a larger theme involving three generations of Jewish-Americans and the defeat of their hopes for America. The only non-Jew in the novel is a black janitor.

Doctorow's Jewishness is not just a fact; it is the key to his personal interpretation of the history he has fictionalized, for he orients himself in it by his concern for the Jewish immigrants, whether they be Houdini, Tateh, or Emma Goldman. His views of the three cases are pertinent: Houdini "never developed what we think of as a political consciousness" because he could not "reason from his own hurt feelings." His obsession with escapes speaks to the immigrant experience of repression and to the function of show business as an opiate of the people. Tateh's upward mobility sacrifices his solidarity with the workers and compromises his artistic aspirations when he achieves affluence in making escapist movies. Emma Goldman, when arrested and asked for her views about Coalhouse Walker, simply says, "Wealth is the oppressor. Coalhouse Walker did not need Red Emma to learn that. He needed only to suffer." It is a radical perspective, married (in contrast to the usual socialist realism) to a modernist interest in technique, one that calls attention to its own fictionalizing.

In an interview, Doctorow has spoken of his admiration for Goldman's prophetic kind of Jewishness and of his growing up in "a lower-middle class environment of generally enlightened, socialist sensibility," stemming from his Russian grandfather's radical humanism. Indeed, *Ragtime*'s image of what historians used to call "the Progressive era" is notable for the conspicuous absence in it of persons drawn from the large, ideologically mixed group of non-immigrant native reformers, who were active in the period. Teddy Roosevelt appears in *Ragtime* only as a greedy big-game hunter, and Woodrow Wilson is seen only as a man "who wore rimless glasses and held moral views. When the Great War came he would wage it with the fury of the affronted."

Ragtime's image of the past is vulnerable to John Lukács's criticism that Doctorow's interest in America is in "*things* American—altogether on a different level from his knowledge of Jewish-American *thoughts*." His remoteness from the non-Jewish characters is indicated by the fact that (except for Walker) they have no particularizing names. What is most American about *Ragtime*, Lukács suggests, is its pictorial imagination and a rapidly moving clipped style, like the comics and the movies. Doctorow himself has spoken of his experiments in narrative discontinuity as being "akin to television—discontinuous and mind-blowing." It is curious that this experimental vanguardism in technique and this radicalism in political ideology should be akin to the mode of a mass medium. It testifies to the extent to which the 1960s marked the process in which, as Gerald Graff has pointed out, "the antinomian disparagement of 'bourgeois values' is celebrated by the agencies of publicity, exploited by the manipulators of cultural fashion, and emulated in personal conduct—an additional reason why the ante of provocation and radical experiment must continually be raised if the arts are to justify their vanguard credentials. . . . The point seems to have been reached at which artistic intransigence is indistinguishable from celebration of the dynamisms of mass society." *Ragtime*'s immense popularity illustrates his point.

Doctorow's sense of having a particular place to stand in Jewish-American radicalism, as a resource for his art, does not square with the boy's nihilistic metaphysical meditations in *Ragtime*. They may serve to rationalize Doctorow's fictionalizing of the historical material, but the material itself is viewed from the standpoint of the political sympathies that he acknowledges in the interview. The tension between the boy's meditations and his creator's responses in the interview defines the ambiguous quality of *Ragtime*'s point of view. It has led one perceptive critic to say that his art is "committed yet unconvinced," written out of a Jewish biblical view that "history is redemptive—and also out of Modernist doubt."

Twain's conflict is analogous to Doctorow's because of the tension between his view of history as redeemed by the American and French revolutions and his despair of majority human nature on whose good judgment democratic republicanism depends. The Yankee can assure the reader at one point that "there is plenty good enough material for a republic in the most degraded people that ever existed . . . if one could but force it out of its timid and suspicious privacy," but in the end he finds that the Arthurian masses are sheep. That disappointment could be explained, however, by the immense historical gap between his project and the society in which he is a stranger. But Morgan's ideological conflict intersected with his creator's self-division, the sense of having a separate "dream self." The artistic result for his novel was a lack of control reflected in its loose, rambling, repetitive, and anecdotal structure in contrast to the controlled and skillful braiding of historical and fictional lives in Doctorow's tale.

The competing elements in Hank Morgan are significant, however, because they are not just the author's. His sympathy for the oppressed majority and his deep suspicion of its judgment and ability would be competing themes as well in the Progressive movement itself, which often joined indignation against the trust, the political boss, and the sweatshop with a passion for organized efficiency. Hank Morgan has the artistic burden of having to carry more meanings than Doctorow's stylized characters. The Yankee contains a multitude, incorporating the showman, inventor, rationalist, entrepreneur, democratic reformer, dictatorial imperialist, and disenchanted romantic in his identity. This amplitude of meaning, however, is also what gives a modern resonance to Twain's fantastic version of history, which might otherwise simply have been reduced to what it is in its worst stretches—a heavy-handed tedious assault on monarchy and aristocracy. It is Hank Morgan's complexity that makes it possible for a contemporary reader to think of Twain's story as the precursor of a more sophisticated and more disenchanted form of black humor.

Twain needed a successor to go beyond his own speculative history. His literary sense of America, for all its close familiarity with a rich variety of American experience, lacked any appreciation for the immense process of immigration. It is historically symbolic that the year in which Twain began writing his story about the Yankee was the year that Emma Goldman emigrated from Russia to America, her romantic imagination stirred by anarchist literature and history. When the novel was published, she was moving to New York to join the anarchist movement. One of the important literary consequences of immigration was the development after the Second World War of many influential and highly accomplished Jewish-American novelists. Doctorow's *Ragtime* is one sign of that coming-of-age; and, among the historical figures in his book, Emma Goldman is the heroine. *Ragtime* is also a sign of the extent to which a Jewish grandchild of the immigrants can become what Mark Twain was, a popular interpreter of America to itself. Hank Morgan, meet Coalhouse Walker and Emma Goldman.

Doctorow in *Ragtime* cites Freud's remark that "America is a mistake, a gigantic mistake." Another Jewish-American novelist, Saul Bellow, referred to the remark in a speech, given shortly after the publication of *Ragtime*, to the Anti-Defamation League when accepting its America's Democratic Legacy Award. (Curiously enough, Bellow's *Henderson the Rain King* seems also to be partly inspired by Twain's fable: a Connecticut pig-farmer journeys to a fabulous Africa, encounters a primitive society, and becomes involved with a king.) Bellow used the occasion to counter Freud's judgment with the philosopher Morris Cohen's belief that "the future of liberal civilization was bound up with America's survival and its ability to make use of the heritage of human rights formulated by Jefferson and Lincoln." If this stirring confidence is missing from both Twain and Doctorow, it is partly explained by the difficulty in the late 1880s or in the Nixon years of hearing any trumpets sounding in the corridors of power for that great tradition. The final despair of Hank Morgan and Coalhouse Walker draws on that silence.

CHRISTOPHER D. MORRIS

Illusions of Demystification in Ragtime

Ragtime recounts and intertwines three main stories: of an upper middle-
class family identified only as Father, Mother, Mother's Younger Brother, and
the little boy; of Tateh, a Jewish Latvian immigrant; and of Coalhouse
Walker, a black pianist. The unnamed family is outwardly happy and prosperous, but over the course of the novel the three adults become estranged.
Tateh begins as an impoverished socialist but becomes an entrepreneur and
successful film-maker. Coalhouse Walker is humiliated by Irish firemen;
when his fiancée dies as an indirect result of Walker's search for justice, he
and a few confederates avenge themselves in acts of violence that eventually
lead to his death. In addition to these three connected plots, the novel
contains a number of characters and incidents from the years 1906 to 1914,
the chief temporal setting.

   Ragtime is the first of a series of works in which Doctorow experiments
with narration; more specifically, in this novel, *Loon Lake, Lives of the Poets,*
and *World's Fair,* the principal narrator cannot finally be determined, either
as "omniscient" or as an identifiable character. By detaching discourse from
any ultimately determinable source, this series of experiments may attest to
the severity of previously explored narrative predicaments; it shows in new
ways the delusion of the self as the autonomous manipulator of language; it
shows the writer orphaned by writing. At the same time, these narrational

From *Models of Misrepresentation: On the Fiction of E. L. Doctorow*. © 1991 by the University Press
of Mississippi.

innovations explore alternatives to the specter of eternal return. Of course, from the existence of experiment, no sure motive and no sure author can be deduced; indeed such an impossibility becomes a subject of these later works, perhaps because *Ragtime*'s experimental quest for alternatives is in the end disappointed.

The undecidability of the narrator of *Ragtime* is the result of the generic names assigned to the primary family: Father, Mother, Mother's Younger Brother, and the little boy. The first three names appear to imply that the narrator is the little boy, the only child in the family. However, throughout the novel the little boy is referred to in the third, not the first person, as though he is not the narrator. The anonymous narrative voice of *Ragtime* appears to be the voice of an American writing in about the year 1975, a person familiar with American cultural history and one who is given to both irony and rhetorical flourish. With one exception, this narrative voice refers to itself as the editorial "we" when generalizing about history ("This was the time in our history"). The exception to this practice occurs near the end of the novel, when Father's death at sea, in the sinking of the *Lusitania*, is recounted: "Poor father, I see his final exploration. He arrives at the new place, his hair risen in astonishment, his mouth and eyes dumb. His toe scuffs a soft storm of sand, he kneels and his arms spread in pantomimic celebration, the immigrant, as in every moment of his life, arriving eternally on the shore of his Self."

Some critics conclude, on the basis of this passage, that the narrator is the little boy grown up. This inference can be supported by other internal evidence; for example, the narrator's knowledge of a visit from Houdini comes from "the family archives." The full implications of this inference will be analyzed later; for now it is important to emphasize that the identification remains only inference: nowhere is the "I" explicitly identified as the little boy. Because the reader acquiesces to the convention of an anonymous narrator telling a story about characters known as Father, Mother, Mother's Younger Brother, and the little boy, the introduction of "I" instead of "we" does not remove the mystery. As other critics have maintained, the exceptional use of "I" can still refer to an anonymous narrator who names only an object of his narrative, not necessarily a relative.

The ambiguity does not end there, for a third possibility is that the narrator is the little girl, Tateh's daughter Sha. Since the Yiddish words for father and mother are Tateh and Mameh, she occupies a position in the narrative equivalent to that of the little boy. If Sha is the narrator, then the scene in which she and Jung mutually experience a moment of recognition or telepathy makes more comprehensible the narrator's otherwise inexplicable condemnation of Freud. Also, if Sha is the narrator, then the vivid detail in her recollection of a chance meeting with the little boy becomes more comprehensible. There is yet a fourth possibility, that the editorial "we" refers to both Sha and the little boy speaking together. At the end of the novel, in Atlantic City, the two children are depicted as ideal, telepathic playmates, in the spirit of Goethe's "elective affinities" or Shelley's complementary lovers. Although this possibility cannot be dismissed, it obviously creates new problems in examining the exceptional use of "I."

Geoffrey Galt Harpham captures the radical quality of Doctorow's experiment when he refers to "the unplaceability of [the novel's] narrative voice." In fact, the narrational uncertainty is an enigma that forces the reader to concentrate on the issue of pronoun references. The identity of the narrator can be decided only by the conferral of equivocal referents to the pronouns "I" and "we," linguistic shifters without inherent meaning. Four different interpretations of the novel can flow from the four different identifications of the narrator; at the same time, each ends in contradiction, for to adopt one is to exclude others equally plausible: male pronouns exclude the female; singular pronouns exclude the plural; the three specific attributions (the boy, the girl, both) exclude the anonymous narrator; and vice versa in each case. This wholesale indeterminacy, which mandates error in interpretation, forces the reader to entertain the possibility that the whole concept of a narrator may be only the fabrication of novels.

In order to read the novel, however, ultimate uncertainty cannot be tolerated; some attribution of a source to the words must be made. One act of naming that respects the enigma is to consider the narrator "double," that is, *simultaneously* two different entities, a specific attribution and a separate, anonymous voice. In fact, such a practice could find some support in the novel's many images of duplication, especially in this description of the little boy's gazing at himself in the mirror: "He would gaze at himself until there were two selves facing one another, neither of which could claim to be the real one." If no determinable source for this sentence (or for others in *Ragtime*) can be settled upon, then it embodies the very doubleness it describes. It suggests that an integral Cartesian self is not the originator of discourse but that, instead, a story can be told by *two equally unreal entities*. In this way, the novel's two unreal sources seem to demystify the illusion of a single consciousness as narrator.

Nevertheless, the demystification is only *seeming*, since in any practical reading it is next to impossible to posit unreal, plural sources. In the next few paragraphs, the awkward "narrator(s)" and "they" are used to refer to the narrative voice. (It is understood that this procedure is already in error. In this state of indeterminacy, to name at all is already to err; any "insight" afforded by the problem of the novel's narrator(s) is made possible, after all, only by a prior blindness.) The reader is falsely demystified in the attempt to interpret characters as well as narrator(s), but that delusion is anticipated in the narrator(s). For example, the very first pages of the novel try to represent the ragtime era: "Everyone wore white in summer. Tennis racquets were hefty and the racquet faces elliptical. There was a lot of sexual fainting. There were no Negroes. There were no immigrants."

After one page of further description, centering on the murder of Stanford White by Harry K. Thaw, the narrator(s) write: "Evelyn fainted. She had been a well-known artist's model at the age of fifteen. Her underclothes were white. Her husband habitually whipped her. She happened once to meet Emma Goldman, the revolutionary. Goldman lashed her with her tongue. Apparently there *were* Negroes. There *were* immigrants."

The narrator(s) now speak from the vantage point of a completed narration, from knowledge supposedly derived from the tale, because they refer to the meeting between Evelyn and Emma, which has not yet been narrated. At the same time, the futility of their own "learning process" is obvious in the irony and self-mockery that accompanies their supposed demystification. Paul de Man's two-stage process is evident here: first, the reader believes in a demystification; next, that demystification is perceived as only a construct. What will be the value of narrating (or reading) *Ragtime* if the illusions it depicts can be destroyed only by new illusions?

In fact the narrator(s)—whether anonymous or specific—never learn; illusions persist until the end. Consider first the case of the anonymous narrator, whose continuing blindness is brought home to the reader on the last page, in the description of the origin and nature of Tateh's new films. Tateh gets his idea for the films one day while watching the three children (his daughter, his stepson, and Coalhouse Walker III) playing together in his California backyard. The narrator(s) endorse the films' sentimental depiction of a "society of ragamuffins, like all of us, a gang, getting into trouble and getting out again." Of course, the "vision" of these new films is a gross misrepresentation of the bulk of the action of *Ragtime*, which tells of violent, incurable racial and ethnic conflict, but the narrator(s) identify themselves with the gang of ragamuffins, thereby accepting Tateh's Pollyannaish vision and revealing a blindness to the events of their own completed narration.

Now suppose the narrators are identified specifically, that is, as the boy, the girl, or both. In this alternative, either or both specific narrators, in their California backyard, serve as the very model for the cinematic misrepresentation that Tateh, in ignorance, perpetuates. There is no retrospective denunciation of this irony. If error is generated and perpetuated in this way, then narrating is misrepresenting, learning is illusory, and the circularity of error is inescapable.

Illusory demystifications also afflict the major characters in the three principal plots. Within the New Rochelle family, Father is at first depicted as the embodiment of the unexamined pieties of his day, benign capitalism and patriotism, which—as we seem to learn—mask exploitation, racism, and sexism. He is a manufacturer of the signifier of these illusions, the American flag, which draws credulous immigrants in ships to New York Harbor. Over the course of the novel, Father undergoes two seeming transformations. The first occurs during his trip to the Pole with Peary, when his adultery with an Esquimo woman appears to teach him a new knowledge of female sexuality, but despite this knowledge, he quickly becomes emotionally and sexually estranged from Mother. A second false lesson grows out of his contact with Coalhouse Walker, which seems to teach him American racism, but despite this knowledge, Father commits himself even more faithfully to the patriotic dimension of his business; eventually his firm supplies the government with advanced munitions. In both cases Father's supposed demystification is only apparent; he remains in thrall to the false values symbolized by the now-discredited flag he manufactures.

Mother also undergoes a seeming demystification. After she is forced to assist in the management of Father's flag-making company, Mother no longer holds the world of business in awe. As critics have noted, Mother seems to become, simply through practical experience, a working example of the abstract doctrines of women's liberation espoused by Emma Goldman, but this supposed learning process does not lead to her independence and autonomy. Instead, Mother's liberation from Father's sexism is finally accomplished through her enchantment with another man, another manufacturer of (and believer in) illusions, Tateh. Tateh's new false identity, as Baron Ashkenazy, adds to the sense in which she is again seduced as soon as she flees from Father's demystified values. It is as if one set of illusions can be exposed only when they are exchanged for the new.

Such empty learning is obvious in Mother's Younger Brother, whose life first has meaning for him when he is dazzled by the glitz of Evelyn Nesbit. The memorable scene in which Mother's Younger Brother observes her from a closet recalls the story of the intrusion of Actaeon into the bath of Diana, an allusion suggested by other details as well. For this intrusion, Actaeon is punished by being transformed into a stag that is later hounded to death by his own dogs; like him, Mother's Younger Brother becomes a kind of prey, possessed by self-destructive delusions. First the spell of Evelyn herself victimizes him, but he recovers from this mystification with the aid of a new belief system, Emma Goldman's anarchism, which propels him into the causes of Coalhouse Walker and Emiliano Zapata. Mother's Younger Brother believes that in adopting Goldman's anarchism he has demystified the American political system. But the self-contradiction in anarchism is made clear by Goldman's highly organized, very unanarchic way of life: a small but telling example is her habit of having a change of clothes and a book ready in case of imprisonment on short notice. A *purely* "anarchic way of life" may not be possible. In order to help Coalhouse Walker, Mother's Younger Brother and Walker's anarchic confederates must be highly disciplined. As a munitions expert, Mother's Younger Brother has sophisticated technical skills; moreover, this intellectual prowess appears in blueprints later put to use in maintaining American state power—the opposite of anarchy. In any case, Mother's Younger Brother's false belief in his demystification of politics becomes clear in the suicidal final stages of his career when he loses his hearing just before dying in Zapata's cause.

Insofar as the boy may be considered solely as a character, his education follows a familiar literary path of imaginative and sexual awakening which holds forth the prospect of exchanging innocence for reliable knowledge. From his beginnings in a nearly solipsistic absorption in his own small world, the boy becomes aware of the world through examining its detritus—the oil-stained letter from Father, the silhouettes of Evelyn Nesbit discarded by his despondent uncle. He passes through moments of usual childhood belief in the omnipotence of thought. He becomes aware of his mother's sexuality. By the end of the novel, the boy experiences a relationship of ideal intersubjectivity with Tateh's daughter Sha. So outlined, the boy's maturation is an apparent demystification, a movement from innocent illusions, through engagement with the world, to love, and yet this demystification vanishes whenever the reader recalls the possibility that the boy alone narrates the events. When this thought obtrudes, a whole series of new considerations rapidly destroys confidence in his learning. As a sixty-year-old cultural historian, the grown boy endows himself, in retrospect, with preternatural powers concerning the assassination of Archduke Franz Ferdinand. He reconstructs his parents' sexual relations with detail bordering on the obsessive or voyeuristic; he blandly narrates Tateh's erotic attraction to his mother while his Father sleeps. On other occasions he is ironic; by kidnapping young men, he writes, Harry K. Thaw was "beginning to work out his problems." He inserts dogmatic opinions about cultural history, makes generalizations about history without supplying evidence, and concludes by imagining himself as part of a happy "society of ragamuffins." In short, study of the boy as narrator suggests that he has shed the illusions of youth only to acquire new ones in maturity.

If the experiences of the New Rochelle family suggest deceit in the idea of learning, they are no more its victims than are Tateh or Coalhouse Walker. Some of the illusions have already been noted which change Tateh from a starving Jewish socialist—one who adheres strictly to Hebraic codes governing adultery—into a pseudonymous, seducing director of films that misrepresent his country and his past. Although Tateh sees his progress as a movement away from the mystifications of politics and class conflict, the reader sees that he gains success only by renouncing his heritage and accepting a vision of America that contradicts his own suffering. Tateh does not regress from an earlier, authentic perception to later illusion; on the contrary, nothing in the novel suggests that his treatment of Mameh, his denunciation of Evelyn Nesbit, his flight from the strike of Lawrence, or his work on flip-books represents either progress or regress. Indeed, critics believe that these episodes, too, can be interpreted as symptoms of blindness in Tateh. Thus his life may be regarded as a series of false demystifications, the shift from one illusion to another.

Of all of the major characters, only Coalhouse Walker seems a probable candidate to embody an authentic demystification. The music he plays gives the novel its presiding metaphor and principle of organization; it recalls the nonverbal alternatives to delusion tested in Red Bloom's jazz and Billy Bathgate's songs. Walker's belated courtship of Sarah seems a direct expression of human dignity. His revolt against racial humiliation appears to be designed to demystify, to expose contradictions in the heart of the political and economic systems. His insistence on the particular—his car and Willie Conklin—seems to give the lie to other characters' absorption in theory and fantasy. As long as readers concentrate on the Coalhouse plot by itself, the novel provides a seeming anchor by which to judge the circularity of its other characters' behavior: whatever the excesses of his revolt, it is a response that at least confronts a world that other characters avoid or flee. The novel's movement toward climax proceeds inexorably. The precipitation of an ultimate disclosure is promised in the still tableau of Coalhouse bending over the plunger wired to blow up the Morgan Library, to explode the decadent repository of Western metaphysics. The considerable intellectual recourses of the novel—its critiques of enlightenment, of capitalism, of the melting pot, of America itself—are evidently at stake in the moment of Coalhouse's silent surrender. If the lives of other characters remain mystified, then this moment may bring truth. Such is the expectation wrought.

The story of Walker is drained of this potential for signification, however, the moment the reader sees it intertertextually, as the adaptation of Heinrich von Kleist's "Michael Kohlhaas" (1808). Coalhouse now appears not a representation of an authentic mode of existence but of only another representation. As a sign his putative referent—racial or human justice, the dignity of man—is replaced by another sign, Kleist's Michael Kohlhaas. Likewise Sarah now recalls Kohlhaas's wife Lisbeth, Booker T. Washington, Luther, Conklin, Junker von Tronka. Since Kleist's story, in turn, is based on a previous text (a medieval chronicle of incidents in history befalling one Hans Kohlhasen), there is now the prospect of even further regress. As recent studies suggest, interpreting Kleist is no simple matter. The famous "deadpan" narrator of "Michael Kohlhaas" provides a foretaste of this difficulty in his initial remark that Michael Kohlhaas was "one of the most upright and at the same time one of the most terrible men of his day." If Coalhouse is derived from a Michael Kohlhaas who is undecidable from the outset, then contemporary interpretation will only commit once more, in modern trappings, the necessary error of interpretation exposed in the execution of Kohlhaas. Instead of escaping the circularity afflicting other characters' phony learning, Coalhouse Walker, too, becomes a manifestation of Nietzsche's "eternal reiteration of the same thing."

Once this moment of intertextuality occurs, the problem of narration becomes a new morass. Whether Coalhouse's story is being told by an anonymous or nonanonymous narrator, the narration now loses its once-supposed anchor in the real. If the story of Coalhouse/Kohlhaas is told by the boy or the girl grown old, or both, the novel's credibility collapses: earlier suspicions of their illusions are confirmed; they become palpable fiction writers. Even if the Coalhouse/Kohlhaas story is told by an anonymous narrator, its meaning in *Ragtime* now depends on a prior interpretation of Kleist's story; but that story's narrator, like its critical history, warns that secure interpretation may be impossible. Once again, the very moment that insight into *Ragtime* appears to be approachable, blindness is evident. The reader sees in fleeting moments of demystification only phantasm.

Inducing this momentary illusion of learning is one of the exertions of art. In *Ragtime* the perils of that effort are dramatized in Houdini, who has been analyzed as a figure for the artist. Houdini follows in the tradition of the artist-as-performer, which was begun with the image of the clown in "The Songs of Billy Bathgate." In addition, he continues the depiction of the artist as struggling with the representation of death in ways observable in Blue and Daniel. Like his predecessors, he strives to demystify but only spellbinds and, in so doing, shows the limitations of art in the crucial test case of representation, death.

Even before the death of his mother, Houdini's feats are geared to defy mortality. After escaping from sealed milk cans and chains, Houdini asks to be buried alive but finds he cannot escape. Nevertheless he continues to be fascinated by events that seem to defy death; he pays homage to a sandhog who somehow survived an explosion during the construction of a tunnel under the East River. After the death of his mother, Houdini's acts become frightening as he risks death with even greater intensity. Houdini's art raises the Heideggerian issue of the fallacy in representations of death. In this way, Houdini also resembles Blue: death is the end point and origin of their quests. And like Daniel, Houdini feels driven to display his artistry in the composition of a death scene. In retrospect these representational efforts were doomed from the outset. In Houdini's case, it becomes obvious that death cannot be truly represented by artifice (if only because no successful performance could be iterable). Thus, even in his harrowing performances, Houdini can only repeat an artifice that can never "more closely approximate."

This futility also haunts other representations. After his mother dies, Houdini arranges framed photographs of his mother in his New York brownstone "to suggest her continuing presence." He puts a picture of his mother on the very chair in which she posed for it. He hangs a picture of her entering the house inside his door. This futility is not confined to visual representations. A delusion of presence is induced by the music-box songs his mother once loved and "the redolence of her wardrobe." These are pathetic models of misrepresentation.

In this delusion Houdini nevertheless tries both to perfect his own art and to find a "genuine medium" to make the absent present. Even as he persists in this delusion, he works to demystify the artifice of others, his colleagues or competitors in the art of deathly illusionism. Desperate to make contact with his deceased mother, Houdini hires a detective agency to investigate the claims of spiritual mediums; he casts about for some scientific means of reaching his mother. Like his performances, these efforts at enlightenment cannot succeed, because they assume that the absent can be represented. For the reader of Houdini (as of Blue and Daniel), death uncovers the dysfunction of language.

Whatever its dysfunction, there seems to be no alternative to the artifice, whether the illusions of Houdini or such fiction as *Ragtime*, to which they allude. This sense of the absolute necessity for illusion-making and illusion-believing is conveyed by the narrator's comment that today "nearly fifty years since [Houdini's] death, the audience for escapes is even larger." In this famous aside the narrator makes self-canceling statements about illusions; audiences, like readers, are gullible, but the narrator—the fiction-writer of the Coalhouse/Kohlhaas story, for example—is busy writing the "escape." What Miller calls "varnishing"—the authorial assertion of a center that reveals, instead, its own incipient collapse—is once again disclosed. Like Houdini, the narrator demonstrates that both writer and reader, performer and audience, are escape artists. It is as if the attempt to represent must neccessarily delude with the false promise of escape, in the face of a necessity.

If escape from delusion is impossible, the events of human history become repetitions, duplications of attempted escapes and failures. This is, again, the "burdensome thought" of Nietzsche's eternal return, which haunted Doctorow's earlier work. In *Ragtime* the eternal return is "the duplicable event," a phrase that links reiteration in history with narration.

The phrase first appears in an account of the ragtime era: "All across the continent merchants pressed the large round keys of their registers. The value of the duplicable event was everywhere perceived. Every town had its ice-cream soda fountain of Belgian marble. Painless Parker the Dentist everywhere offered to remove your toothache. At Highland Park, Michigan, the first Model T automobile built on a moving assembly line lurched down a ramp and came to rest in the grass under a clear sky."

The duplicable event is here associated with a seemingly inexorable loss of individuation—a kind of cultural entropy of the sort depicted in the novels of Thomas Pynchon. The imminent homogenization of America will be accompanied by an equivalence of people and of things mandated by Henry Ford's application of the principle to industry: "not only that the parts of the finished product be interchangeable, but that the men who build the products be themselves interchangeable parts." Both passages suggest that behind the apparent diversity of men, of machines, and of environment lie only the monotonous repetitions of history.

Of course, repetition is a structural principle of the plot. Harry K. Thaw has two trials. Evelyn Nesbit bathes Tateh's daughter, Sha; then Emma Goldman, in turn, ministers to Evelyn's body. Theodore Dreiser repeatedly tries to find the perfect alignment in his room. Admiral Peary searches for the precise position of the North Pole. To win back Sarah, Coalhouse repeats his Sunday visits. Tateh cries twice for his daughter and makes numerous silhouettes of Evelyn Nesbit. J. P. Morgan finds evidence of the same doctrine of reincarnation in Rosicrucianism, in Giordano Bruno, in the Hermetica. Scott Joplin rags are heard in New Rochelle and Atlantic City. The first explosion at a fire station is followed by a second. These explosions are framed by the tunnel blast that nearly kills a sandhog and by Younger Brother's detonations in Mexico. Booker T. Washington's mediation is followed by Father's. Coalhouse Walker's ruined Model-T is replaced by a rebuilt one. Tateh's films are made in series, as sequels. This list only begins to suggests the extent of repetition in the novel. The futility and monotony of such repetition suggest that history signifies nothing at all.

This suggestion is supported by the novel's many scenes of imprisonment and false liberation. Houdini's numerous escape attempts result only in
the persistence of his delusion that human effort may produce some correct
understanding of death. The futility of Houdini's imprisonments and escapes
is repeated in the imprisonment and eventual release of Harry K. Thaw,
events that purport to distinguish madness from sanity but obviously do not.
Like the incarceration of Susan in *The Book of Daniel*, the institutional distinction between madness and sanity in *Ragtime* is shown to be fictional. The
saddest example of phony freedom is the experience of immigrants, who are
first "arranged on benches in waiting pens" after landing in New York. The
presumed further liberation of the immigrant can be tracked in Tateh; the
novel's imagery suggests that Tateh's life in New York is also a kind of prison
from which he makes several escapes—first to Lawrence, Massachusetts, then
to Philadelphia, Atlantic City, and California. However, each of his attempts
at human or spiritual liberation lands him in a new mirage world: the "Hollywood ending" of *Ragtime* repeats the Disneyland climax of *The Book of Daniel*
and anticipates the dream pavilions of *World's Fair*. In *Ragtime* the duplicable
events means the movement from one imprisoning illusion to another. Each
promise of demystification turns out to be false, a model of misrepresentation.

A similar effect is created by the many empty coincidences in the novel.
Readers agree that the novel teems with them. For example, Tateh got his
start on a career in film-making by designing flip-books for the Franklin
Novelty Company in Philadelphia. The same company manufactured a
cheap pamphlet that taught Henry Ford the doctrine of reincarnation. Stanford White planned the home of Mrs. Stuyvestant Fish, who hired Houdini
to entertain guests at her party; White's assistant, Charles McKim, designed
the Morgan Library. In Egypt, J. P. Morgan sees the same New York Giants
baseball team that Father took the little boy to see at the home ballpark. Such
intersections of independent plot lines seem portentous, but in the end they
reveal nothing. Equally teasing are the accounts of Freud's visit to America
to lecture at Clark University in Worcester, Massachusetts, and of Theodore
Dreiser's artistic depression following the publication of *Sister Carrie*. Such
coincidences seem to invite interpretation; indeed, critical discourse about
the novel, including the one now in progress, has been drawn to them as loci
of meaning, but Arthur Saltzman aptly summarizes the mystifying effect of
this lure: "If we are gratified by the connections our narrator makes for us
. . . we are still disheartened by how seemingly fruitless those connections
are." By themselves, coincidences express nothing other than their existence;
the impulse to make them represent creates new error.

This de Manian delusion in reading is underscored by a second reference to the duplicable event, one that further links the repetitions and coin-

cidences of history to narration. It occurs as the boy perceives the "instability of both things and people." In a kind of radical solipsism, he acknowledges no permanent reality separate from his own perception. The movies and his grandfather's stories are images of an importance equal to his hairbrush or his window, which seem to conform to his will. He listens to the Victrola and plays "the same record over and over, whatever it happened to be, as if to test the endurance of a duplicated event." In this passage the boy—one of the putative narrators—occupies himself in a *double* repetition: the recorded song is of course a "duplication," and the repeated playing duplicates it. Whatever the narrator's identity, narration and reading may resemble the repeated playing of the recorded song; both are double duplications that have the effect of testing art's "endurance." The open-ended "playing" of the song is like the potentially infinite, repetitive sequence of reading and interpretation. Only in this logical necessity can it be said that the duplicated event of art endures.

The novel seems to endorse the boy's version of the eternal return, as meaningless redundancy, especially when that idea is contrasted with more obviously mystified versions, such as J. P. Morgan's belief in reincarnation. According to Morgan's doctrine, divinely inspired leaders reappear throughout history to lead people and to inaugurate new epochs. In a secret room in his Library, Morgan propounds this theory to Henry Ford. He finds evidence for it in Rosicrucianism, Giordano Bruno, and the Hermetica. The first such leaders, Morgan confides, were the Egyptian pharaohs. In the belief that he and Ford are modern avatars of those demigods, Morgan invites the industrialist to accompany him on a trip to the Pyramids. In the end, Ford subscribes to the theory, with some ironic detachment; and though Morgan travels to Egypt alone, the two become sole members of "The Pyramid."

In this famous fictional meeting, Morgan and Ford accept a theory of history as the eternal return which resembles the Nietzschean doctrines of the *Übermensch* and cyclical history set forth in *Thus Spake Zarathustra*. That Morgan sees himself as an *Übermensch* is suggested by echoes of the Nietzschean hero: "He knew as no one else the cold and barren reaches of unlimited success. The ordinary operations of his intelligence and instinct over the past fifty years had made him preeminent in the affairs of nations and he thought this said little for mankind. . . . I have no peers, Morgan said. . . . It seemed an indisputable truth. Somehow he had catapulted himself beyond the world's value system."

Morgan's philosophy of the eternal return is formidable indeed. Like Emma Goldman's anarchism, it has the potential—if endorsed by the novel—to justify such radical actions as the revolt of Coalhouse Walker or Mother's Younger Brother's terrorism. In addition, Morgan's version of the *Übermensch* could provide intellectual sanction for Harry K. Thaw's murder of Stanford White or for Tateh's abandonment of his earlier Hebraic code. In short, Morgan's Nietzscheanism proposes a transvaluation of values by which any individual action could be justified. With so much at stake for interpretation, the novel's treatment of Morgan's theory must be carefully evaluated.

The contradiction in Morgan's "practical Nietzscheanism" is made apparent in his meeting with Ford and in his trip to Egypt. In the meeting, Morgan says he suspected Ford might be an embodiment of a divine mission when he noticed a resemblance between Ford's features and the mask on the sarcophagus of Seti the First. In other words, an underlying belief in representation is a condition of Morgan's Nietzscheanism: an *Übermensch* must be discernible. The shakiness of this assumption is evident enough in the resemblance Morgan claims to have found. Ford's deflating reply—that the doctrine of transmigration may be apprehended without the trappings of Morgan's intellectualism—further gives the lie to the existence of the necessary signs, from manuscripts, pamphlets, or physiognomy, that Morgan valorizes.

Morgan's historical Nietzscheanism is undermined in the laughable account of his trip to Egypt. There, he spends the night in the King's Chamber of the Great Pyramid, hoping to learn the disposition by Osiris of his ka, or soul, and his ba, or physical vitality. These lofty aspirations are brought up short when the experience yields only two results: he dreams of a former life as a peddler, and he is bitten by bedbugs. Confused, Morgan reasons as follows: "He decided one must in such circumstances make a distinction between false signs and true signs. The dream of the peddler in the bazaar was a false sign. The bedbugs were a false sign. A true sign would be the glorious sight of small red birds with human heads flying lazily in the chamber, lighting it with their own incandescence. These would be ba birds, which he had seen portrayed in Egyptian wall paintings. But as the night wore on, the ba birds failed to materialize."

Morgan's pathetic distinction between true signs and false signs recalls Blue's wish, in *Welcome to Hard Times*, for the "good signs" of spring that keep life going, and as with Blue, the wish is circular. Notice that Morgan's desultory gropings for meaning are prompted by previous representations, the ba birds in the Egyptian wall paintings. Of course, the fallacy that human destiny in history is readable in resemblances and recurrent signs is fundamental to many doctrines other than Nietzsche's; it is evident in Calvinist "signs of election" or the historiography of Thomas Carlyle, for example.

Thus in the character of Morgan, the novel exposes the impoverishment of this tradition, that an "eternal return" can be read in history.

By contrast, the little boy's version seems less mystified; he is content to register the empty repetitions of the world without conferring meaning on them. In this aloofness—a kind of refusal to read—the boy separates himself from all of the other characters, not simply Morgan, who cannot tolerate a condition of uninterpreted redundancy. The boy resists the hermeneutic need to assign a meaning to repetition, preferring instead to see himself and the universe as part of history's dumb metamorphosis: "It was evident to him that the world composed and recomposed itself constantly in an endless process of dissatisfaction . . . the boy's eyes saw only the tracks made by the skaters, traces quickly erased of moments past, journeys taken."

This cold, ontologically neutral view of change is also expressed in the boy's fascination with the eternal return in baseball: "[Father] turned to his son. What is it you like about this game, he said. The boy did not remove his gaze from the diamond. The same thing happens over and over, he said. The pitcher throws the ball so as to fool the batter into thinking he can hit it. But sometimes the batter does hit it, the father said. Then the pitcher is the one who is fooled, the boy said."

The boy's acceptance of deception and pure repetition seem to fit the plot of *Ragtime*. Moments of insight, supposed climaxes, and turning points are revealed, in retrospect, to be hollow: Evelyn Nesbit seems to galvanize the lives of Tateh and Mother's Younger Brother, then runs off with a dance-hall musician; Coalhouse Walker brings official New York to a crisis, then dies, his confederates and Mother's Younger Brother dispersed to other causes; the marriage of Mother and Father gradually deteriorates; the obsession behind Houdini's quest to pierce the veil of death recedes, and he is last seen repeating old escape tricks; the sensational murderer, Harry K. Thaw, returns to march in an Armistice Day parade. Far from ratifying the idea that history has a meaning, the inconclusive action of *Ragtime* makes time appear random and open-ended, in keeping with the tradition of *Big as Life* and Doctorow's other novels.

But this conclusion is also incorrect, confounding character-narrator and author. Recall that as character in his California backyard, the boy served as a model for Tateh's misrepresentation, and that as narrator, the boy never learned. So the false impression of insight must be amended again. The boy's view of time, history, and change is no loftier than that of the other characters; it is only another illusion that reading, afterwards, discovers.

BERNDT OSTENDORF

The Musical World of Doctorow's Ragtime

What could E. L. Doctorow have had in mind when he chose *Ragtime* as the title of his best-selling novel of 1975? No more than a loose metaphor for an age if we go by the published literary criticism; for most of it focuses on narrative technique and the book's success or failure as a historical novel. It is time therefore to start reading the book completely, beginning with its title and the epigram by the black composer Scott Joplin.

Ragtime refers to a particular music, now considered timeless. But the term also identifies that era in the history of American music from 1896 to 1917, when Ragtime set a new agenda in popular music and ushered in a social revolution. While the first strains of this "novelty music" were heard as early as 1896, the ragtime "craze" began after the turn of the century. The time frame of Doctorow's novel extends from Stanford White's murder in 1906 to America's entry into World War I in 1916. The memory of the young boy, the principal narrator, reaches backward to 1902, when the house in New Rochelle was built, and forward to the marriage of Tateh and Mother in 1917, which happens to be the year of the Russian Revolution and of the first jazz recording. Doctorow's novel, then, covers the exact period when historical ragtime was a dominant style of American popular music.

Ragtime's historical significance and current meaning are not identical, and the novel's epistemology is inspired by this difference. Historical ragtime

From *American Quarterly* 43, no. 4 (December 1991): 579–597. © 1991 by the American Studies Association.

was pioneered by blacks and initially resisted by the Victorian musical establishment. But after 1900 ragtime lost its association with black musicians and became a "white" music by national adoption. Hence black sounds entered the American mainstream in whiteface, as it were. James T. Maher writes: "The straight line from plantation music to the earliest recorded jazz (1917) runs through ragtime: the impact of Negro syncopation is the major force in the Americanization of our popular music." After 1917 ragtime was replaced by jazz and Tin Pan Alley and gradually lost its status as the queen of popular music.

The more recent renaissance of ragtime began in the early seventies with a best-selling classical record of Joplin rags, recorded by Joshua Rifkin, a classical pianist with degrees from Juilliard and Princeton. The rehabilitation of ragtime by the musical establishment would have pleased Joplin, who had always insisted that his compositions should be listed under classical music. But ragtime soon reasserted its crossover appeal and went slumming again. The success of the musical score of the film *The Sting* restored ragtime to the popular market and expanded its contemporary audience considerably. However, it also helped to increase the distance from historical ragtime and to obscure further the role of its creators. The film score of Joplin's music was nominated for two Oscars, but the awards were given not to Joplin, but to Marvin Hamlish, who arranged the music for the film.

If the ragtime renaissance of the seventies, which undoubtedly inspired the naming of the novel and helped to launch it to best-seller status, was a belated recognition of the music both in the classical and popular markets, it also constituted a subtle form of collective repression. A renaissance filters out the blood, sweat, and tears of the historical place and time that it evokes, while it foregrounds current, often nostalgic desire. This renaissance lifted ragtime out of its context and turned its history into metaphor or image (a key word in the novel). The historical music became the vehicle of a nostalgia for history with a set of associations quite different from the webs of significance in which the original producers and consumers were caught. The "rearrangement" of black-derived ragtime in our structure of feeling, credit for which goes to the rearranger, mirrors the previous, "mistaken" adoption of this black foundling and its successful career in white ragtime schools and publications. Understandably, the current nostalgia did not recognize that ragtime was in its time a revolutionary and an embattled black music and that one of its proud black creators died poor, alone, and maddened by the lack of public recognition. Indeed, the current "trivialized" recognition of ragtime as part of a throwaway musical culture may have shifted attention away from the story of ragtime which *Ragtime* tries to tell.

Doctorow articulates a justification for the "rediscovery" of ragtime and its age through the boy narrator, who not only "treasures anything discarded," but also is particularly interested in "meaning perceived through neglect." This editorial aside invites us to read the novel as an attempt to reconstruct the conflict-laden musical universe at the time when ragtime entered into the mainstream of American music and to restore to consciousness what was repressed in the renaissance of ragtime. This reading is supported by a telling detail from Doctorow's biography which he elaborated on in his novel *World's Fair*. Doctorow's father ran a record store in Manhattan that served a mixed clientele of whites and blacks, and his uncle, a once famous jazz musician who had fallen on bad times, passed his knowledge of music history on to his nephew.

The "historical" novel *Ragtime*, then, is a form of biographical-anthropological fiction that apprehends and portrays, from the historical moment of the 1970s, the world of human desire and action of the turn of the century—history in the mode of participant observation over an interval of seventy years. This narrative stance, which deliberately merges past significance and present meaning, met with a mixed reaction from the novel's critics. Though the book was a popular success and received high praise, it was also called the most overrated novel of the year. Historians in particular found it antihistorical, anachronistic, frivolous, and irresponsible, a charge which, as this essay will argue, can only be upheld by readers deaf to the musical message.

The disagreement over *Ragtime* hinges on the question of truth in historiography and historical fiction. Historian Cushing Strout, who has written the most articulate critique of the novel, praises Hawthorne's, Twain's and Dos Passos's historical fictions, even those that bend empirical facts for the sake of a moral point, but finds little to praise in *Ragtime*. On the one hand, Strout argues, *Ragtime* as narrative lacks an integrating, objective point of view. On the other hand, he faults the author for having obvious political, that is, subjective interests, namely to give the black protagonist Coalhouse Walker Jr. more dignity and power than is his historical due. Strout argues that "its unannounced anachronisms make incredible this tale of a ragtime pianist . . . All these details are in a contemporary idiom at odds with the era of ragtime." Most objectionable of all, Doctorow mixes "fidelity to historical details in 1902" with his own inventions. Therefore "the ragtime era is as frivolously manipulated as if it were only a tune." The book, he continues, represents an attack on neutrality, objectivity, and impartiality as virtues in historiography, and it boils down to a cheapening of historiographical truth by obscuring the line between history and fiction. It is a "subversion of the conventional form by its deliberate affronts to the historical imagination." Indeed, Doctorow breaks all conventions: "it is too historical for farce, too light-hearted for the rage of black humor, and too caricatured for history." Last but not least, it is irreverent and populist: "appropriately this book was promoted in the media like a popular song, whatever his own intentions may have been." This list of sins against Clio's purpose adds up to a summary statement of Doctorow's aesthetic.

Hardest to swallow for Strout is Doctorow's loss of faith in the truth of historiographical "fictions," to which the latter pleads guilty in his essay "False Documents." There Doctorow merely radicalizes certain doubts that have inspired modern novelists and historians since Flaubert and Nietzsche: like them, he entertains a philosophical skepticism towards all man-made narratives. Like them, he doubts the "dogma of immaculate perception" (Nietzsche) embraced by a Rankean historiography which purports to narrate history "as it actually was." Like them, he realizes that all narrated facts are socially constructed and therefore charged with human interest beyond their mere facticity. Inevitably, our modern historical consciousness is a product and victim of the market of ideas. It has become—like the world it reflects—industrialized, that is, saturated with ready-made, prepackaged and widely disseminated narratives of the social and historical sciences. One might add on a critical note that the philosophy that fuels Doctorow's doubt is not exactly revolutionary and has in its turn become a bit of an industry.

Doctorow's epistemological agnosticism towards "objective" history explains the absence of an objective, integrating point of view. He argues in "False Documents" that an "objective historiographical" point of view" unburdened by the benefit of hindsight is the greatest fiction of all. Instead we are prisoners of the contemporary, enmeshed in narrative agendas not of our making. Therefore Doctorow presents a confusion of voices and narratives vacillating between the past and present and mixing real and invented figures. Yet, the moral center of the narrative consciousness is firmly anchored—how could it be otherwise?—in the subjectivity of the author rather than in a historical time. This conscious moral orientation in the present (*Commentary* called his a position of Jewish radicalism) implies a recognition of the inevitability of our historical place. There is no escape from our perspective even when we naively believe, like Strout, in the possibility of an objective stance in the past unburdened by knowledge of events to come. The boy's words to Houdini "warn the Duke" (of the impending assassination which would ignite World War I) are indeed anachronistic, but intended as a warning to us of the impossibility of escape from the hermeneutic prison.

It could be argued that Doctorow shows more respect for a "truth of the heart" by insisting that all narratives, historical, fictional, and biographical, are written from contemporary points of view and have to be decoded as fictions of their time. In Walter Benjamin's words we are prophets of the past with our backs to the future. Strout's parting shot in calling the book as irrelevant as a ragtime tune does not bode well for a serious reading of the musical story.

But even if we disregard the epistemological tack of the novel and merely insist on historical accuracy, *Ragtime* is true enough to salient, though neglected facts of American music history. For it picks up some of the zany contradictions of ethnicity and class at that particular juncture in the development of American popular music. By the 1970s certain historical and cultural results of that ethnic and class mix had become manifest, notably in the emergence of ethnic agents and agendas in all fields of inquiry, and novelists of historical fiction would profit from the benefit of hindsight. Given his background, Doctorow himself is one "result" of the mixture of ethnicity and class he describes. In this sense, *Ragtime* is "autobiographical" because it identifies Doctorow's social and epistemological place both in America's real and narrative history as a result of the very forces of history and historiography which the novel captures. Doctorow chooses the narrated bits of predigested history carefully; sometimes just a symbol or an icon of the age will evoke a revisionist controversy over historical meaning.

A good example of his metonymic style is his handling of three icons of the age: the upright piano, the Model T Ford and film. Of the three the piano may serve as the best example. It is of special significance since the assault of black ragtime on white respectability used the queen of instruments, the piano, which was considered a Victorian "moral institution." According to the *New York Times* of the day "the pianoforte more than any other single object will be looked upon in the years to come as the emblem of the Victorian age." The production figures bear this out. In 1909, the year when some of the most important events in the novel unfold, the sales of upright pianos reached an all-time peak. It was also the year when Congress passed a copyright law to secure income for composers from music serialized on piano rolls. The choice of a black pianist as protagonist of the novel is not incidental. The musical world of Coalhouse Walker Jr., Scott Joplin, and James Reese Europe connects with the industrial world of Henry Ford and J. P. Morgan via the Model T Ford, the principal incarnate of relentless serial production. The third icon of the age, the moving pictures, represented by Tateh and his inventions, highlights the role of visual representation in the age of mechanical reproduction.

The narrative mirrors the spirit of automation; its components are "moveable parts," namely the case studies, personality typing and composite social portraiture from history, sociology, and psychology that have settled into conventional wisdom. These recycled narrative units are in Doctorow's words "industrialized forms of storytelling," which he brings into his own, jagged order and which he dots with cynical or compassionate asides. This creates an effect which might be called the narrative equivalent of syncopation. The overall organizing principle is, as in ragtime, a system of contradictions, most abstractly between being and becoming, or between metamorphosis and stasis, a system which fans out into all sorts of concrete oppositions. In terms of narrative timing there is both a forward drive and a holding back, an "accelerando" and "ritardando." The novel moves, in Doctorow's own words, "at an absolutely relentless pace." Yet at the same time the voice of Scott Joplin urges us in the epigram: "Do not play this piece fast. It is never right to play Ragtime fast. . . ." Surely the human agents may be divided into those that resist speedy transformation and would rather hold on to eternal, biological, or deterministic master plans (Father, Morgan, Ford), and those who favor "bricolage" such as Tateh, the "artist," who decides to arrange "his life along the lines of flow of American energy," and Mother, who gladly adjusts to liberating innovations. On its most metaphysical level the novel is a meditation on the psychopathology of the culture industry caught between a desire for progress and a dread of change so typical of modernization in the Progressive era. It is necessary to take another look at the entire musical story the novel tells.

The years from 1896 to 1917 mark the period of intense modernization in American culture. In music and in industrial production, and surely in their unique fusion that gave us American popular music and its cultural industry, this is a transitional period. By 1896, industrial production had nearly consolidated, but there was not yet a culture of consumption to match it. By the 1920s, however, the mass cultural industry was firmly in place. In terms of music history, then, ragtime fits snugly between the older era of sheet music and the modern age of the player piano, the record player, and the radio. The music by Stephen Foster and Charles Harris written in the late nineteenth century required a publishing network, song pluggers and a musically literate audience. The music of the 1920s by Irving Berlin, George Gershwin, and Harold Arlen reached, via records and radio, a large multiethnic audience that no longer needed literate skills. The dominant sound technology of the ragtime era, that is, piano rolls and player pianos (one of which, in the novel, is taken by Peary to the North Pole), is of a transitional nature. Piano rolls and the player piano (which were marketed on a large scale after 1902) marked the beginning of the age of automation in the reproduction of sounds. These sounds are forever inscribed in the rolls, which may be produced in series and *en masse*. Yet the rolls require as a sound carrier the old venerable piano, which has to be activated by human effort. The production of player pianos had risen constantly from the introduction of the Pianola by the Aeolian Company in 1902, to 1923, when 56 percent of all pianos were automated. Piano sales tapered off after 1909 and declined drastically in the 1920s when the improved recording technology facilitated not only the recording by microphone and the reproduction of performed music by relatively cheaper record players, but also its dissemination by radio. By 1929 production figures were down to 35 percent of the earlier high in 1923.

Ragtime is transitional in yet another sense. Before 1896 popular songs were all of one generic kind—they were essentially based on the European *lied* tradition or on waltzes and marches. Though there were new and unheard (black) strains in Stephen Foster's minstrel-derived songs, they did not mark a radical departure from the European models. Besides, his innovations did not catch on, nor did they settle into the racist tradition of coon songs. In classical music there was no American-born classical composer of note with the exception of Louis Moreau Gottschalk (whose influence on Joplin can be heard by the discriminating ear), and he was ignored. The classical canon was dominated by Europeans. The class division between classical and popular musical cultures deepened increasingly as classical music, in the epithet of Lawrence Levine, became "sacralized" toward the end of the century. With the coming of ragtime and jazz, however, two indigenous American musical grammars arose which straddled, or ignored, these class and cultural barriers and which held great appeal for the new ethnics, particularly for Jews. Neither jazz nor ragtime produced an exclusively mass cultural or elitist type of music. To be sure, both could be trivialized for mass cultural purposes, yet they also allowed the highest musical achievement. Both jazz and ragtime were indeed commodified (which accounts for one of the most egregious misjudgments of Theodor W. Adorno who dismissed jazz as *essentially* proto-fascist), but ragtime and jazz also yielded a crop of superb creative artists, and inspired many classical composers including Charles Ives, Maurice Ravel, Claude Debussy, Igor Stravinsky, Darius Milhaud, and, quite clearly, George Antheil and Kurt Weill.

In terms of cultural history then, ragtime marks a transitional phase in the coming of age of an Afro-American musical aesthetic which would find its classic form in jazz. Gunther Schuller writes:

> rhythmically 'ragging' melodies and themes was only one step removed from loosening them (musical pieces) up even further through improvisation and melodic embellishment. Thus, many of the earliest jazz musicians were essentially ragtime players, or,

to put it more precisely, musicians who were transitional in the progress from a relatively rigid, notated, non-improvised music (ragtime) to a looser, more spontaneously inventive perfor- mance style (jazz).

The Afro-American aesthetic initiated by ragtime and jazz does not so much represent a specific genre of music, but rather projects a world view, namely a uniquely urban, modernist attitude of improvisation, invention, and "brico- lage." After the pastoral and small town tradition of nineteenth-century song, America acquired in ragtime a music in tune with city life and its new ethnic populations.

Until the turn of the century, the musical canon of the United States was largely dominated by Europe. Classical music was imported from Italy, France, and, toward the end of the century, increasingly from Germany. Musical taste was primarily determined by German cultural custodians such as Theodore Thomas, Anton Seidl, Karl Muck, and their American allies, and American boys and girls who were musically disciplined by the *Klavier Schule* of Siegmund Lebert and Ludwig Stark which by 1884 had seen seven- teen editions. Among immigrant workers the European song tradition was alive. Bright, the Irish maid in *Ragtime*, listens to John McCormack's "I Hear You Calling Me," a typical example of imported ethnic folk music, some of which survived the ravages of industrialization better in America than in Europe. Up to the turn of the century American popular music, with a few notable exceptions such as Stephen Foster and James Bland, consisted of songs imported from Europe or of songs written by immigrant songwriters such as Victor Herbert and Rudolf Friml, who are mentioned in the novel as Peary's favorites. Herbert's "Gold Bug" was an all-time favorite in America, but it would be hard to identify what is "American" about it. Even second- generation songwriters such as Harry Von Tilzer or Paul Dresser, the fat and prosperous brother of Theodore Dreiser, wrote a slightly Americanized copy of European song. Von Tilzer, for one, composed beer garden waltzes such as "Down Where the Würzburger Flows" (which he followed with "Under the Anheuser-Bush"), and Dresser joined the ranks of the "shameless motherlovers" with his immortal air "I Believe It For My Mother Told Me So." Other jingles from their pens are "The Letter That Never Came," "The Convict And The Bird," and "The Outcast Unknown."

An all-time hit and therefore representative of musical taste in the early 1890s was "After the Ball" (1892) by Charles K. Harris, an East European Jew who in all likelihood had changed his name. This was terribly senti- mental stuff. The lyrics tell of a little girl who climbs upon her old uncle's knee and asks "Why are you not married?" Then he tells the story "I had a sweetheart once, but I caught her kissing another man at a ball," where-upon he breaks the engagement only to find out much later, when it was too late to make amends, that the man his sweetheart kissed at the ball was her brother. The song is a perfect Victorian vehicle of sentimental schmaltz, made up of frustrated desire, the negation of bliss, stiff moral principles, and a hearty dose of self-denial in the tradition recorded by Leopold von Sacher-Masoch.

This world of rarified Victorian virtues that Father and Mother live in inspires Doctorow to savage satire. Sex is taboo and, when encountered, causes fainting spells. Procreation continues—after a fashion—with a bad conscience on the part of the male and with clenched fists, closed eyes and a prayer on the lips of the female. Much later in the novel, after Mother learns to swing, she begins to push back, much to the surprise of Father who thought this was a somewhat gauche habit of Eskimo women. Father is the image of prosperous frustration: he drops out of Harvard (a Harvard inter-ruptus) then becomes a frustrated explorer with Peary and Henson (the latter, a black, ousts him from Peary's graces). The account of Father's sexual encounter with Eskimo women is by no means fanciful fiction. Members of the Peary expedition left their traces in the gene pool of the Inuit, and thanks to Henson's high pigmentation his offspring was traced in Northern Green-land. Harvard University recently invited Henson's son and grandchildren for a commemoration of the black explorer. However, Peary's entire enter-prise has been called into question. Recent scholarship expresses some doubt that he ever made it to the North Pole, to the center that holds. Doubly frus-trated Father returns to a life defined by the sudden appearance of a deserted black baby, whom Mother takes in, followed by the mother of that baby and by Coalhouse Walker Jr., the father, who upset the harmony of the previous, Victorian world. Before Father fully appreciates what has happened to his life-style he sinks with the *Lusitania*, taking his world, his culture, and his weapons with him. "*Untergang des Abendlands.*"

John Philip Sousa, also mentioned in the novel, gave America its impe-rial and ceremonial music, such as "President Garfield's Inauguration March" of 1881. His name should alert us that ethnics were not entirely innocent in the creation of such music. Sousa's father was Portuguese, his mother Bavarian. His repertoire, though clearly indebted to European mili-tary music, included pieces with a new beat and "American" melodies. Though critical of ragtime and wary of the "menace of mechanical music," he reacted to audience demands and flirted with a variety of American tradi-tions, among them black music or, at least, whatever part of it transpired through the minstrel mask. A recording from 1905 called "Silence and Fun: A Ragtime Oddity" is not ragtime and to our ears not particularly odd. Sousa sounded much better than the very early recordings allow for. Although this type of marching music was a European derivative, it represented, at its best, an American improvement of a European tradition. Sousa's brand of music, it should be said, was not without influence on Joplin and other ragtime composers.

Then came ragtime. The music had a new musical grammar, marked by syncopation, which, as its detractors pointed out, could be found in music before the ragtime craze. However, the "constant collision between internal melodic and underlying rhythms was its *raison d'être*, not one of many stylistic features." This permanent tension in melody and rhythm reflected and spoke to a different libidinal structure. It mirrored the contradictions of urban living and projected a new urban attitude that the French call "*Je m'en foutisme*" (I don't give a damn). In 1896, a tune with recognizable ragtime features and a jaunty melody hit the charts. The lyrics of this ragtime song shed the maudlin sentimentality so popular before and were recognizably closer to the tradition of Afro-American humor: "You've Been a Good Old Wagon, But You Done Broke Down," a tune that would later become a favorite of Bessie Smith. It is significant that this song had not only a verse, but also—and this may be read as a black touch—a "chorus" and a "dance." The composer and author was one Ben Harney, who has remained a somewhat mysterious figure. Yet, whatever we know or don't know about him makes the actions of Brother in the novel (who "blacks up" as a radical inversion of a minstrel Sambo) seem not so strange after all. Harney was introduced on the cover of the song as "the Original Introducer to the Stage of the New Popular Rag Time in Ethiopian Song." Eubie Blake, a black ragtime pianist, claimed that Harney was a black man who had passed for white, prefiguring James Weldon Johnson's "ex-coloured man," another fictional ragtime pianist. Others say Harney was a white man who passed for a black man passing for white. Harney left no record that would clearly establish his genealogy. Whatever his pigmentation may have been, the historical fact of this confusion marks an important threshold in American culture: the eruption of black rhythms into the mainstream of music and the gradual takeover by blacks of its musical grammar.

Ragtime was the musical "high yeller" black baby left at the doorsteps of white folks who gladly adopted it, some of them not even realizing it was black. There is another significant historical fact: Ben Harney's ragtime song was published by a company of second-generation German Jews by the name of Witmark. Julius Witmark (who would correspond to Tateh in the novel) actually served as a midwife to bring this new child, black song, to the light of day. Eubie Blake, for one, was a Witmark author, and, though never overly fond of ragtime, he played it then and into our days as demonstrated by the recording—at the age of ninety in 1979—of his "Charleston Rag" (1917). Like Coalhouse Walker Jr. he belonged to a new breed of blacks who were willing to challenge the system of overt and covert racism. Ford and Father were suddenly surrounded by clever Jews and uppity Afro-Americans.

Race relations were at an all-time low at the turn of the century. The year of Harney's hit was also the year of the *Plessy vs. Ferguson* decision of the Supreme Court which cemented segregation. In the musical market, writes Sam Dennison, "cover illustrations adorning sheet music of the 1890s became more colorful and more insulting to blacks than at any other time in the history of American popular song." Therefore the range of "revolutionary cultural possibilities" for Afro-Americans was clearly limited. We tend to judge the black agents of this era negatively when compared to those of the Harlem Renaissance or the Black Cultural Revolution of the sixties whose achievements in "advancing the race" were more visible. But to be "black and proud" was much harder in 1896. The first and hardest job, and this is what ragtime was all about, was to overcome the unthinking racism of minstrelsy inscribed in musical taste as in cultural behavior.

Times had already changed, if ever so subtly, by 1906. Coalhouse Walker Jr. was the representative of a new group of urban blacks. One has to read the novel carefully for the many subtle data of musical history. On Coalhouse's first visit to the house in 1909 he is asked by Father to play one of the popular "coon songs." These were popular tunes of the day which had emerged with minstrelsy and which made seemingly innocent fun of blacks. Coalhouse Walker Jr. quite firmly refuses. He also carefully wipes the keys of this middle-class white piano (produced by the Aeolian company) before starting to play. For a first demonstration of his talent he does not select a tune already popular with white audiences, but pointedly chooses "The Wall Street Rag" by Scott Joplin, a new composition hot off the presses in 1909, which foreshadows Walker's later challenge to the capitalist system embodied by the J. P. Morgan Library. Later on, as a concession to white folks, he encores with a well-known hit, "Maple Leaf Rag." All this on an upright piano which, to the chagrin of his white hosts, he judges "badly in need of a tuning." Times had changed and were, perhaps, from Father's point of view, already out of tune. Though the "new negro" was a few years hence, there was already a new breed represented by figures such as George Walker, the brothers James Weldon and J. Rosamond Johnson, Bob Cole, Will Marion Cook, and James Reese Europe. Their historical role has not been properly acknowledged by mainstream historians of American culture. These young blacks represented a recognizable urban cohort that was subversively active in the creation of new types of *American* popular entertainment. The irony and the subversion lie in the fact that the Americanization of music through ragtime resulted in the blackening of the American musical grammar at the worst possible moment in race relations. And to add ethnic insult to nativist injury immigrant Jews were its midwives or secondliners. Most American music in the twentieth century is of course black-derived, but ragtime marks that crucial moment when black music began to set the agenda. Before it was "Swanee River" and "After the Ball," now it was "Alexander's Ragtime Band" by Irving Berlin and "Shuffle Along" by Noble Sissle and Eubie Blake.

This brings us to a second theme of the novel, which also captures the chief ambition of black ragtime players between 1900 and 1917. Frederick Douglass defined the black political agenda as the quest for literacy and freedom. These quests are reflected in ragtime; ragtime is a composed, that is, literate, music. Though a popular genre in terms of its public appeal, ragtime draws its rules of composition and performance from the discipline of the classical tradition. Implied in this music was a quest for freedom from the shackles of minstrelsy (both as a form of oral, unsophisticated entertainment and as a form of servile behavior expected of black musicians). White patrons of minstrel shows continued to ask for Tambo and Bones on the public stage and would have cared little for well-groomed and literate black pianists. These black musicians, however, whose expressive repertoire was limited by the tyranny of white expectation, began to divorce themselves from the spirit of minstrelsy by creating alternatives to minstrel music. This divorce was not easy; and for a long time ragtime was simply taken on board by minstrel shows as a welcome new feature. Coon songs were played as rags and ragtime songs retained the "jingle with the broken tongue," as Paul Laurence Dunbar called the pseudoblack dialect in which white readers expected him to deliver his poetry. But latent in the music was a new revolutionary option which would eventually mature and graduate from the minstrel show.

Undoing the shackles, the corsets, the encrustations, opening the closets—this is a major theme of the novel. Houdini turns escape (from his working-class Jewish background) into a compulsive art, Evelyn Nesbit throws off her corset, so does Mother, quietly. Toward the end of the novel when the rain makes her garments cling to her body, her mature sensual form is visible to an appreciative Tateh who has by this time in the novel overcome his rigid orthodox mores. Ragtime stood for more than just musical change: for its white listeners, at any rate, it connoted doing away with self-denial. And this liberation concerned culturally determined libidinal structures, in short, rhythm. Why else would Doctorow send Freud and Jung through the Tunnel of Love?

We may reconstruct the libidinal charge of ragtime at this historical moment *ex negativo*, from the reaction to ragtime by mainstream classical musicians. Today ragtime may seem innocent enough, just the thing for encores in classical concerts, for music students bored with Clementi or for film scores. But we are children of the musical and libidinal liberation that ragtime set in motion. For us, as for the little boy, "there seemed no other possibilities for life than those delineated by the music." The reaction to ragtime by established musicians in the early part of this century was related to the pervasive feeling of decline common among the ruling classes, as expressed in Madison Grant's *The Passing of the Great Race* of 1916. From their perspective, ragtime had to appear as a pathological, immoral, patently sexual, and subversive instrument of decline. The composer Daniel Gregory Mason thundered: "Let us purge America and the Divine Art of Music from this polluting nonsense." Hans Muck, the director of the Boston Symphony Orchestra, concurred, "I think that what you call ragtime is poison. . . . A person inoculated with the ragtime fever is like one addicted to strong drink." Others charged that it led to permanent brain damage or that it would wreck the nervous system. "Its greatest destructive power lies in its power to lower the moral standards." A man named Walter Winston Kenilworth wrote a letter to the Paris editor of the *New York Herald-Tribune* in 1913 which was later reprinted in the *Musical Courier.* It sums up negatively what the novel is all about:

> Can it be said that America is falling prey to the collective soul of the negro through the influence of what is popularly known as "rag time" music? . . . If there is any tendency toward such a national disaster, it should be definitely pointed out and extreme measures taken to inhibit the influence and avert the increasing danger—if it has not already gone too far . . . The American "rag time" or "rag time" evolved music is symbolic of the primitive morality and perceptible moral limitations of the negro type. With the latter sexual restraint is almost unknown, and the widest altitude of moral uncertainty is conceded.

A New England music critic concurred and, in jumbled prose which mirrors his nativist *angst*, continued the argument by defining the role of the Jew in this nefarious plot to destroy Aryan America:

> Ragtime is a mere comic strip representing American vices. Here is a rude noise which emerged from the hinterlands of brothels and dives, presented in a negroid manner by Jews most often, so popular that even high society Vanderbilts dance to it. All this syncopated music wasn't American, it is unamerican.

> The Jew and the Yankee stand in human temperance at polar
> points. The Jew has oriental extravagance and sensuous bril-
> liance. However, ragtime is a reflection of these raucous times; it
> is music without a soul.

These apocalyptic reactions are by now familiar in the history of jazz and
popular music. They articulate a latent fear of instability and libidinal
freedom associated with the threatening Other, represented at this time by
blacks and Jews.

To white cultural custodians ragtime may have heralded the decline of
the West, to black middle-class musicians, most of all to Scott Joplin and
James Reese Europe, it was a conscious departure from debasing minstrelsy
and an entry into serious, literate, and classical black music. We witness a
misunderstanding across the racial divide over the meaning of black musical
emancipation, a drama of mistaken motives and cross purposes. For the
white musical power structure the "libertinism" of ragtime threatened to
destroy the moral fiber of the nation and indicated a lowering of moral standards; for blacks its acceptance as serious music was part of a political
struggle for dignity. Coalhouse Walker Jr. is the pianist in Jim Reese
Europe's Clef Orchestra, which was the finest black brass band, dance and
symphony orchestra of the time and the first black orchestra to storm the
citadel of high culture, Carnegie Hall, in 1914.

Within larger orchestras the piano has always been a central instrument. The pianist in the orchestra is the arranger; he can read, and he is in
charge of literacy. Coalhouse Walker Jr.'s job gives us his professional
profile within the black culture of the day. His status is furthermore
apparent in that he is one of the first motorists of the brand-new Model T
Ford which came off the production line in 1909. Could it be that
Doctorow is having a bit of fun here in connecting the two icons of the
novel, the piano and the Model T? One of the two historical pianists of the
Jim Reese Europe orchestra in the first decade of the century and
cofounder of the Clef Club was a fellow by the name of Ford T. Dabney
who has a good number of compositions to his credit.

Mastery over the piano and ownership of the Ford Model T are
symbols of the new achievement and the new dignity, the new spirit of
human possibility and human principle which Walker represents. His reply
to the spirit of interracial practical joking enacted by the Irish firemen in
Ragtime and by innumerable white comics in blackface is a firm "we are no
longer amused, we are a serious people." In this he resembled not only
Michael Kohlhaas, but also, closer to home, black artists James Reese
Europe, Bob Cole, George Walker, and Bert Williams, who had to work on

the borderline between minstrelsy and serious black music, or the pianist Eubie Blake, and last but not least, Joplin, who created the most memorable compositions in ragtime and whose life is a dramatization of Walker's purpose. For Walker's subsequent behavior in the novel, the sequence of incidents leading to the bombing of the fire stations and the wiring up of J. P. Morgan's library, there is no historical parallel, but it may be taken as an objective correlative—in present day terms—of the deep symbolic hurt and anger of urban blacks such as Joplin.

Joplin was a serious artist who wanted nothing more than to be recognized as a composer of serious music. "Do not play this piece fast. It is never right to play ragtime fast." This exasperated warning, which Joplin had printed on many of his compositions and which Doctorow chose as the epigram of the novel, is crucial. It is a sentence loaded with musical and historical meaning. Why would Joplin make such a fuss over those interpreters who play his music as if the name set a fast metronome? Joplin prefaced an edition of his music without any of the modesty which in those days was expected of blacks of any station:

> What is scurrilously called ragtime is an invention that is here to stay. That is now conceded by all classes of musicians. That all publications masquerading under the name of ragtime are not the genuine article will be better known when these exercises are studied. That real ragtime of the higher class is rather difficult to play is a painful truth which most pianists have discovered. Syncopations are no indication of light and trashy music, and to shy bricks at "hateful" ragtime no longer passes for musical culture. To assist amateur players in giving the "Joplin Rags" that weird and intoxicating effect intended by the composer is the object of this work.

Joplin complained that imitators tended to Taylorize his music, giving it the sound of a machine, when in fact syncopation and its "weird and intoxicating effect" upset the regularity of a mechanical beat. "Play it slow until you catch the swing" he advised those of his pupils, who like Admiral Peary were proud of pumping out the "Minute Waltz" in forty-eight seconds.

Joplin's warning may have been the first inadvertent acknowledgement of a basic difference between European-American and black music making (which may also imply a difference between a modern-technocratic and a preindustrial sense of time). Due to the improvement of instrument technology and due to the premium placed on *technical* mastery, a tacit context seems to have developed among Western musicians in the period of modernization to step up the speed of music—performances which have given us Zez Confrey and Liberace in popular music, and Glenn Gould in the classics. Indeed it has been in the realm of technical mastery where white imitators of black jazz musicians have succeeded best, namely in doing fast numbers; where many break down is in ballads and blues. The difference lies not in the *choice* of pace, but in "timing" on the one hand and in "attack" or "sound" on the other, which show up best in slow numbers. Afro-American timing, attack and sound, which are part of a rhythmic grammar (hence related to dance), have not too often been the forte of white jazz musicians (particularly those with classical training), yet it is the essence of what is called black "soul." Joplin's dogged insistence on correct timing therefore has black cultural nationalist implications.

It also brings to the foreground a contradiction between the conflicting goals of political emancipation and of the quest for a black cultural identity, which surfaces for the first time in American culture during the period. The dilemma was that before ragtime could be accepted beyond a black ethnic horizon, it had to shed just enough of the roughness of the (black) country and adopt just enough of the sophistication of the (white) city without losing its "innovative" appeal. Ragtime had to adapt to or "compromise with" the tyranny of classical musical norms to the extent of becoming competitive and compatible within a larger market. A black cultural pioneer such as Joplin, whose goal was the political emancipation of his music, had to master these norms through the music, yet not succumb to their hegemony by a slavish compliance with the dictates of a Western metronome. His political balancing act was to retain as much of the Afro-American pace and sensibility as the market would accept. Hence, his dogged insistence on "timing" (that is, on saving the dance) as the important Afro-American cultural marker. Is it surprising then that Joplin, whose score of *Treemonisha* was at best sketchy and incomplete, left most elaborate instructions for the choreography of the dance number "Real Slow Drag" in his opera?

Ragtime is revolutionary by introducing an Afro-American structure of feeling to Western music and dance. To attract promoters Joplin had, shortly before his death, staged a concert version of his opera. It failed miserably. After that *Treemonisha* was never performed in full and was practically forgotten until the 1960s when music historian Vera Brodsky Lawrence reissued the works of Joplin, and then Robert Shaw and the music department at Morehouse College produced a first hearing in 1972. Gunther Schuller saw to it that the opera was performed by a professional company. Vera Brodsky Lawrence writes in the liner notes:

To early twentieth century America it was unthinkable, inadmissible, and intolerable that a black composer—worse yet, a black composer of vulgar ragtime—should attempt to invade the inviolably white precincts of white opera. Publishers, however willing to issue Joplin's highly salable piano rags, turned a deaf ear to the outrageous concept of publishing his full-length opera. Who would buy it? Or perform it? Apparently nobody, for producer after producer and publisher after publisher successively rejected *Treemonisha*; and Joplin, who with each refusal became more compulsively determined to see the work published and staged, committed himself irretrievably to the tragic and futile quest that was to obsess and possess him for the remaining decade of his life.

Here is a musical Michael Kohlhaas. The ragtime pianist Coalhouse Walker Jr. is clearly a representative of the ragtime age. But should we take Joplin's ambition to be accepted as a classical composer as seriously as Coalhouse's demand to be respected as a citizen? Was Joplin not rightly forgotten? After listening to Gunther Schuller's and the Houston Symphony Orchestra's rendition of "Real Slow Drag" who would need further proof of Scott Joplin's talent? Clearly Joplin is a master of choral composition and brings to opera the complicated rhythms and the call and response patterns of black folk music, indeed "verse," "chorus," and "dance." And his detailed instructions for the choreography set the stage for jazz dance. Had he been given recognition and support he might have built up a sizeable *oeuvre* which would have preceded *Porgy and Bess* by decades and which would have established him as the first black cultural nationalist. Moreover, the black opera *Treemonisha* was a logical step in the quest for literacy and freedom implicit in ragtime. The libretto of the opera reflects Joplin's abiding belief that the black path to dignity and civil rights lay through education. (Like the black baby in the novel, the heroine of *Treemonisha* was found by her foster parents as a baby under a tree, hence the name Tree-Monisha.)

Scott Joplin died in 1917, a frustrated and angry man. Even a cursory look at Joplin's work and biography would have laid to rest the claim that the novel's sense of history is contrived or that Coalhouse Walker Jr. is "in no way typical of the prewar years." The novel merely translates Joplin's anger and frustration as a creative Afro-American of his time into action and plot understood in our time. We ought to take the author's choice of a musical title seriously.

JOHN G. PARKS

Compositions of Dissatisfaction: Ragtime

Tragedies end in funerals, comedies in marriages. Doctorow's *Welcome to Hard Times* and *The Book of Daniel* may be called tragedies of history. Blue, of *Welcome to Hard Times*, lives long enough to tell the story of his destruction while also bearing witness to the persistence of his dream and his hope. The pieces of his life as well as his story await the next settler. While burying his past, Daniel, of *The Book of Daniel*, is enabled to live on, to reenter or reconnect with history bearing some knowledge of the plural nature of truth, which his electrical narrative opened up. *Ragtime* may be called a comedy of history. While many people die, it ends in a marriage symbolizing some new and rich possibilities for America's future, after its innocence is lost.

If the narrative of *The Book of Daniel* challenged the monologic power of the regime with its polyphonic quality, the narrative of *Ragtime* is a virtual carnival. A carnival is a popular occasion when all hierarchies are overturned, oppositons blurred, when the "jolly relativity" of all things reigns. The stable, the authoritative, the serious are loosened, mocked, subverted. The carnival, Mikhail Bakhtin shows, had a shaping effect upon literary genres, an effect he calls "carnivalization." This term is useful in describing the "jolly relativity" of Doctorow's *Ragtime*, a text that resists organicism through the interplay of multiple voices, historical and fictive. Similarly, Frederick Karl likens the narrative of *Ragtime* to a Barnum and Bailey circus. The novel

---

From *E. L. Doctorow*. © 1991 by John G. Parks.

approaches what Roland Barthes calls a "plural text," a text that calls the reader not merely to consume the meaning but rather to produce it. As Doctorow's epigraph to the book from Scott Joplin warns: "Do not play this piece fast. It is never right to play Ragtime fast. . ."

In his attempt to reopen the Isaacson case, in *The Book of Daniel*, Daniel struggles to find or make connections between two radicalisms—the Old Left of the 1930s and the New Left of the 1960s. Using the metaphor of electricity Daniel locates "currents" and "resistances" and "circuits." He seeks a way to resist historical and cultural duplication as well as the current of continuous change. Doctorow, in *Ragtime*, continues with his exploration of these themes but in a different historical era, this time the first two decades of the twentieth century. The little boy says: "It was evident to him that the world composed and recomposed itself constantly in an endless process of dissatisfaction." The novel explores the changing compositions of history—replications and changes—and, as always in Doctorow's fiction, the possibilities of moral growth in history. One of the historical personages in *Ragtime*, Henry Ford, who made history with his assembly line techniques ("He had caused a machine to replicate itself endlessly"), is reputed to have declared that "history is more or less bunk," a view Doctorow's novel seeks to challenge with a prophetic vision of social injustice.

Two excerpts of the novel were published in 1974 in different issues of *American Review*, a journal published by Bantam. In July of 1975 the complete novel was published by Random House, then celebrating its fiftieth year in publishing. The producer Dino De Laurentiis secured the movie rights, and the Book-of-the-Month Club featured *Ragtime* as its main selection. The novel became a best-seller in hardback and Bantam bought the paperback rights for $1.85 million. The initial reviews were almost unanimous in praising the novel, some even predicting that it would win the National Book Award and a Pultizer Prize. In fact, it was awarded the first National Book Critics Circle prize for fiction. However, some critics had second thoughts. A novel that was making that much money raised questions about its worth as literature—a kind of perverse logic in American culture. A second wave of reviewers tended to downgrade the novel's literary value. Roger Sale, in the *New York Review of Books*, called the novel "all surface." Jeffrey Hart, in the *National Review*, accused the novel of sentimentality and questioned its moral vision. Writing in *Commentary*, Hilton Kramer condemned the leftist ideology of the book. British critics denounced the book as little more than a comic book. Among its defenders, however, was John Seelye, writing in the *New Republic* in 1976, who called the novel "a literary equivalent of a time bomb." This ambivalence about the novel's worth makes for an interesting case in cultural reception. Nevertheless, more considered essays in scholarly journals have treated the novel positively as an important work of contemporary fiction.

The central metaphor of the book, of course, is that to which the title of the book points—ragtime music. Despite moralistic attackers, ragtime music, which emerged from the black community, became immensely popular and flourished in America around 1897 to 1917. One of the most important innovators of ragtime music was black composer Scott Joplin, whose "Maple Leaf Rag" was a national hit, and who is described as influencing Doctorow's Coalhouse Walker in the novel. Ragtime music is characterized by its syncopated rhythm—the treble hand on the piano accenting second and third beats of a measure, improvising as it were, and the bass hand playing a steady, precise, and regularly accented beat. The effect is a consequence of the mixture of the formalized and the improvised. As such, the music captures well Doctorow's sense of the Progressive Era—repetition colliding with change, convention with innovation. The nervous, driving energies of ragtime reflects an age never quite realizing itself, never quite gaining control of the many forces of change to which it gave birth.

In addition to the music of ragtime, the title of the novel also refers to another image—the rags associated with poverty. There are a number of passages in the novel, as William Matheson shows, where the term *rag* is used. Father sees an immigrant ship coming into New York harbor and thinks: "a rag ship with a million dark eyes staring at him." At society balls for the poor, the rich guests come dressed in rags. Tateh flees the Lawrence, Massachusetts strike and leaves his rags. Zapata's peasant army wears rags. Also Jacob Riis, the reforming photographer of the poor, creates an ethnic map of New York City, which he describes using an analogous term: "You have a crazy quilt, . . . a crazy quilt of humanity." And, at the end, Tateh imagines a series of films about "a society of ragamuffins, like all of us, a gang, getting into trouble and getting out again." Such a reference is fitting for a novel attacking social inequality and injustice, and advocating the acceptance of a pluralistic society, "a crazy quilt of humanity," the positive political vision of the novel.

Ragtime describes not only the age the novel is concerned with, but also the style of the novel, its narrative flow. George Stade describes the narrative effect well: "The rhythm of the sentences and events in the novel is the verbal equivalent of ragtime. The left hand pounds out the beat of historical change. It modulates from the WASP to the immigrant to the black families as through the tonic, dominant and subdominant chords upon which the right hand builds its syncopating improvisations. These are variations on themes provided by representative figures and events of the time." The sprightly energy of the sentences, the shifts in scene, the blending of the fictive and the historical, the parallels and coincidences, the repetitions and innovations—all work together to show a world of change. Despite Scott Joplin's warning in the epigraph, it is hard not to read the novel fast. In interviews upon publication, Doctorow says that he wanted the novel to be accessible, especially to people who do not usually read books. To John F. Baker in *Publishers Weekly*, Doctorow says that he "was very deliberately concentrating on the narrative element. I wanted a really relentless narrative, full of ongoing energy. I wanted to recover that really marvelous tool for a novelist, the sense of motion." Contributing to the sense of motion of the narrative, and reflecting Doctorow's sensitivity to the developments in optical technologies in this century, is his use of cinematic devices—framing, abrupt shifts, and the like. The novel is very visual and moves from the static reproductions of the silhouettes to the volatile images of the new motion pictures.

All this narrative energy, what Geoffrey Harpham calls "the process," gives rise to criticisms of the novel as shallow, superficial, and all surface. Such criticisms, in part, are based on assumptions about fiction that really do not apply to Doctorow's novel. The book does not intend to be a dense study of character. Its pastiche quality intends to challenge conventional notions of plot. Its idiosyncratic blending of fact and fiction intends to challenge the privileged status of historical discourse. It is a text that illustrates Doctorow's ideas of history as spelled out in the "False Documents" essay: "There is no history except as it is composed. . . . That is why history has to be written and rewritten from one generation to another. The act of composition can never end." The novel is not about the ragtime era, but about how people view that era, how one might compose and recompose it. For Marxist critic Fredric Jameson, this narrative pastiche is evidence of the postmodern loss of the historical referent—a loss of connection between the writer's and readers' now and the past, and hence, a "crisis in historicity." The historical subject remains out of reach to us, problematizing interpretation. For this reason, Jameson sees Doctorow as "the epic poet of the disappearance of the American radical past, of the suppression of older traditions and moments of the American radical tradition."

In any event, the ever-changing narrative surface of *Ragtime* is part of the "meaning" of a book concerned with changes. As the little boy learns from Grandfather's stories from Ovid: "the forms of life were volatile and that everything in the world could as easily be something else." This "principle of volatility" the boy finds illustrated everywhere, including the replicating image of himself in the mirror. In one sense, then, the novel is a novel of faces, of people "making appearances" on the icy surface of history. To remain the same is to remain in the past. From the movies he likes so much, the boy learns that "moving pictures depended on the capacity of humans, animals, or objects to forfeit portions of themselves, residues of shadow and light which they left behind." The attempted imposition of self onto history leads to defeat, while self-sacrifice or forfeiture enables survival and moral growth, though, of course, no triumph is guaranteed.

Unlike the intense narrative of *The Book of Daniel*, the narrative voice of *Ragtime* is cool, ironic, distancing. To whom does such a voice belong? For over three-hundred pages the narrative appeared to be an omniscient third person, but in the third to the last paragraph the narrator becomes first person, identifying himself as the Little Boy who is introduced in the long first paragraph of the book, and who then loses his capitalized status for the remainder of the book. As Constance Pierce suggests, the appearance of that "I" signals the need to reread the novel with a new set of expectations. That "I" unites the beginning and the end of the novel and merges fiction with history and social responsibility. The novel is the tale of the little boy grown up; it is his composition. In a real sense, moreover, the novel is a product of a warning read back into history after a terrible catastrophe—in this case, World War I, the ending of American innocence and the real entry of America into the twentieth century. The little boy tells Houdini to "Warn the Duke" at the end of chapter 1, a warning that, of course, cannot be given and, hence, cannot be heeded. Yet it is a gesture of freedom that, since he is an artist, needs to be made. For Pierce, this gesture creates the authority of the narrator while it displaces history, and makes history accessible only through the composition of the narrator-artist, which raises issues of the indeterminacy of meaning, literary as well as historical.

What the reader has in *Ragtime*, to use a helpful distinction of Warner Berthoff, is not a historical document in which the "problem is verification," but rather a fictional document in which the "problem is veracity." And the truth–value of this composition is largely dependent upon the believability of the narrator whose identity the reader discovers at the end. The narrative is at some pains to establish the credentials, as it were, of the narrator—his sensitivity, his perceptiveness, which is a concern of most of Doctorow's narrators. In the first chapter we are told about the little boy: "He had reached that age of knowledge and wisdom in a child when it is not expected by the adults around him and consequently goes unrecognized." Later the reader is told: "He was alert not only to discarded materials but to unexpected events and coincidences." Again: "He saw through things and noted the colors people produced and was never surprised by coincidence." The boy's composition is a challenge to a view of history that forecloses the imagination and moral freedom. It is his testing of "the endurance of a duplicated event," like baseball where "the same thing happens over and over." For the boy, sensitive to the volatility of all things, certain forms of recurrence are a source of security. He tries to contain change within certain recurring frames, but the frames are volatile as well. Only the "motion picture" offers an artistic solution for historical volatility.

One of the most intriguing and appealing aspects of *Ragtime* for most readers is Doctorow's playful blend of fact and fiction. He does not just set his story in a particular historical frame for purposes of fictional decoration. Instead he puts history into his fiction, not changing the "facts" of history, but rather imagining new "facts." Doctorow says that he wrote "about imaginary events in the lives of undisguised people." This blending, in often very humorous ways, of real and imaginary people gives his novel the feel of an "inside view" of history, stories not told in the schoolbooks. But the effect is not to trivialize history, but rather to demystify it, to promote a new historical self-consciousness. It does not sentimentalize the ragtime era, nor does it create nostalgia for a bygone age. In fact, if anything, the novel is antinostalgic, forcing the reader into a critical confrontation with injustice, past and present. Nevertheless, Doctorow's insistence upon a personal view of history puts him in league with a number of writers in his generation, such as John Barth and Thomas Pynchon, among others, for whom, as David Lodge puts it, "Art can no longer compete with life on equal terms, showing the universal in the particular. The alternatives are either to cleave to the particular—to 'tell it like it is'—or to abandon history altogether and construct pure fictions which reflect in an emotional or metaphorical way the discords of contemporary experience." Lodge's alternatives are perhaps too distinct to account for Doctorow's imaginative blend of fact and fiction. In any event, a good deal of the serious fiction since World War II reflects what Barbara Foley calls the writer's "fundamental alienation from history" and a corresponding skepticism about the so-called objective nature of history and reality.

Despite the skepticism in Doctorow's vision of history, *Ragtime* intends to be taken seriously as social and political criticism. As such, it follows in the rich tradition of John Dos Passos's *U.S.A.* Like *U.S.A.*, *Ragtime* offers a radical critique of the Progressive Era and makes use of most of the same events and persons—Henry Ford, J. P. Morgan, Big Bill Haywood, the Lawrence textile strike, Teddy Roosevelt, and much more. But, as Barbara Foley points out, despite the many parallels, the treatment of history in each novel is different. Dos Passos subordinates his fictional narrative to the framework provided by the actual historical agents and events, which he portrays through his newsreels, biographies, and Camera Eye sections—devices quite innovative at the time. In Doctorow, however, history is subordinate to his fictional narrative, which, as I have noted, reflects his view of the nature of history as narrative. John Seelye describes Doctorow's departure from Dos Passos well:

What Doctorow has done, in effect, is to take the materials of Dos Passos' *U.S.A.*—a sequential series of fictional autobiographical and historical episodes—and place them in a compactor, reducing the bulk and hopelessly blurring the edges of definition. And yet the result is an artifact which retains the specific gravity of Dos Passos' classic, being a massively cynical indictment of capitalistic, racist, violent, crude, crass and impotently middle-class America.

In addition to Dos Passos, as Seelye reminds us, Doctorow borrows from other radical novels—Henry Roth's *Call It Sleep*, George Milburn's *Catalogue*, and Heinrich von Kleist's *Michael Kohlhaas*. The result is a highly entertaining and selective treatment of a turning point in American history that seeks to alter the ways we perceive our past and, hence, the ways we understand ourselves. As Seelye comments: "We should realize the implications of Doctorow's dissertation, for in the manner of the classical historical romance, it is a reshaping of the past to fit the matter of the moment."

As a contemporary historical romance, the novel is a syncopation of a number of oppositions and tensions: degeneration and regeneration, static forms and volatile images, repetition and change, history and fantasy, self and other, rich and poor, white and black, WASP and immigrant, narcissism and self-divestment, journeys outward and journeys inward, departures and arrivals. These tensions are exhibited in the interaction of the fictive families and the historical personages. The novel chronicles the lives of three families—an upper-middle-class white protestant family, an immigrant Jewish family, and a black family. Separated at the beginning due to class, racial and ethnic differences, they are brought together through a series of chance and accidental occurrences so that, by the end, they become one family. Only the black family is given names—Coalhouse Walker, the ragtime pianist, Sarah, and their son, Coalhouse Walker III. The other two families are designated by capitalized role names. Thus, the white family includes Father, owner of a fireworks and flag business, Mother, Grandfather, Mother's Younger Brother, and the little boy. The Jewish immigrants are known as Tateh, Mameh, and the Little Girl, whom Tateh calls "Sha" at one point. Only one of the fathers and one of the mothers survive the tumult of the era, who manage to direct their lives along the current of American energy and generate a new history.

Earlier I noted that, as the little boy's book, the novel is the result of a warning from the present read into the past. The present, of course, knows what the past does not. The warning therefore functions as a hidden clue to a possible destiny, to what ought to have been known if people were more morally perceptive and courageous. But it does not seek to create sadness or

despair about historical failure. Rather, it seeks to quicken the moral imagination as it confronts the present. Accordingly, as Emily Miller Budick insists,
"Dotorow's moral fiction of history is intended directly to effect social and
moral change." Placing the novel in the historical romance tradition, Budick
sees it as a "fantasy of reality" that recovers its connection with history. The
action of the novel begins with an interruption of a recurring event—Mother
and Father's weekly coitus. The cause of the interruption is the little boy's
virtual summons of the famous escape artist Houdini. From the outset the
historical is brought into the fictional. In addition, Houdini is a fitting image
for all the characters—historical and fictive—who seek to escape from historical reality by imposing upon it their own narcissistic visions. Budick argues:
"Like most of the characters in *Ragtime*, Mother and Father flee the reality of
difference and change which is the uninterrupted intercourse of history." Only
a consciousness that is historical, that faces the responsibilities and limitations
of time and place can avoid the pitfalls of self-absorption. Historical consciousness is regenerative, whereas narcissism leads to degeneration and disaster.

The idealized world of Mother and Father in their nice house in New
Rochelle cannot avoid the incursions of history. A world where "there were
no Negroes. There were no immigrants," turns out otherwise. Despite his
following the call of Theodore Roosevelt to lead the vigorous life, Father
is the least able to adapt to change. Overtaken by history, the proud and
confident explorer is, at the end, a diminished man, frustrated by failed
quests and helpless to control events swirling about him. Because of
Father's activities, the reader learns that "the marriage seemed to flourish
on Father's extended absences." But after failing to locate the pole with
Peary, Father returns, seeing himself as a "derelict, a man who lacked a
home," and both he and Mother realize that "this time he'd stayed away
too long." In his absence Mother has grown strong and confident. She has
rescued and taken in a black child and his mother. She has run and
improved Father's business. Trying to recover the place he vacated among
his family, Father realizes sadly that "there was nothing he had to tell
them." Father has the most difficulty in coping with the presence of Sarah
and her baby and the visits of the ragtime musician Coalhouse Walker,
whose pride and dignity befuddle Father. After expressing irritation over
the strange courtship occurring under his roof, Mother rebuffs him saying:
"There was suffering, and now there is penitence. It's very grand and I'm
sorry for you that you don't see it." Trying to escape from real history,
Father finds there is much that he cannot see.

Inheriting a history of neglect, abuse, and exploitation, Coalhouse
Walker embodies the claims of a new history upon America, especially upon
the white middle class as represented by Mother and Father. For some critics,

the whole Coalhouse Walker episode is anachronistic, taking a late-1960s black radical and placing him in the ragtime era—such a thing just could not have occurred at that time such critics feel. Such criticisms would be more valid if the novel were a conventional historical novel. But as part of a historical romance the episode works well. Plus, a closer examination of Coalhouse Walker may reveal a different consciousness from the radicals of the black power movement of the sixties. As Emily Budick argues, despite the justice of Coalhouse's claims, his action "reflects a private vendetta conceptualized wholly in terms of self. He wants *his* car returned as it was. Walker does not manage to link his vision of personal justice to larger social claims and aspirations." Conversely, Maria Diedrich argues that Walker does indeed take a position larger than a personal vendetta. His second letter to the New York press refers to his being "President, Provisional American Government," and when he meets with Booker T. Washington in the Morgan library, he tells Washington that "we might both be servants of our color who insist on the truth of our manhood and the respect it demands." Moreover, Walker's followers call themselves "Coalhouse," which also suggests a larger claim than one man's injury. In any event, Walker's violent action is no match for the entrenched power of the Morgans and Fords. Even so, the Coalhouse Walker episode functions as the major catalyst for the action of the novel.

The Coalhouse Walker episode lays bare the racism beneath the genteel surface of the Progressive Age. The main source of Doctorow's portrayal of Coalhouse Walker is the German writer Heinrich von Kleist's 1808 novella *Michael Kohlhaas*, which was itself based upon a historical incident from late-medieval Germany, and which further blurs the boundaries between fiction and history. The name Coalhouse is obviously derived from Kleist's protagonist. In Kleist the incident involved the attempt of an honest horse dealer to obtain justice when his horses are wrongly confiscated. In Doctorow it is Coalhouse's new Model T Ford that is trashed by local volunteer firemen led by Chief Willie Conklin. Both protagonists seek every legal means to obtain justice before becoming vigilantes. The use of the Model T also links the story to George Milburn's novel *Catalogue*, as Seelye reminds us. Both protagonists are victims of the falseness and hypocrisy of their social systems. Doctorow's use of the Model T Ford in the incident also links the episode to the character of Ford who had just discovered how a machine can duplicate itself endlessly. Owned by a proud black man, who "didn't act or talk like a colored man," the car reveals the virulent connection of racism and class in American society. The injustice transforms an artist into a revolutionary, whose stance leads to the dissolution of Father's family.

As the patriarch of the WASP family and the embodiment of the values of an older America, Father is portrayed as ineffectual in dealing

with a world where there were indeed Negroes and immigrants. Father is the
only child of a man who made and then lost a fortune. His father "had
produced in his only son a personality that was cautious, sober, industrious
and chronically unhappy." Yet he went to Groton and then to Harvard for
two years, where he heard lectures by the great William James. "Exploration
became his passion: he wanted to avoid what the great Dr. James had called
the habit of inferiority to the full self." But what that "full self" means never
comes to Father, his incessant outward explorations seeking escape from his
internal conflicts and contradictions. On his trip to the pole, Father is
repelled when he sees an Eskimo woman enjoying sex. Later he feels guilt
after taking an Eskimo woman to bed. Returning home "gaunt and hunched
and bearded," Father fears Mother's growing passion. It is as if Father is in
retreat from the new century, while Mother is in step with it. When Coalhouse goes on his rampage, Father wonders whether they had lost control
over their lives. "We are suffering a tragedy that should not have been ours,"
he tells Mother, which is clear indication of Father's moral limitations.
Increasingly, Father feels "by-passed by life, a spectator at an event." Despite
his limitations, Father is not without honor; he does what he can. He bails
Coalhouse out of jail; he serves as a negotiator during the crisis at the
Morgan library; he tries to keep his family safe and intact.

Even so, some of the harshest judgments of Father come from Mother's
Younger Brother. Early in the Coalhouse episode, Younger Brother says to
Father: "You speak like a man who has never been tested in his principles."
Later, after Younger Brother is fully radicalized and a member of Coalhouse's
gang, he tells Father: "You are a complacent man with no thought of history.
. . . You have traveled everywhere and learned nothing." So it would seem.
Yet Father, if not a hero, is not the real villain of the piece; he is only one
chord that plays itself out in the shadows of history. With his family
dissolving, Father throws himself into his new weapons industry and awaits
"the final alignment" that will precipitate the war. Fittingly, Father goes
down with the *Lusitania* while secretly shipping weapons to England. The
little boy, his son, makes the final judgment:

> Poor Father, I see his final exploration. He arrives at the new
> place, his hair risen in astonishment, his mouth and eyes dumb.
> His toe scuffs a soft storm of sand, he kneels and his arms spread
> in pantomimic celebration, the immigrant, as in every moment
> of his life, arriving eternally on the shore of his Self.

Forever arriving. Never to take possession of the full self and hence a pawn
of history. What would have made a difference? What did he lack and why?

Such are the questions a son's judgment upon his father raises for the reader.

If the currents of history overcome two of the fathers, they lead the third father to success. While Coalhouse Walker's fate is being sealed and Father's family is being dissolved, Tateh and his family struggle in the fish-smelling Lower East Side just to survive. Mameh is banished from the family for taking money from her employer for her sexual favors. Tateh ekes out an existence on the streets as a silhouette artist. As with the other two fictive families, Doctorow has this one intermingling with historical figures. The notorious Evelyn Nesbit by chance discovers the Little Girl and visits her often, and virtually dedicates herself to helping the family. As a Jewish Socialist, Tateh attends lectures by Emma Goldman. The character of Tateh allows Doctorow to reveal the dark underside of the ragtime era—the exploitation of labor, women and children, the terrible living conditions captured in photographs by Jacob Riis. Failing to make a living selling his silhouettes, Tateh takes the Little Girl and travels to Lawrence, Massachusetts, to work in the mills. When the workers go on strike and IWW leader Big Bill Haywood comes to town, violence threatens to break out and does when the workers try to send their children out of town until the strike is settled. Tateh and his daughter by chance escape on a train heading to Philadelphia. It is at this point that Tateh's life finds a different trajectory. Embittered by poverty, Tateh loses his faith in revolutionary or collective change. "From this moment, perhaps, Tateh began to conceive of his life as separate from the fate of the working class." Tateh reenacts the myth of the self-made man, like the heroes of Horatio Alger novels. Arriving in Philadelphia with little more than the shirt on his back, he recapitulates the humble beginnings of Benjamin Franklin, enshrined for posterity in his influential *Autobiography*. To make this connection clear, the reader learns that Tateh sells his "movie books" to the Franklin Novelty Company. The narrator tells the reader: "Thus did the artist point his life along the lines of flow of American energy."

The uncompromising Coalhouse Walker dies for his convictions. Tateh discovers how an entrepeneur can make it in America. Is this compromise a sellout? Or does it suggest a way of social transformation that is more effective than collective revolutionary action? Like Daniel, Tateh becomes a self-progenitor, he creates himself by becoming Baron Ashkenazy the successful filmmaker. "His whole personality had turned outward and he had become a voluble and energetic man full of the future. He felt he deserved his happiness. He'd constructed it without help." Thus, Tateh's discovery of the motion picture, and his abandonment of the static, essentially premodern silhouette, aligns him with the truly modern metamorphosing energies of the twentieth century. The movies show volatility within frames and offer people a vision of difference and otherness, and hence the chance to understand themselves. Both ragtime music and movies are democratizing forces in American culture. As Budick says, "They provide what static and stabilizing images cannot, the possibility for sympathetic self-divestment and identification with the other." The marriage of Tateh and Mother at the end represents a new historical composition, which points to a pluralistic American future, and is perhaps the only composition worthy of survival. What image of our future will or can survive the catastrophe of the Great War? It is Tateh's idea for a series of films about an interracial group of children—like the Our Gang comedies—who get into and out of trouble. It is this vision that offers an alternative to the view of history as a machine, "as if history were no more than a tune on a player piano." Moreover, such a vision is regenerative and morally responsible.

In one sense, *Ragtime* is about the death of the father, of patriarchy, at least of a certain kind. By the same token, it signals the emergence of woman into the new equation of the twentieth century. The voice and influence of Emma Goldman is strong throughout the novel, speaking for the freedom of women from physical and economic and political servitude. Evelyn Nesbit comes under her care and influence. Even Mother has one of Goldman's books at her bedside. Mother awakens to her passions and her strengths and is thus able to participate in the generative forces of history.

The little boy, one recalls, loves coincidences. The book is filled with them—chance meetings, unexpected incidents, accidental occurrences. Perhaps they are fitting for an age undergoing transformation, an age discovering relativity and the principle of uncertainty. As a musical meditation upon history, the novel shows two views of history in opposition. One is the view of the narrator, where history is seen as volatile and unpredictable. The other is the view held by J. P. Morgan, where history is repetition, reoccurrence. Morgan invests a small fortune into research that will support his theory of reincarnation. He believes that he and Ford are the reincarnations of the historical elite. When Morgan tries to interest Ford in his Egyptian projects, Ford shows that he holds, literally, a two-bit version of Morgan's ideas. Ford read about reincarnation in a pamphlet he bought from the Franklin Novelty Company. Ford is too busy duplicating machines to accompany Morgan to Egypt. Morgan continues his quest alone, hoping for a sign from the ancient gods. His night alone in a pyramid proves fruitless, except for the bedbugs. But such historical narcissism is doomed to failure, as is true of the ceaseless escapes of Houdini. No matter how hard he tries, Houdini cannot compete with the "real-world act." No matter how often he "defies death" he will still die—the earth will prove too heavy at last. Houdini is another frustrated quester, condemned by his art to imitate life. Only the little boy and the girl, in playing the serious "burial game" at the beach, are allowed a glimpse of rebirth. Obsessed with rebirth, Morgan, Ford, and Houdini see history almost wholly in terms of the self, an immature and infantile philosophy of history, one that is static and degenerate. Such a philosophy is a futile attempt to escape the moral responsibilities of finite life lived in historical process. But the Morgan-Ford-Houdini philosophy of escape endures, as the narrator says: "Today, nearly fifty years since his death, the audience for escapes is even larger."

Reality, history, will not be pinned down. History refuses to succumb to the impositions of the human ego. Dreiser turns his chair all night "seeking the proper alignment." Admiral Peary does not locate the exact spot of the North Pole: "On this watery planet the sliding sea refused to be fixed." Only a novel like a motion picture can hope to catch the experience of history. Such is *Ragtime*.

Reminiscent of Mark Twain's *Puddn'head Wilson*, the narrator recalls Freud's judgment of America after his visit: "America is a mistake, a gigantic mistake." There is much in the novel that might support such a view. But the "jolly relativity" of this carnivalesque novel may keep most readers from such a harsh verdict.

DOUGLAS FOWLER

Ragtime

It is one measure of the singularity of *Ragtime* that it can be described as being at the same time a tragicomical novel starring American historical personages and also a sort of prose cartoon strip starring allegorical Everypeople purposely drained of biographical reality—a novel that is at once history, cartoon, political fable, and fairy tale. Some of the novel's events took place historically and some merely ought to have. Some of its events are painfully real and some of its events are charmingly magical. The tone in which the novel is told is sardonic and urbane and directed along a privileged wavelength of attitude and allusion, and yet the prose itself is intentionally flattened, declarative, chilly. Doctorow called the voice he used "mock historical-pedantic," and Stanley Kauffmann observed that "the absence of quotation marks on direct dialogue gives the book the visual effect of a saga discovered, rather than of a novel written." It is a prose that seems intentionally parodic of the eighth-grade American history textbook, but with a text the real textbooks would not tell. And yet if the purpose is didactic, the manner is playful, ironic, self-aware, and brushed with the supernatural.

Doctorow's central intention seems to be to depict the invasion, from below and within and without, of a smug and secure American WASP family, circa 1908–1915, a family which is a microcosm of American self-conception at about the turn of the century. The novel is indeed a family and national

From *Understanding E. L. Doctorow*. © 1992 by the University of South Carolina.

Bildungsroman—an account of the nature of the American national character and the transformation of its identity. Such an ambition in such a form struck some critics as pretentious.

For example, the reviewer for *Time*, R. Z. Sheppard, spoke irritably of Doctorow's narrative hybrid as an unsatisfactory mix of domestic comedy and cosmic portentousness: "As if Clarence Day had written *Future Shock* into *Life with Father.* Doctorow's images and improvisations foreshadow the 20th century's coming preoccupation with scandal, psychoanalysis, solipsism, race, technology, power and megalomania."

A more sympathetic response came from *The New York Times Book Review*, where George Stade described the novel's texture as "absorbing rather than annotating the images and rhythms of its subject, in measuring the shadows of myth cast by naturalistic detail, in rousing our senses and treating us to some serious fun." *Ragtime* is indeed serious fun, perhaps one of the finest didactic novels written about the American experience. There is much to learn, and Doctorow realizes that a useful simplification is the best first step in teaching anything.

It is 1908, or thereabouts—Doctorow is not going to be pedantic and literal in his use of chronological sequences, or in fact with any other dimension of his novel. He has claimed that history belongs to the novelists and the poets rather than to the social scientist: "At least we admit that we lie." At this moment in American history the President of the United States, Teddy Roosevelt, the Rough Rider, has just finished giving the monarchies of the Old World a lesson they will not soon forget at San Juan Hill in Cuba. Protestant Anglo-Saxon American has just annexed Hawaii and put down the Philippine insurrection, so the little brown brothers and sisters of the Third World have been instructed in just what is good for *them*, too. (When McKinley seized the Philippines, he wrote "there was nothing left us to do but to take them all and to educate the Filipinos and uplift and civilize and Christianize them, and by God's grace do the very best we could by them, as our fellow men for whom Christ also died.") In 1908 the Wright brothers are only five years past running a bicycle shop in Dayton, Ohio, and it will be almost half a decade until the Panama Canal is completed and the Model T Ford mass produced at the great factory in River Rouge. In 1908 America is still a small town three thousand miles wide.

But of course there are masked tensions under the small-town surface. This is Doctorow's crucial point and the moral substance of his novel. In 1908 America was still pretending.

> "In normal lives," T. S. Eliot wrote, "misery is mostly concealed. . . . In the Puritan morality that I remember, it was

tacitly assumed that if one was thrifty, enterprising, intelligent, practical and prudent in not violating social conventions, one ought to have a happy and 'successful' life. Failure was due to some weakness or perversity peculiar to the individual; but the decent man need have no nightmares."

Doctorow's "decent man" is called only Father, and as the story opens he has succeeded in the business of life just as Ben Franklin and Thomas Edison and Abe Lincoln indicated a penniless young American male should succeed. In fact, in 1908 Father sounds like figment out of Horatio Alger's daydreams. Educated at Groton and Harvard for a leisured but empty life, Father was fortunately forced to become a self-made man when his own father's investments failed after the Civil War. Now he manufactures fireworks and flags and patriotic paraphernalia and has done so well at it that God has rewarded him with a gold watch chain across his vest, a good digestion, a substantial income and a fine New Rochelle house, and a "large blond" wife and a son in sailor suit—in about that order of importance. He is a big-game hunter and an amateur explorer of real accomplishment, too, for the decent American man in the first decade of this century wants to be as much like Theodore Roosevelt as he can manage.

There is of course a Mother in the family, and Mother will learn a great deal about herself in the course of the action—revelations that will both startle and please. There is a maternal Grandfather in the family, too, about whom the reader never learns much other than that he is a sort of faded academic relic. There is the sailor-suited little boy of about nine or ten years, an artist-in-embryo (and perhaps an authentic clairvoyant) to whom no one but Doctorow and the reader pay the slightest attention. There is also Mother's Younger Brother living here in the big New Rochelle house, a moody, rudderless youth of perhaps eighteen in a white linen suit and a straw boater pining away for the infamous artist's model Evelyn Nesbit. The noted architect Stanford White has just been murdered for making Evelyn his mistress (an event that really transpired in 1906), and Mother's Younger Brother can think of no one other than Evelyn and schemes to have her for himself (and since Doctorow is writing a fairy tale as well as a history text, he will).

Nightmare genii are about to penetrate the shell of this smug American microcosm whose official belief is that "there were no Negroes. There were no immigrants." After Doctorow gets through with it, America is not going to be able to pretend any more. By an accident that is not quite an accident, Harry Houdini, headlining in Manhattan, appears at the house one empty summer afternoon. This is wonderful. The little boy, like all little boys, is fascinated by the great escape artist's powers, and it is the first of the novel's magical events that Houdini's chauffeur-driven 45-horsepower Pope-Toledo auto just happens to break down in front of the house. Doctorow is setting in motion one of his most imaginative and intricate ghost machines. The car is only overheated, and while the chauffeur replenishes the radiator the magician spends a few moments in the family living room, just long enough to discover that Father has been chosen by Admiral Peary to join his third assault on the North Pole (an event that actually transpired in 1909).

The great magician Houdini will turn out to be one of Doctorow's most intriguing presences (he will also commandeer J. P. Morgan, Henry Ford, Sigmund Freud, and Emma Goldman, along other once-real people), and the author gives the reader a clue to the magician's profound self-contempt when we see that Houdini reacts with admiration to Father's Arctic adventure and dismisses his own feats of derring-do as just legerdemain to thrill children. "The real-world act was what got into the history books," as he bitterly observes to himself later, when he has abandoned the real world altogether in pursuit of contact with his dead mother's ghost on the other side of death.

Just as Houdini is about to drive away from the New Rochelle house, Doctorow inserts into the scene a detail that will turn out later in this novel to be a clue that there is an organizing energy lying below the surface of the novel's world. It is the first instance of Doctorow's demonstration of a cosmic design beneath the outward, random look of things.

> The little boy had followed the magician to the street and now stood at the front of the Pope-Toledo gazing at the distorted macrocephalic image of himself in the shiny brass fitting of the headlight. Houdini thought the boy comely, fair like his mother, and tow-headed, but a little soft-looking. He leaned over the side door. Goodbye, Sonny, he said holding out his hand. Warn the Duke, the little boy said. Then he ran off.

Almost halfway through the novel Houdini will have his chance to indeed "warn the Duke." Tragically, he will miss it. Houdini does not yet sense that the boy's words are an authentic signal to him from the Other Side, and the magician's recognition of their supernatural identity only comes much later and will even then be incomplete. And so the historical consequences of missing that signal from the beyond will be severe, for the Duke that the boy was urging him to warn turns out to be Archduke Franz Ferdinand, heir to the Habsburg throne in Austro-Hungary, who will come to an airfield in Germany to witness with his "stupid, heavy-lidded eyes" Houdini giving demonstrations of airplane flight for the Prussian military. If the Archduke could have avoided getting assassinated at Sarajevo on 28 June 1914, the course of world history would surely have been less tragic. But Houdini misses his cue, and the Duke is drawn along toward his own extinction and the flashpoint of historical catastrophe.

Doctorow is not quite done with this signal from the Other Kingdom, for in the novel's final pages we hear the little boy's warning from 1908 one last time. At almost the moment that the Archduke *really is* shot to death in the Balkans, Houdini is thrilling a Manhattan midday crowd with one of his most dangerous and audacious escapes. Dangling in a straitjacket upside down from a cable twelve stories over the pavement of Times Square, he undergoes "the one genuine mystical experience of his life":

> He was upside down over Broadway, the year was 1914, and the Archduke Franz Ferdinand was reported to have been assassinated. It was at this moment that an image composed itself in Houdini's mind. The image was of a small boy looking at himself in the shiny brass headlamp of an automobile.

It was a swashbuckling turn toward narrative hyperconsciousness that rescued *The Book of Daniel* from the flatness that had so disappointed Doctorow in his first draft. Simple two-dimensional lifelikeness will no longer interest him as a writer, and he will never again construct a novel like *Welcome to Hard Times* or *Big as Life*. From *Daniel* on, his novels became acutely aware of themselves as artificial, self-referential texts. Here in *Ragtime* the author and the reader share an awareness of design and destiny of which the characters are only fitfully aware. A close look at some of the novel's small particulars reveals a tracery of coincidence, correspondence, and the supernatural surrounding its characters and events.

Thus, it is not really a coincidence that Mother has one of Emma Goldman's books on a woman's right to contraception on her bedside table, that Houdini glimpses Harry Thaw in his cell, that J. P. Morgan's library was designed by Stanford White. Or that Father and his little boy will in chapter 30 attend a New York Giants baseball game at the Polo Grounds and then that those very same Giants appear again in chapter 40, where they will infuriate J. P. Morgan as he emerges from the Great Pyramid after a harrowing night trying to communicate with primal energies from beyond death and finding his solitary vigil interrupted only by Egyptian bedbugs. These subtle tracings show the reader that although the purpose of Doctorow's tale is moral instruction, the technique of its telling is playful, ironic, multidimensional, as self-aware as a puzzle inviting us to solve it. Like Joyce's *Ulysses* or Nabokov's *Pale Fire*, *Ragtime* is a novel which invites the reader to discern a pattern in its structure that its characters in their world of ink and paper cannot achieve the elevation to perceive. Close reading reveals that the entire circuit of characters in the book is linked with major or minor—in many cases minute—connections.

An example of a major connection, though still a connection that the characters involved do not themselves ever fully apprehend, is the linkage of coincidence which binds the New Rochelle family with two other families featured in the novel: those of the black musician Coalhouse Walker and his wife Sarah, and of the immigrant Jew Tateh and his never-named daughter. Myth and politics have seldom been so minutely interwoven, and the net of connections seems to vitalize the book's subsets of character and incident just as real nerves conduct impulses into living tissue. The circuit is detailed and elaborate.

Mother's Younger Brother ingratiates himself with Evelyn Nesbit and has a short, doomed love affair with her. She jilts him out of impatience with his devotion: "She loved him but she wanted someone who would treat her badly and whom she could treat badly." Evelyn is almost always weak, greedy, exploitative in her relationships with the men who desire her so desperately, but there is one pure, passionate love in her that is wholly unselfish. This is her nonsexual fascination with a beautiful little Jewish girl. Evelyn falls in love with the girl, whom she glimpses in the Lower East Side streets on her chauffeur-driven way back from visiting in his Tombs jail cell her mad millionaire husband, Harry K. Thaw, awaiting trial (eventually dodging it by means of an insanity defense) for murdering Evelyn's lover, the architect Stanford White.

The nameless little girl's father is a destitute, Yiddish-speaking silhouette artist Doctorow will only call Tateh—Yiddish for "father"—who is identified thus as the ghetto analogue to the WASP Father of New Rochelle. Tateh, his rigid sexual puritanism outraged by the mere thought of the defilement, has just expelled forever from their tenement rooms his wife, Mameh, for daring to offer to sell herself as a prostitute to keep the three of them from starvation. He is half-mad with mourning (to him, his wife is dead), and frenzied with the consequences of his conscience. In analogy to the WASP Mother of New Rochelle adopting the black washergirl Sarah and *her* baby, Evelyn expresses some urgent, motherly love hunger in herself by befriending Tateh and his beautiful child. For a time Tateh tolerates her intrusion into their lives because of its benefits to his daughter, but he despises Evelyn as the most infamous sexual adventuress of the era—her picture is everywhere—and she recalls to him all too vividly his castoff wife's willingness to barter sex for bread: "My life is desecrated with whores," he tells her in Yiddish. He will not stand for it long.

Through her connection with Tateh and his daughter, Evelyn meets the historical anarchist Emma Goldman (Doctorow will show the reader the chain of linkages that will lead away from this meeting, too). But Tateh, anticipating with horror the inevitable brutalization of his child in the Manhattan slum jungle and fearing for her corruption at the hands of the infamous society whore Evelyn Nesbit, simply steals away one day with his daughter on a northbound trolley, no destination in mind and some thirty dollars hidden in his pockets and shoes.

If Doctorow rejoiced in exploiting what he called "disreputable genre materials" like the Western and science fiction for his first two novels, here in *Ragtime* it might be suspected that he is commandeering for his vehicle a creaking pushcart right out of Yiddish melodrama. After all, the situation could hardly be more charged with potentially mawkish sentiment: penniless immigrant father, immaculate lovely daughter, Lear and Cordelia as orphans of the storm. But Doctorow's storytelling powers make the situation work because he convinces us of its reality. "Nothing is as good at fiction as fiction," Doctorow observed for a symposium on the importance of fiction for *Esquire*. "It is the most ancient way of knowing but also the most modern, managing when it's done to burn all the functions of language back into powerful fused revelation. . . . You will experience love, if [fiction] so chooses, or starvation or drowning or dropping through space or holding a hot pistol in your hand with the police pounding at the door. This is the way it is, it will say, this is what it feels like."

Doctorow does not hesitate to revise some history for political effect. But first he organizes his episodes by means of synchronicity and magical correspondence. This is the method with which he links his forty short chapters and his half-dozen subplots. At their transfer station in New Rochelle, Tateh and his daughter glimpse none other than Mother and her sailor-suited little boy, and the little girl seems to find some nameless magical connection in the lad's face. But for the moment nothing comes of her inarticulate apprehension of the presence of fate.

Transferring again and again, Tateh and child make their way by interurban trolley up into Massachusetts (total fare: $3.40), where Tateh finds work at a factory woolen loom in Lawrence and sequesters his daughter inside their unheated rooms to keep her free of the world's vile touch. The immigrant factory workers, outraged by the exploitations by the Lawrence textile concerns, initiate a violent strike. (The real strike in Lawrence did not occur until 1912, but the effect Doctorow knows he can achieve is simply too good to miss). The International Workers of the World sends its most charismatic orator, the historical Big Bill Haywood, to encourage the strikers, and Tateh, despite his fears for his daughter's safety, finds himself committed to the labor struggle out of admiration for the agitator's eloquence. Tateh, beaten by the police strikebreakers, manages to hoist himself onto the departing child's train, and eventually he and the girl end up in Philadelphia. "From this moment, perhaps, Tateh began to conceive of his fate as separate from the fate of the working class." For $25 apiece he contracts to create for the Franklin Novelty Company what they call "movie books"—flip the edge of the book pages with your thumb and a little one-reeler takes place before your eyes.

And so when next we see him fifteen chapters later, Tateh has become that most fantastic of truly American successes, the movie mogul complete with jodhpurs and white linen cap, and that most preposterous of truly American parodies, the ersatz aristocrat complete with bogus title and fake accent. No one unmasks him and the past does not rise up to destroy his celluloid castle—far from it. He has "invented" the movie serial (Doctorow's real father turned down a chance to star opposite Pearl White in *The Perils of Pauline*, preferring to keep his secure job in a bank, so this may well be an instance of Doctorow's revenge on facts). And Tateh has secured for his daughter a luxurious life that perhaps will compensate for the expulsion of her mother and the years of poverty. He will even get to marry a lovely Christian woman and live happily ever after—in Hollywood, of course.

Still, one interviewer was so disturbed by Doctorow's failure to administer moral justice to Tateh that he asked the writer if he had "been tempted to condemn [Tateh] for abandoning his working-class ideals." Doctorow's response to the query is revealing because it is so tough and unsentimental, and it is a response worth keeping in mind when the reader comes to assess the moral implications of *Loon Lake* and *Billy Bathgate*:

> "No, I love that character, but also understand him," Doctorow replied. "I was making an observation in my treatment of him, that very often a man who begins as a radical somehow—with all his energy and spirit and intelligence and wit—by a slight change of course can use these gifts to succeed under the very system he's criticizing. . . . As compassionate as we feel for Tateh and as much as we love him, here's a man who has betrayed his principles and sympathies and gotten ahead that way."

By coincidence—always a highly charged term in *Ragtime*—Tateh, now calling himself Baron Ashkenazy, meets the New Rochelle family at the Jersey shore. Tateh's daughter and Mother's small, quiet son become inseparable on the beach, and "the Baron" charms the family, especially Mother, whose blond beauty intrigues him. History soon contrives to separate them all—even though history will eventually contrive to bring some of them back together. Father is called to New York to deal with Mother's Younger Brother's role in the occupation of the Morgan Library by Coalhouse Walker and his band. The morose young idealist has turned his passion for Evelyn Nesbit Thaw into a commitment to radical justice. He comes under the influence of the radical Emma Goldman, and his commitment to social transformation and his skill with anarchist explosives will eventually kill him.

And war is in the air, the Great War of 1914–1918. The ragtime era will end with a bang, not a whimper. The family does not quite comprehend why Fritz von Papen of the German army should be so interested in examining the particularities of the Jersey shoreline, but it is with foreshadowing details like this that Doctorow signals that the great catastrophe of the war will reach out to their lives quite shortly. Mother's Younger Brother will soon die with Zapata's peasant forces in the Mexican Revolution.

Father discovers that the young man's legacy to him includes blueprints for no fewer than seventeen ordance devices of futuristic design, for Mother's Younger Brother turns out to have been a combination of Leonardo da Vinci and Tom Swift who had secretly created designs for grenade launchers, land mines, sonar-directed antisubmarine depth charges, infrared sights, and so on, weapons some of which are "so advanced that they were not used by the United States until World War II." At once good American patriot and good American profiteer, Father converts his factories from fireworks to munitions in anticipation of America's entry into the conflict and secretly conveys to both the American and Allied high commands Mother's Younger Brother's astonishing blueprints for death. Father is himself killed along with 1,194 others aboard the *Lusitania* on 7 May 1915, when the German submarine U-20 torpedoes the vessel off the coast of Ireland, the episode which made inevitable America's involvement in the war. "Mother wore black for a year," and then Tateh, ingenuously revealing to her that he is not a baron at all but a simply a very rich Jewish socialist from Latvia, asks and receives her hand in marriage.

Although the social convulsion which leads to the occupation of the Morgan Library and a dozen deaths originates in race hatred, and although the novel offers no evidence at all that America can solve its racial crisis (quite the contrary), Tateh, the perfect American entrepreneur, extrapolates from a idyllic scene just outside his window in California the movie gimmick that will mark his greatest success. "He suddenly had an idea for a film. A bunch of children who were black and white . . . little urchins who would have funny adventures in their own neighborhood, a society of ragamuffins."

Tateh is seeing, of course, Our Gang, one of the gauziest American fantasies of them all, and his vision of the commercial possibilities of this happy racial detente forms an ironic coda to the thematic burden of the novel, which indicates that America's racial crisis is deep and probably insoluble. The very existence of the "schwartze child" in Tateh's triptych is in fact one of the novel's most crucial plot devices and the fulcrum of its moral scheme. But to explain the significance of the child it is necessary to return all the way back to chapter 9. *Ragtime* is that kind of book.

While Father is gone on his expedition to the North Pole, Mother discovers in the family garden a living baby who turns out to be the illegitimate offspring of a neighborhood washergirl called Sarah and a black ragtime musician, Coalhouse Walker. Doctorow told an interviewer that he'd heard the true prototype of this story from his wife, and "I found myself using it in *Ragtime*, where I never knew in advance what was going to happen."

What does happen sets in motion the entire march of events that forms the moral scheme of the novel. It is a tale of race and of property, those two enduring American obsessions. Coalhouse Walker, the musical gentleman "of color" whose refusal to be racially humiliated infuriates a certain sort of white ("he had created himself in the teeth of such feelings"), comes weekly to see his lover and the child he had sired. With each visit he passes the rowdy Irish crew of the Emerald Isle Engine Company of volunteer firemen. The sight of an uppity black man driving a Ford automobile through these lily-white precincts does not sit well with them. Pretending to be charging him a toll for the use of the road into New Rochelle, the firemen end up defiling and eventually destroying Coalhouse's car. He demands restoration or restitution. These are refused. Then Sarah is badly injured when she tries to reach the Republican candidate for vice-president, Sunny Jim Sherman, in order to ask him to intervene on her lover's behalf. One of Sherman's military bodyguard strikes her savagely with his rifle butt. When Sarah dies of pneumonia brought on by her injuries, Coalhouse sets out to exact a terrible vengeance on WASP America.

With dynamite and shotgun Coalhouse ambushes and assassinates a half-dozen of the racist firemen. Now the black man the press calls the "killer arsonist" lays siege to New York, murdering more firemen and taking for a hostage something far dearer to the white American's heart than the mere life of any of our citizens—property. In this case Coalhouse and his rebel band, the "Provisional American Government" (and we hear in our mind's ear echoes of the IRA's Provos), occupy and threaten to dynamite the collection of treasures Pierpont Morgan has accumulated in the marble library building he has caused to be erected as his own monument on 36th Street. Coalhouse's ordnance man is Mother's Younger Brother, lately the chief designer at his brother-in-law's fireworks factory, and with this defection compounding Mother's adoption of the black orphan child

Doctorow signals that the smug WASP New Rochelle Everyfamily of 1908, transformed by compassion and outrage, has been changed forever. This disillusion even includes that holiest sacrament of American life, business itself—for if, as Calvin Coolidge claimed, the business of America is business, even that central mystery is exposed "for the dreary unimaginative thing it was" when Mother commands for a time the family enterprises during Father's Arctic adventure.

The domestication of yesterday's radical visions is central to America's political evolution, Doctorow feels, citing as illustration for his claim the fact that Emma Goldman's outrageous proposal that abortion simply be made available to any woman who wanted it had become in the eight intervening decades since her deportation from these shores the orthodoxy of today.

In the Coalhouse Walker subplot of *Ragtime*, Doctorow has literalized this political insight. Radicalism is not only "part of the family"; it is the basis for the formation of the family—in this case, the radical family of ideology which inevitably replaces the feeble family of genes, habit, and decorum that is the American middle-class legacy, Eliot's "decent" life of gentility and inhibition. Mother's Younger Brother is simply Artie Sternlicht from *The Book of Daniel* writ large.

Realizing that he will inevitably be destroyed for his bloody vigilante presumption ("a ceremony of vengeance in the manner of the ancient warrior"), Coalhouse demands that the racist fire chief of the Emerald Isle company, Willie Conklin, be given over to him for blood justice. This is not done, nor does Coalhouse really expect it to be. Then Booker T. Washington, the living embodiment of social humility as the cost of economic advancement for the black race, meets with Coalhouse under the flag of truce and admonishes the revolutionary to see that his intransigent demand for revenge is dragging to their deaths the half-dozen young blacks and the young white man in blackface, Mother's Younger Brother, solely in order to satisfy the claims of his own vendetta.

In order to save his men, Coalhouse softens his demands to a simple and symbolic restoration of his automobile, for he will not give up his life without transforming its loss into a moral lesson about the rights of a black. Negotiations are completed, and fire chief Willie Conklin is made to assemble an entire Model T from its disparate parts at curbside in front of the Morgan Library. But of course Coalhouse and his men realize that the completion of the automobile will signal the musician's destruction, for at that moment he has promised to give himself up to the authorities. The grim climax of the novel occurs as Coalhouse is shot to death in the street by "a squad of New York's Finest armed with carbines."

Behind the geniality of its temperament and the cheerful audacity of its method, the novel is surely a dark, violent prophecy from out of the age of which it is written to the era that will come to read it—our era.

For *Ragtime* Doctorow has invented a style which, by its seeming *negation* of style, manages to throw into relief the slightest nuance of irony he applies to character, episode, description. Without seeming effort the novel catches up on the quicksilver of its small, radically curved surface a micro-cosmal concentration of the American world during the first decade of our century, a world that convinces with the accuracy of its miniaturization and the authority of its dramatic metaphor. Doris Grumbach spoke for a number of American reviewers when she praised Doctorow's "adroit cleverness" in plotting and the subtle humor just beneath the simplicities of its "Dick-and-Jane-and-Spot prose." And like many of her colleagues in the American literary community, she saw nothing wrong with Doctorow's reinvention of historical incident as a technique to highlight the inner truth of the ragtime era, "the world of simplicity and optimism at the turn of the century" when it might have still been possible for America "to make peace between classes and races in this country."

Reviewers for such important publications as *The New York Times, The Village Voice, Newsweek, Saturday Review,* and *The New Yorker* awarded the novel high praise when it was brought out in 1975 and post-Vietnam America was in a revisionist mood. For example, George Stade claimed in *The New York Times Book Review* that Doctorow had achieved an impressive breakthrough in his invention of a technique that could capture "the fictions and the realities of the era of ragtime." Eliot Fremont-Smith said in *The Village Voice* that Doctorow's novel was "simply splendid" on one level and yet also "complicatedly splendid" in its deeper levels of meaning, implication, and irony, "a bag of riches, totally lucid and accessible, full of surprises, epiphanies, little time-bombs that alter one's view of things." Writing on the novel for the *Washington Post,* Raymond Sokolov called it "brilliant and graceful" and said that it was Doctorow's marvelous trick to "throw the knowns and unknowns together in a racy plot that uses conventional history as its main premise and spins on outward from there in a zany extrapolation . . . [that turns] history into myth and myth into history."

Even critics who disapproved of *Ragtime* as a pretentious fairy tale admired its animation and charm and conviction. For example, Hilton Kramer disliked Doctorow's Leftist political bias; *Ragtime,* he claimed, "distorts the actual materials of history with a fierce ideological arrogance." But Kramer praised the book's "delectable aesthetic surface." Like many of his colleagues, Walter Clemons in *Newsweek* was pleased rather than disturbed by Doctorow's reinventions of episode and encounter, finding an

they felt that Doctorow had attempted a serious political seduc-
r the cover of an appealing, pseudo-naïve narrative manner. Thus,
Raban conceded that *Ragtime* "is a consistently bright, thoroughly
ook," but he was annoyed by the political bias, by what he felt were
caricatures, by Doctorow's gleeful alterations of historical reality,
e opportunistic relocation of the story from character to character,
episode. In Raban's final analysis the novel was "a cunning, fragile
ards. Its major interest lies in the way in which it suggests a recipe
ntemporary bestseller. It is written to be read fast."

ther British reviewer, Paul Levy, announced that he was speaking
st all British critics" and "several thousand common readers" when
ically identified the *real* plot of *Ragtime* as its sales campaign, and
hat Doctorow had failed to live up to the splendid promise of *The*
aniel. Levy described *Ragtime*'s construction as "a little nostalgia
tle noble left-wing sentiment there, and the lashing of semen when-
eader's interest threatens to wane." He cited the author's alterations
as its gravest fault and linked this sentimental falsification to the
'the book's natural constituency of trendies."

likely that critical reaction to the book will continue to be divided
issue of its political vision of America and, as one type of response
sion, the right of an artist to alter and invent a fable "truer" than
ts. As Roger Sale crystallized this phenomenon in *The New York*
Books, Doctorow's procedure was to lay out "impudently and
distorical actions which did and didn't happen," and implicitly
at his creations in *Ragtime* carried a poetic truth formerly
1 from us by our complacent allegiance to "mere" facts. Clearly,
and hype that surrounded the initial appearance of the novel were
t a fad. But the novel that remains in the aftermath of the fad is
ing achievement.

exhilarating freedom in the book's presump

fiction and history is magically dissolved.

details because I *wanted* them to be true. . .

of *Ragtime* make it enormous fun to read.

rhythms sound the neat, sad waltz of *Gats*

disfigured promise that the best American nc

And Stanley Kauffmann's response in *Saturd*

as an authentic modern masterpiece: "*Ragtim*

of art about American destiny, built of fact a

music heard and sensed, responsive to cinem

datum. . . . Doctorow saw ways to fuse i

dramatized history, to distill an era. . . . Thi

seem simple, is complex and rich."

    But the novelist's meddling with object

reviewers uneasy. They doubted that invented

events fixed in historical reality. And pe

sheathed his radical politics and racial pe:

deadpan, "pseudo-pedantic" style, in the man

adults, some critics reacted negatively. From

Ragtime has provoked striking instances of cri

Doctorow's most controversial book.

    For example, in a review in *Commentary*

message he felt was concealed beneath the no

realities of Mr. Doctorow's political romanc

American life, and its celebration of a radical a

it were, in the quaint, chromatic glow of a T

ened and made more decorative in the prc

similar charge in a review in *The American .*

taking "gross liberties with history in the nar

the reader to indulge himself in a radical chic

the airs of revolutionaries, in purely fantasy an

Writing in *The Atlantic*, Richard Todd called

book of the year" largely because of what he f

ical message. Predictably, the conservative *Nat*

ical bias of the novel, and even while praising

medium," Jeffrey Hart noticed that Doctoro\

house Walker and Emma Goldman: "Both o

from the moral skepticism in which Doctoro

Irish. . . . The serious danger to Doctorow as a

    Some British reviewers also objected to th

melodrama Doctorow built into his tale. Lik

reviewer

tion und

Jonathan

readable

its facile

and by t

episode

house of

for the c

   An

for "alm

he sarca

claimed

Book of

here, a l

ever the

of histor

needs of

   It

along th

to that

mere fa

Review

gravely

assert

conceal

the fam

partly j

an endu

JOHN WILLIAMS

Ragtime *as Historical Novel 1977–85*

The most recent edition of that reliable tool for English majors, Holman and Harmon's *A Handbook to Literature* (1992), has retained its explanation of the historical novel from 20 years before. It reads in part:

> The classic formula for the historical novel, as expressed by Scott in his numerous prefaces and introductions to the Waverly Novels, calls for an age when two cultures are in conflict; into this cultural conflict are introduced fictional personages who participate in actual events and move among actual personages.

The only change is a lengthened list of novelists who write in the genre. To standard names such as Thackeray, Tolstoy, and Cooper, the editors have added Barth, Mailer, and Doctorow. It may be mere coincidence that the description of the work by these men withholds clear approval: "historical novels *have been attempted*" by these writers (emphasis added); on the other hand, this phrase may indicate the uncertain status accorded Barth's, Mailer's, and Doctorow's efforts. In the case of Doctorow, journal articles that began to appear in the late 1970s concerned more than just his use of Kleist. Along with that flurry of source studies and extending beyond it, the larger issue of Doctorow's view of history, its process, and its representation

From *Fiction as False Document: The Reception of E. L. Doctorow in the Postmodern Age.* © 1996 by Camden House.

in fiction occupied a small group of critics who were now paying attention to his corpus of four novels, soon to be five with the publication of *Loon Lake* in 1980.

Together, these novels (excluding the almost always neglected *Big as Life*) constitute a survey of American history from the late 1880s to the 1960s. As we have seen, reviewers noted either with dismay or delight Doctorow's use of history, and that issue dominated the slowly but steadily growing number of articles in scholarly publications. Instead of focusing on arguments about Doctorow's fidelity to fact, critics in journals broadened the scope of debate to reopen theoretical questions on the relationship between fiction and history, questions that could not be contained by those two terms alone.

In a famous distinction in book nine of the *Poetics*, Aristotle says that history narrates "the thing that has been," whereas the poet writes about "a kind of thing that might be." As a result, fiction (poetry) "is more philosophical and more significant than history" because it is "more concerned with the universal, and history more with the individual." By "universal" Aristotle means general human nature; by "individual" he means the factual, or specific events in time. In other words, Aristotle seems to claim for art a better way of knowing than mere accuracy. Its very freedom from the need to reproduce specific historical circumstances with exactitude allows it to derive meaning from those circumstances.

This distinction appears in various guises throughout literary history, and can be taken as a defense by artists, indeed, by all humanists, against the recurring criticism of art as either immoral or irrelevant. Sidney's depiction of the "golden world" of poets relies on Aristotle (as well as Plato) to defend fiction as purveyor of a higher truth than other disciplines. The Romantic poets employ similar logic and diction to make their case for the superiority of poetry to science or history. As we shall see, this claim energizes much of the affirmative Doctorow criticism. By the time his critics took up the issue, however, centuries of debate on the exact nature of literature and the upheavals of twentieth-century thought had complicated Aristotle's distinction considerably. When Doctorow critics discuss his use of history, they often bring with them complicated baggage from romantic, modern, and post-modern attempts to define fiction against a range of literary and non-literary discourse.

Common to all these major sensibilities has been the view of fiction's oppositional stance. Since the industrial revolution and rise of the modern bureaucratic state, artists have often viewed the factual record, including history and the disciplines, to be under the control of governments or agencies indifferent or hostile to human freedom. Seen in this light, literature, always subversive in some ways, takes on an adversarial function unique to the modern age, at least in the eyes of its practitioners, filling in gaps left by philistine official documents. Though perhaps sentimental in retrospect, Frederick Henry's refusal in *A Farewell to Arms* to mouth patriotic abstractions illustrates a sense of modern mistrust of institutionalized language, what Bakhtin called monological or authoritative discourse (1981).

In American criticism, several strands of oppositional theory weave the background for extant commentary on Doctorow's historical fiction. First, modernism, as much debated as its essence may be, includes a sense that fiction goes beyond, even outside history as a way of knowing. The seminal writers of this period produced work based on mythic, timeless structure. Eliot's well-known praise of *Ulysses* illustrates the point. According to Eliot, Joyce had triumphed because as an artist, he had found in myth "a way of controlling, of ordering, of giving a shape and a significance to the immense panorama of futility and anarchy which is contemporary history" (1923). This retreat into artistic form was inherent in the school of criticism Eliot helped create. The New Critics became infamous for trying to install literature, especially poetry, as a "verbal icon," separate and independent from other genres such as history.

The noble aim of purer expression, of order in disorder, was not the only goal of the attempt to create a separate status for literary discourse. As Terry Eagleton, among others, makes clear, the development of New Critical practice and theory which followed was motivated in large part by a desire to provide a model of analysis competitive with the dominant mode of knowledge—science. Science was the epistemological enemy but also the professional rival of literary studies in the relatively new world of "disciplinary" academia (1983). In order to survive as a legitimate discipline, literary criticism must have precise analytical tools. This twin engine still drives English studies: it is both a humanistic alternative to scientific knowledge and a competing discipline that measures its stature in terms of new theory and a formidable jargon. Doctorow criticism proves no exception, as it has tried to find its niche in the poststructuralist world while exploring Doctorow's canon for humanistic themes.

Despite its emphasis on form, modernism produced its share of critics who did more than promote the autotelic art object. Lionel Trilling (1950), for example, emerged as a champion of modern fiction, celebrating its ability to capture the complexity of human beings in particular cultures at specific historic points. Although no New Critic, Trilling does stand with them in the battle to preserve a distinct place for literature among modes of knowledge, the array of nonfiction discourse that Doctorow himself has called the "industrialized forms of storytelling" (*Drinks Before Dinner* 1979).

Trilling's interest in fiction's potential as a way of understanding culture was shared by a number of influential critics during this same period. Together, F. O. Matthiessen, Perry Miller, R. W. B. Lewis, Leo Marx, and others created a brand of cultural criticism known as American Studies, which, according to Gerald Graff, became a distinctive approach in the 1930s and flourished after the Second World War (1987). It discovered in literature sustaining myths that attempted to define the American experience. Certainly not monolithic in its concerns, American Studies fostered not only a sense of American "exceptionalism," but, as Giles Gunn argues, used American fiction to show how the great experiment in democracy and freedom could "go awry" (1986). Thanks to the persuasive scholarship of books like Matthiessen's *American Renaissance* (1941) and Marx's *Machine in the Garden* (1957), critics of American fiction have inherited a set of literary and cultural motifs. For example, when David Emblidge (1977), whose essay will be discussed later, argues that Doctorow's work is a critique of the idea of progress, he employs the strategy initiated by Matthiessen in his seminal work and furthered by Marx's *Machine in the Garden*. As we shall see, Emblidge in fact builds his argument by using the writers that Matthiessen helped to canonize. Although one may agree with Graff that American Studies failed in its attempt to reorganize knowledge of the national culture (1987), its body of work did wed New Critical close reading with interest in the relation of literature to history and society, proving an influential model for critics of Doctorow.

By the time critics began to respond to Doctorow, however, neither traditional cultural critique nor New Criticism had survived intact the assault of French theory. The older notions of analysis, whether emphasizing form or historical critique, depended on the special status of the literary text as a separate and superior language. As Lee Patterson (1990) points out, formalist attempts to establish the independent status of literature were undermined by the advent of poststructuralist thought. New Critical emphasis on the special language of literature broke down under the assault on distinctions among types of discourse. In this new wave, beginning in the late 1960s, differences between subjective and objective cultural analysis disappear; history is no less interpretive than literature. For example, Hayden White (1973) concludes that historians use the same tools as any novelist; consequently the claims of history on the truth are far more provisional than positivists would have us believe. If this view, in its leveling of discourse, restores the authority of fiction as a kind of history, Patterson points out that it could also mean a loss of literature's special "ontological status," leaving a functional one that arises from the unique interplay of culture and language. Patterson's remarks support a New Historical approach to literature that would study texts embedded in the social structures they describe. In this retooled historicism, neither literature nor criticism can stand apart from history as purer expression and therefore more universal truth; the humanities are encompassed by the same historical conditions that operate to render discourse part of the larger cultural text. Patterson admits the danger of seeing culture as only a text; such a view may lead back into the hermeticism of pure deconstruction. He does not mention a related danger, however. In New Historicism's attempt to see fiction as a social practice, it can fall prey to the de-humanization of texts, that is, viewing literature primarily as the site of social or linguistic effects to the detriment of the old human themes and concerns. To put it another way, poststructural demystification of literary discourse sometimes has the effect of robbing it of its power to speak of culture and history with the mimetic authority first suggested by Aristotle.

Of course, it can be argued that one of the major benefits of recent critical theory has been to open literature to new readings, to heretofore unexplored historical influences and interpretations. If the evolving concept of fiction's relation to history has expanded the limits of permissible critical topics, if it has opened the possibility of hearing previously silenced voices, it has also threatened to close off more traditional approaches if they seem associated with mainstream moral or social themes. Harold Bloom's theory of influence notwithstanding, recent theorists often seem unconcerned with or disdainful of universal human experience. Following Susan Sontag's dictum, many postmodern critics want not to interpret the text but to "show how it is what it is" (1966). According to much theory, human agency has little to do with how the text becomes what it is. Language and culture are seen as impersonal forces that "construct" not only a text but what we call reality, even the human subject, a view that may alter our basic notions of what it is to be human.

Critics of the 1970s inherited, then, an unsettled legacy that had called into question key assumptions behind Aristotle's claim for the superiority of fiction over history. The mimetic theory behind his elevation of fiction implied the possibility of consensus on the truths imitated by poetry. The lofty role for literature painted by romantics and moderns alike—as guardian of basic human values and dreams based on transmission of intuitive knowledge—had been tarnished by postmodernism's skepticism.

Writing near the beginning of this tumultuous scene, Warner Berthoff (1971) addresses in part the expectations of post-World-War-Two culture. He notes the demise not only of traditional humanism but of the modernist creative spirit as well. Literary studies need wider justification, he says, but in the process of rebuilding a rationale, a "tougher and deeper humanism of mind" may emerge. The burgeoning business of literary theory—he has structuralism and its analysis of narrative in mind—might expose a basic human need for "fiction-making," a realization that "the fundamental forms of our knowledge [are] narrative and fabulous." In other words, narrative involves humans in a cognitive process; or, to put it more strongly, narrative constitutes a way of knowing. We are back to Aristotle's hint that history is inadequate to understand the possibilities of corporate human life. Like Berthoff, Murray Krieger realizes a void left by the loss of objectivity: "Imagination collapses history into the categories of human form: in effect it turns history into a fiction" (1974). Both critics sought in the early days of postmodernism to retain humanist ideas for literary study and have continued to assert the powers of art to fill the void of skepticism, accommodating the value of fiction to new theories about history and language.

Berthoff's essays, collected in *Fictions and Events*, represents a cautiously optimistic attitude about the relativist perspectives in the new theory and retains a sense of fiction's value for life. His Aristotelian distinctions between literature and history expand to include the idea that fiction should move us away from history toward myth, that mysterious accretion of central cultural stories necessary for redefinition of contemporary life. Berthoff exalts fiction's role in history as providing a coherent design, and, as I suggested earlier, this spirit informs much of the positive criticism of Doctorow. However, the prevailing view of Doctorow critics tempers celebration of his reimagined history with insistence on the dark insights of his cultural critique and the problematic status of literary and critical language in relation to history. From the early journal essays, then, history in Doctorow's novels, especially *Ragtime*, was put to a variety of uses.

Making *Ragtime* Do Theoretical Work

Almost twenty years after its publication made Doctorow's career, *Ragtime*, with its problematic view of history, remains his most popular and most discussed work. These two decades furnish a case study of the progress and dilemma of contemporary criticism as well. Although other topics are addressed in the more than fifty essays and five books devoted in part or whole to *Ragtime*, the majority of reviewers and critics alike return to its use and view of history. In turn, questions of history involve the function and status of not only historical novels, but of all fiction. The unsurprising arc of *Ragtime* criticism begins in the relatively early stages of postmodern skepticism, struggles to find in the novel a useful relation to history, and proceeds to yield to notions that neither history nor fiction has an unquestioned status or function. In the process, critics display the increasing influence of poststructural style, an accoutrement of so-called epistemological skepticism. In short, *Ragtime*'s professional readers enact the spectacle of a discipline in transition and no little disarray: possessing the impulse to find significance but rapidly losing the language and professional sanction to give it voice.

The remainder of this chapter attempts to detail the first decade of this transition. Criticism of *Ragtime* will be its main focus because the issue of history became so associated with that novel. After examining the reception of *The Book of Daniel* and *Welcome to Hard Times*, I will take up the second decade of *Ragtime* criticism, with its triumph of poststructuralist approaches, in chapter four.

Even though discussion of *Ragtime* and to a lesser extent *The Book of Daniel* would dominate until the early 1980s, it was obvious even in the first essays that the success of *Ragtime* had sparked interest in other Doctorow work. For example, David Emblidge (1977) traces the theme of "progress as illusion" in *Welcome to Hard Times, The Book of Daniel,* and *Ragtime.* In his view of these novels, history is recurrence, an ominous pattern of apparently hopeful surface activity or change disguising a repetition of dashed hopes and brutality. Interestingly, Emblidge connects this theme with the American literary tradition, specifically Hawthorne, Fitzgerald, and Melville. He compares the description of the cemetery of Hard Times to the opening of *The Scarlet Letter.* Both scenes suggest that society begins by recognizing death and crime. As for the echo of Fitzgerald, Emblidge sees Blue, the entrepreneurial mayor of Hard Times, as lamenting a lost dream comparable to Jay Gatsby's. Speaking of recurrence in *Ragtime,* Emblidge characterizes Doctorow's view of history as "Melvillian" in its pessimistic assessment of human nature. Later critics would trace the theme of recurrence to European sources—primarily Nietzsche—rather than American ones, but Emblidge is the first to note what would become a dominant subject for Doctorow's critics.

The survey style of Emblidge's essay, a tactic that naturally becomes more prevalent with Doctorow's growing body of work, eschews any close reading to support the comparisons. In fact, the comparisons are general enough to apply to many modern novelists who take as their province the ideals of America. Along with the previously mentioned Matthiessen, Alfred Kazin had noted in 1942 the profound alienation of the American writer from the culture that sustained him. Still, Emblidge is among the earliest to attempt to secure a place for Doctorow in the great American tradition of cultural critique. To do so, he compares Doctorow to writers from the romantic period. In fact, few have compared him to the realistic or naturalistic writers whose work we associate with the historical subjects of his first three major novels: the settling of the West (*Welcome to Hard*

Times), American radicalism (*The Book of Daniel*), and the social and racial unrest of urban ethnic life (*Ragtime*). In spite of these typically realistic or naturalistic themes, no early essays invoke the names of Norris or Dreiser. Instead, at least in Emblidge, comparisons center on Doctorow's affinity with writers whose imaginative worlds predate the events considered in his novels but who, like him, seem in their work to question mainstream views of America.

Emblidge follows the lead of reviewers in assigning thematic importance to Doctorow's use of musical imagery, not only in *Ragtime* but also in *The Book of Daniel*. The "raga" of the earlier novel, a term supplied by narrator Daniel to label one of his summaries of the McCarthy era and defined by Emblidge as a form of Hindu devotional music, as well as the ragtime of the later work, feature an insistent foundational beat from which we are distracted by gaudy variations. The variations symbolize the illusions of history and the beat is the ominous fact of recurrence. With several variations of their own, critics who see Doctorow as productively subversive of complacent American ideology would later repeat Emblidge's explanation of the ragtime metaphor in essays throughout the eighties and into the nineties.

Other articles on *Ragtime* in the 1970s took a more theoretical approach to Doctorow's use of history, attempting to answer the questions raised by reviewers about the relationship of fiction to history. In 1979, both Constance Pierce and Samuel Hux combine the Aristotelian privileging of fiction over history with the postmodern dogma that history is inevitably constructed, not objective, to praise Doctorow's achievement. For Pierce, *Ragtime* is a self-reflexive novel demonstrating that only subjective "reporters . . . be they poets or historians," give us access to history. In her version of the ragtime metaphor, the major accent represents history, always being displaced by the seemingly minor accent of fiction. Likewise, Hux's speculative and discursive essay argues that the historical novel must be taken seriously because it does what a mere recitation of facts cannot—it compels belief. The techniques of fiction satisfy the human need to believe. Its imaginative authenticity alters our perceptions by making plausible suppositions about motive and event that *could* have occurred and "might provide some atmospheric consistency surrounding events we 'know' did occur." This procedure, Hux argues, is different only in degree from the historian's method of speculating about motive and possible cause.

Hux's version of Aristotle-cum-Hayden White welcomes a blurring of lines between fiction and history for the sake of the compelling subjective truth imparted by the former. Thus in *Ragtime*, which Hux uses to illustrate his thesis, the image of Ford and Morgan as "would-be Pharaohs," convinced of their imperial destiny, merges with and even displaces whatever facts about the two men may be known to the reader. Although Hux does not use the word "myth" (in fact he does invoke the term "saga") to describe his notion of how fiction works, his insistence on the human mind's almost primitive need for belief beyond facts suggests Berthoff's view (1971) that fiction in its most effective form becomes myth. Grounded in emerging postmodern challenges to "master narratives," Hux and Pierce push Aristotle's original principle of fiction's superiority to its extreme, or perhaps they simply negate the implied distinction he makes between the two discourses. Sanguine about the possibility of fiction illuminating history, both come close to losing the distinction between fiction and history as separate ontological entities.

This concern drives the first Marxist-influenced reading of Doctorow. Barbara Foley's "From *U.S.A* to *Ragtime:* Notes on the Forms of Historical Consciousness in Modern Fiction" (1978) is significant because it appeared in *American Literature*, the only major publication up until that time to feature analysis of *Ragtime* and the first to feature Doctorow since Barbara Estrin's essay on *The Book of Daniel* in the *Massachusetts Review* (1975). Further, while Emblidge had noted parallels between Doctorow's work and the American literary tradition, Foley makes it the crux of her argument, asserting that *Ragtime* reveals a radically different view of history than its precursor, John Dos Passos's *U.S.A.*

Foley's essay begins by noting the debt owed by *Ragtime* to *U.S.A.* Doctorow's "radical critique of capitalism" echoes Dos Passos's earlier attack. In addition, *Ragtime*'s narrative voice and basic structure derive from the older writer. Both novelists abandon to some extent the traditional mimetic form of realism in favor of intrusive documentary details that confuse fact and fiction. These parallels intend to establish for Dos Passos an influential role in modern fiction, but despite this thrust, Foley's real interest is in the idea of so-called classical historical fiction, defined in Georg Lukács's *The Historical Novel* (1937). Her major shift in the essay, to a critique of Doctorow's departures from Dos Passos, amounts to a defense of Lukács's conception of the genre.

Lukács's work, which follows his more general *Theory of the Novel* (1920), was written in the late 1930s when both Hitler and Stalin loomed large in his consciousness, their presence no doubt lending an urgency to his description of historical novels from his English model, Scott, to contemporary Germany's Mann. Clearly the crisis then taking shape in Europe underscores the important mimetic role of fiction. For Lukács, novels do not merely reflect history; they analyze it. Fiction grows out of broad historical forces that only its particularized form, its wealth of small detail can fully illuminate (1937). Foley notes this principle and makes it the chief distinction between Dos Passos, who allows history to structure his novel, and

Doctorow, who prefers what Foley calls the apocalyptic style, in which fiction delights in deforming history to show the artist's invention or control (1978). Like Lukács, Foley approves of alteration of detail in order to capture the *Zeitgeist*, but Doctorow strays too far from a mimetic model. She cites as an example his invention of Coalhouse Walker, the black musician who becomes a terrorist. This character's anachronistic sensibility and reactions violate Lukács's rule of typicality, that is, that all figures, especially the major ones, should be faithful outgrowths of their time and place. Although Foley does not cite Lukács here, the need for characters to accurately reflect their era is vital for him, since an art divorced from social conditions leads the novelist to create "eccentric" characters whose moral and spiritual trials obscure historical causes. Indeed, Foley concedes that Doctorow's depiction of Walker provides a powerful commentary on racism, but she also implies that the book's 1960s style distorts history. She might have granted that with the Walker episode Doctorow creates his own version of another Lukácsian principle: historical novels should reveal how past epochs become the "prehistory" of the present (Lukács 1937). In other words, the value of a historical novel lies in its ability to show cause and effect. Late in *The Historical Novel*, Lukács claims that the task of contemporary historical novelists is to answer the question "How was the Hitler regime in Germany possible?" For many readers, Doctorow's projection of black militancy into the ragtime era did heighten awareness of how America reached the racial boiling point in the late 1960s.

Foley's larger concern, of course, is not with how well *Ragtime* conforms to Lukács's formula. Underlying the formula, and the Marxist project in its fullest sense, is the belief that history has objective status and purposeful movement. As she is well aware, "apocalyptic" novelists with whom she groups Doctorow reflect the shaky foundations of history as a discipline (1978); in turn loss of historical consciousness threatens the basis for Marxist dialogue. Foley thus praises Dos Passos for making history itself, not specific fictional plots, the centerpiece of *U.S.A.* His work has the "external coherence" of history behind it. Doctorow, on the other hand, subordinates history to fiction because he shares with many of his peers a "fundamental skepticism about the 'objective' nature of historical reality."

Significantly, Foley discusses Doctorow's reliance on the notion of "false documents" as justification for his method in *Ragtime*. Shortly before her essay appeared, Doctorow's own essay, "False Documents" (1977) had been published in the *American Review*. In it he asserts that there is no such thing as objective history. Without acknowledging the essay, Foley notes the idea from an interview of Doctorow, in which he admits borrowing his documentary approach from Defoe, whose *Moll Flanders* among others constitutes a "false document." As a false document, *Ragtime* "lies" with a straight face, as it were—compelling reader credulity by its claims of facticity. Mentioned in the interview and developed more fully in Doctorow's essay, the strategy of the false document exposes an ancient anxiety of the artist: his competition with history for an audience. Art is forced to give its audience something other than the facts, but offers it in the guise of facts. Foley recapitulates Doctorow's rationale in her argument, but what is seen in his essay as cause for celebration of imaginative capacities, represents for her a dangerous loss of faith in the imagination's ability to know reality.

Although she does not use the term, Foley's discomfort with writers like Doctorow who play fast and loose with history for imaginative purposes brings to mind the Marxist epithet "false consciousness," a term denoting blindness to the oppressive features of capitalist culture that prevent social change. Georg Lukács (1956) taught that modernism was infected with false consciousness; Foley intimates that the emerging postmodern fiction may suffer from the same illness.

Although Foley offers close reading of parts of *Ragtime*, she "uses" the novel to examine a theoretical problem. In fact, many critics use this novel, and other Doctorow novels, to discuss emerging critical issues. By the late 1970s, when Doctorow criticism was gathering momentum, traditional formalism (in America that meant New Criticism) had been challenged on many fronts. To leave specific criticism of *Ragtime* briefly for one example of the search for fresher perspectives, Joseph Turner (1979) classifies *The Book of Daniel* as a "disguised historical novel," one of three value-neutral types of historical fiction that he proposes as alternatives to a strictly formalist approach to genre. His system depends on reader response because the boundaries between text and history "threaten to collapse" if only formalist criteria are used. Turner also rejects the Aristotelian distinction between the universal and the particular. Instead, history and the novel must be differentiated by means of how readers respond to specific generic conventions.

Turner admits the difficulty of drawing lines in the first place, so he puts his three types on a continuum from the documented historical novel, which is the closest to narrated history; to disguised historical novel, which sets up fewer reader expectations that the plot will follow history; to the invented historical novel, which is far enough away from history to create few expectations of fidelity to it. In sum, critics cannot afford to see documented historical fiction in a completely autonomous realm because readers never will. Likewise, novelists must be aware of where they are on the continuum.

Turner uses *The Book of Daniel* as a problematic "disguised historical novel." It "self-consciously flaunts its double status," forcing the reader to "engage the disguise." Turner argues that Doctorow's narrator, Daniel, by calling attention to his public identity as child of martyred parents, compels a knowledge of the Rosenbergs—the historical martyrs—before sense can be made of the history Daniel narrates. In other words, once the fictional Daniel makes connections to the Rosenberg trial, he moves the reader toward an expectation of documented history. The narrator's highly idiosyncratic fictional persona, however, pulls the reader toward invented history, with potential confusion the result, although in this case Turner assesses the final impact on the reader as powerful. I will take up the reception of *The Book of Daniel* in more detail in chapter three. For now, suffice it to say that Turner's theoretical concerns apply not only to it but to *Ragtime* as well.

Turner's essay concludes with a second classification that, disappointingly for Doctorow readers, does not include mention of his work. It nevertheless provides a perspective on the issue of Doctorow's use of history in general and suggests a response to Foley's concerns about *Ragtime*. This final classification, borrowed from Hegel, defines levels of historical consciousness, which can be applied, Turner says, to historical novels (without direct correlation to his own three types). The Original mode supplies a "compelling picture of the past." The Reflective approach generates recognition and reconciliation of differences between past and present. Finally, the Philosophical novel examines how or whether history is possible. Based on the self-reflexive content of *The Book of Daniel* and Turner's own comments on its problematic status, that novel would seem to qualify as philosophical. Although *Ragtime* is not mentioned by Turner, his description of what he calls "comic historical fiction" fits the later book. These novels, he notes,

> create their own comic perspectives on history by poking fun at
> . . . generic conventions, playing delightful variations on the
> interaction of their fictions with history, and generally flaunting
> the inescapable artifice of their creations.

Taken together, Turner's comments on the comic and Philosophical historical novels can be seen to justify Doctorow's method. *Ragtime*, like the more sobering *Daniel*, is about the history-making process itself. Foley's perception of Doctorow as undermining objective history may beg the question. As unappealing as the notion may be to Marxists, *Ragtime*'s parody of the historical record announces that texts—both historical and fictional—are part of what comes to be called objective history.

In 1980, the trend of surveying Doctorow's body of work continued in two articles, one using the traditional mimetic model and the other employing the most thoroughgoing Marxist reading of Doctorow to that point. Working from the older interpretive model that assumes literature reflects an extrinsic history, Cushing Strout praises *The Book of Daniel* because it remains within the boundaries prescribed by history (1980). His negative view of *Ragtime* stems from this same insistence on history as a verifiable record not to be tampered with. For Strout, Doctorow fails to match the integrity of one of his own characters: Houdini performed clever tricks based on a tacit agreement with his audience about the difference between reality and illusion. Doctorow's "corrupted" imagination in *Ragtime* confuses its audience. Strout later incorporated this long essay into two chapters in a book called *The Veracious Imagination* (1981), the title suggesting Strout's mimetic emphasis. In the original essay, he echoes Foley's charge that Coalhouse Walker is anachronistic, adding that this violation of the reader's "historical consciousness" trivializes the racial issues raised in the novel. In fact, seeing trivialization as inherent in Doctorow's playful style, Strout intones rather ponderously, "Linguistic omnipotence is an atmosphere in which history cannot flourish."

Although writing as a Marxist, David S. Gross bolsters his interpretation by use of psychoanalytic theory. His essay's title suggests a trend in criticism that would become more pronounced as the decade wore on: the amalgamation of several approaches. In this case, "Tales of Obscene Power: Money and Culture, Modernism and History in the Fiction of E. L. Doctorow" (1980) is not so much *about* Doctorow's work as it is a *use* of Doctorow along with Freud and Marx to speculate about the hidden springs of both literary modernism and American history. The essay, first appearing in *Genre* and later in Richard Trenner's *Essays and Conversations* (1983), actually derives its thesis from Norman O. Brown's *Life Against Death* (1959), itself a synthesis of sociology and Freud that proposes capitalism as the modern incarnation of the devil because it "violates all our moral standards." Humans repress this almost unbearable truth, but all imaginative literature deals with it. As a sign of transgression (modern getting and spending), money is associated with excrement throughout history and in the work of Doctorow.

In fact, for Gross, Doctorow reveals the "hidden sources of malaise in our culture more clearly than most modern writers." Despite the distancing strategies common to modernist fiction (Gross seems indebted to Georg Lukács on this point), Doctorow is clear in two important ways. First, he brings to the foreground repression of our consciousness of money's complete power—it is a "central subject"—and second, "he establishes the connections among money, excrement and power with savage irony."

Gross deals with all Doctorow's novels in the order of their increasing modernist techniques, which, like psychic defenses, encode the truth. The then newly published *Loon Lake* (1980), with its disjunctive narrative voices and plots, its fragmentary shift from past to present, is the most modernist and therefore contains the most difficult code. Its refusal to employ traditional discourse declares implicitly that language has become part of the "same quantifying rationality," the same debasement of all values to money equivalents that infects culture. Modernist experimentation attempts a protest of this condition, but ironically, its authoritative manner imitates the "imperialist mode" of the debased culture and becomes complicit in it.

In other words, experimental style reenacts the same drama that goes on in culture. The more we repress our consciousness of the obscene power of money, the more fragmented and alienated our lives become. Similarly, the extreme fragmentation of *Loon Lake* calls attention to the effects of money-power. The ahistorical style of Doctorow represents money as it acts in history—doing hidden but damaging work.

In making Doctorow's novels into ideological prooftexts, Gross demonstrates the powerful link between Marxist and psychoanalytic theory. They both claim to know the secret causes of human misery; through analysis, both can effect a revolution, if not in fact at least in consciousness. Gross follows other Marxists in projecting the idea of personal repression of unpleasant truth onto the canvas of history. In the same way that individuals repress trauma, capitalistic America has repressed the trauma of reification. Fiction serves as one of the battlegrounds for recovery of important cultural insights. Gross acknowledges that the step from personal to cultural psychology is suspect, but in defense of the practice he makes a point that illustrates the influence of one strand of postmodern thought. Citing Christopher Lasch, himself a leftist cultural critic who mixes psychoanalytic and social categories, Gross insists that critics must "[read] individual personality in terms of cultural forces." Increasingly, criticism in the 1980s would employ similar logic to the point that individual "subjects" are constructs of ideological forces. In Gross's essay, such cultural determinism is offset by a nostalgic ideal of uncorrupted human nature, a precapitalist self untainted by money, all the more tragic in its idealized absence.

The critic, then, armed with the truth about culture, uncovers in the images and plots of fiction what the work may or may not know. Great novels provide their own unearthing of repressed consciousness, of course, making the critic's task easier. Gross sees Doctorow's "historical vision" as demystifying, even obviously so in *Ragtime*, which he surprisingly judges to be the least modernist of Doctorow's novels. Emma Goldman, the real-life anarchist who appears frequently in the first half of the novel as mentor to one of the book's prime victims of capitalism, Evelyn Nesbit, speaks against money's obscene power, and the chief image of it is the pile of excrement placed on the seat of Coalhouse Walker's prized automobile. J. P. Morgan, who is unseen in the novel but orchestrates Walker's death, symbolizes the repressed money-power hidden beneath the nostalgic surface of "school-book histories."

Gross discusses *The Book of Daniel* and *Welcome to Hard Times* in much the same way. For each book he offers imagery read in terms of his thesis: electricity and Disneyland, for example, in *The Book of Daniel* are metaphors for money's centralized and oppressive control over culture. The technique threatens to reduce these texts to allegory, and one is reminded of Christian hermeneuts searching for one more Christological symbol in a biblical text. Gross's singleminded pursuit of a Marxist thesis has drawn little comment from subsequent critics. If his reading, as Richard Trenner puts it, uses "extraliterary language" and an "imposing theoretical structure" (1983), it seems to have either bored or intimidated those with different views.

The "imposing theoretical structure" of Freudo-Marxism, to use Fredric Jameson's term, perhaps obscures the fact that Gross credits Doctorow with a "terrible and negative" vision of twentieth-century America. Even more importantly, Gross argues that such a vision is inevitable if history does its work, because the record always reveals the evil of man's dehumanizing systems. This pessimistic note would be repeated by many of the critics who focused on Doctorow's vision of reality (Thompson 1991), but there were several writers interested not so much in his philosophy of history as they were in his artistic vision. Marxists were not the only ones preoccupied with image and structure.

Ragtime, Film, and History: The Return of the Aesthetic

Along with continuing interest in history as theme and fiction as episte-mology, there was in Doctorow criticism during the early 1980s a series of essays concerned with explicating the novel's major motifs. Generally, these essays share an interest in the significance of film as image as well as its suggestion of new ways to interpret reality. Charles Berryman (1982) announces the mindset of this group when he complains that in their zeal to debate the value of *Ragtime*'s mix of fact and fiction, critics have thus far ignored its complexity of design. Far from abandoning history, most of these essayists seek to show the relevance of patterns of imagery and other ques-tions of style to the historical issues already a part of Doctorow criticism.

Early in *Ragtime*'s reception history, its narrative voice was praised or condemned as distinctive. In this period, its distinctiveness is examined as an artistic device. In one way or another, critics see narrative voice as vital to understanding what Doctorow achieves in rendering history. In fact, Susan Brienza hails his technique as achieving a fusion of history and art (1981) by translating artistic modes of certain characters into narrative ploys that present the past. Barbara Cooper (1980) approaches the novel as a culmination of Doctorow's attempt to find a proper narrative perspective. She surveys the work through *Ragtime* as a "quest . . . to find order in human experience." Each novel until *Ragtime* contains an artist figure; in *Welcome to Hard Times* and *The Book of Daniel* he is a narrator faced with the problem of "knowing how to tell what has happened." In each case, the narrator fails to reconcile his subjective experience with external data, so each fails to fully render experience. In *Ragtime*, however, Doctorow creates "an anonymous narrative consciousness" that renders "characters only in the web of social and cultural forces, not in the ego, but in the flow of American energy and, thereby, creates the novel of context." In a comparison of *Ragtime* to Saul Bellow's *Humboldt's Gift* (1975), Barbara Estrin makes a similar point. Both novels teach that "truth lies in the movement away from panic, in the calm acceptance of calamity . . ." (1982). Bellow's protagonist Charlie Citrine moves toward the "historical distance and personal indifference" of Doctorow's narrator, whose calm lies in the "dismissal of individualized agony." According to Cooper, this larger perspective provides a "new kind of history" for an audience who wants its novelists to be historians.

Although several critics had already called attention to the importance of the ragtime metaphor for Doctorow's new perspective on history, this group in the early eighties paid special attention to the treatment of film as a symbolic and structural device. Cooper argues that the impersonal narrative voice she so admires is based on the art of film, which can "frame" reality in such a way as to reconcile the subjective and objective domains. Film falls somewhere between highly intrusive self-reflexive narration (exemplified in her essay by Vonnegut's *Breakfast of Champions*) and the total detachment of Robbe-Grillet's *Jealousy*. Doctorow's style approximates the camera's ability to combine photographic realism with editorial selection. While Cooper may be guilty of overdoing the analogy, she sets up between camera and writing, her awareness that the book's technique in some way reflects the emerging technology of early film finds support in others. Berryman's exploration of narrative consciousness, while not emphasizing film, does mention it as an analogue to other images of fragmentation in the novel. For him the shattered mirror is the book's crucial metaphor, and the narrator, whom he identifies as the Little Boy of the WASP family, is the agent who understands the interplay between image and reality implied in the act of gazing in a mirror. The Boy's perspective, a feeling of being divided from self, informs the entire book. In her essay,

Cooper discusses the idea of framing in much the same way as Berryman describes the fragmented mirror images—transitory perspectives signaling an age in flux. History by its very nature diffracts the self, Berryman argues, but the difficulty comes in recognizing that it, like film, is a "reel of illusions."

Berryman argues his thesis more effectively than Cooper does hers, probably because his is less ambitious. She perhaps moves from aesthetic concerns (narrative voice) to epistemological ones with too great an ease. That is, she never makes fully clear how the problem of relating an inner world to external reality can be solved by a particular novelistic point of view. She summons this "Cartesian split" (irreconcilability of subjective and objective) as the great problem for artists and by implication human communication in general, but to suggest that writers ought to imitate movies—sketchy portraits in quick succession—hardly seems a solution. In addition, her illustrations lack cogency. It is one thing to say that a certain scene or groups of scenes are like a frame, but to single out Doctorow's scenes as achieving a frame (the proper synthesis of inner and outer perspective) seems questionable. The right excerpts from Vonnegut or Robbe-Grillet could support the same claim for their work. Berryman, on the other hand, avoids having literature address philosophical dilemmas, choosing instead a largely thematic analysis: *Ragtime*'s action is a counterpoint of violence and rebirth that shows the need to transcend self in order to deal with the volatility of experience. Both critics keep alive Doctorow the artist by their emphasis on narrative technique.

Cooper's argument that film is a key metaphorical device in *Ragtime* was followed within two years by similar exploration. Barbara Estrin's comparison of Doctorow's work to *Humboldt's Gift* sees in both books the idea of film as duplicable event, a mass entertainment deflecting the anxiety of the machine age with its own technology: mechanized images that take an audience out of time. Film asserts the existence of its audience by reflecting them in onscreen images (1982). Writing in *The North Dakota Quarterly*, Angela Hague (1982) echoes Estrin; she points out that the duplication inherent in film art answers a fundamental human need to preserve experience. The new technology represented a way "to subject time to rational control." Estrin and Hague attempt to show how Doctorow incorporates these insights into his structure, but Hague's more detailed focus on film as an organizing principle deserves further mention.

Hague points out that Doctorow uses film on several levels. First, as an answer to those who quarrel with Doctorow's historical accuracy, she makes the case that the novel faithfully portrays the connection between the new art of movies and America's immigrant classes. Several reviewers found Tateh, the Jewish immigrant who transforms himself from working-class socialist to regal filmmaker, at best a whimsical and at worst a fraudulent character. According to film historians cited in her essay, however, movies became a form of accessible entertainment and entree into culture for both audience and entrepreneur. Tateh's story is representative of early American film-makers. Using Walter Benjamin and Susan Sontag as support, Hague also contends that *Ragtime*'s depiction of Evelyn Nesbit's career has roots in the actual "commodification" of the actor that occurred when market interests took over the art of filmmaking.

On the philosophical and aesthetic levels, *Ragtime*, as discussed above, explores the way film's manner of presentation reflects a new way of perceiving reality. In its use of moving photographs, cinema suggests both the need to stop time and the inevitability of its flow. In other words, the onscreen illusions of film derive from the most fundamental illusion: eternal life. Hague suggests a third level of significance for the motif when she argues that in film modern America discovered an art form corresponding to its own sense of the country's vast, incomprehensible being. The culture had given up on understanding reality; it wanted only fragments for serial grati-fication. The "hypnotic" prose of the book creates the effect of "the myste-rious opacity of the photographed image." By making film so important as a structural device, Hague concludes, Doctorow has better fulfilled the purpose of *Ragtime*, to render the birth of a new American art form and the popular culture from which it derives.

Hague's remarks on film as a mode of perception recall Cooper's thesis that *Ragtime* triumphs as a narrative perspective transcending the individual ego. Hague, however, connects her discussion to factors of cultural change. The book is not only *about* the turn-of-the-century, its images and style reproduce the era from the "inside," as it were, to approximate the texture of experience. Anthony B. Dawson also examines the style and content of *Ragtime* as cinematic, adding only a more detailed list of filmic devices approximated by Doctorow's prose. His conclusion, that the ragtime era, like the time in which the book was written, was a period of mechanization and discontinuity, is by this time familiar. His most interesting tactic is the use of Walter Benjamin (Hague cites him also) to support the argument that *Ragtime* represents the fundamental change in modes of perception ushered in by film and continuing in modern culture. Since the edition of his work edited by Hannah Arendt (1969), Benjamin has become fashionable among Marxists and other cultural critics. His essay, "The Work of Art in the Age of Mechanical Reproduction," contained in Arendt's edition, is the most often cited among his works. In it he speculates that the old religious "aura" associated with unduplicated works of art has been replaced in the modern world by a more intense style of perception. Dawson mines that theme in his discussion, echoing Benjamin's ambivalence regarding the value of the new duplicable aesthetic experience. What emerges from Dawson's use of Benjamin, and Hague's, is the advocacy of a *postmodern* sensibility. Benjamin's essay has become popular precisely because it suggests what Baudrillard later calls the "hyperreal" (1983) density of contemporary experience: the encroachment of business into art, the increased pace of consumption to match a greater need for instant gratification, the breaking down of barriers between high and low culture, and the increased emphasis on the superficial. Benjamin touches on these and other phenomena presaged by the synthesis of technology, art, and mass culture in the capitalist world. In exchange for the substantive "aura" of high art and religion, modern—read postmodern—man has the endless repetition of recycled images. Hague closes her essay with a rebuke for those who find *Ragtime* derivative: "Doctorow attempts to make the novel, like film, part of a 'new aesthetic' which irreverently appropriates all of art and experience for its material without compromising its artistic independence."

Hague's peroration, as well as Dawson's faithful application of Benjamin's theory to Doctorow, suggest that the appeal of *Ragtime*'s use of film as style and structure lies in the affinity of that medium with the new modes of perception which were emerging among critics in the 1970s and 1980s and which by the end of the latter decade would be widely known as postmodernism. Although other images and symbols were and would be discussed, film is the most compatible with then-current analyses of art and culture. Ironically for literary critics, Hague says that the ultimate significance of cinematic style is that it can tell us nothing about what it represents. Experience is too fragmented to understand; therefore writing based on the art of the movies best represents reality. Benjamin had hopes that film could be subversive of what he considered an exploitative European capitalism precisely because its fragmentation could jolt viewers out of their comfort zones. Although both Dawson and Hague celebrate Doctorow's achievement—Dawson, for example, asserts that the novel's mechanical mode produces a new "aura" out of its own artifice—they seem to acknowledge film as a model for the loss of coherent representation. The implications of that for fiction become more clear as postmodernism achieves a greater influence on what gets written about Doctorow.

MICHELLE M. TOKARCZYK

The American Dream, Insiders and Outsiders: Ragtime

In *Ragtime* we find many of the themes that mark the rest of Doctorow's fiction, but they are expressed in some notably different ways. Like Doctorow's earlier work, *Ragtime* is a historical novel, representing approximately the years 1902 until 1914. It focuses on three families and includes a wide array of historical personages. But as critics have noted, *Ragtime* is as much about the era itself, a period of rapid change, as it is about any families or individuals. Partially for this reason, the position of the narrator is far less defined than in other Doctorow fiction; though the narrator is generally believed to be the Boy, he is never clearly identified as such. This ambiguity in narration leads Christopher Morris to conclude that *Ragtime* is the first in a series of Doctorow novels (the others being *Loon Lake, Lives of the Poets*, and *World's Fair*) in which the narrator cannot be determined as omniscient or as a clearly identifiable character. In detaching language from a source, *Ragtime* and other novels in this series, "show[s] in new ways the delusion of the self as the autonomous manipulator of language." Implicitly, Morris suggests, the novel shows the constructed and indeterminate nature of history, a continual concern of Doctorow's.

As striking as the narrator's ambiguous identity is his distance from the narration; the novel's prose and Boy's relative detachment from the stories he narrates sharply contrast with other Doctorow narrators' pained

From *E. L. Doctorow's Skeptical Commitment*. © 2000 by Peter Lang Publishing.

engagement. These narrative choices themselves reflect another strategy on Doctorow's part to indirectly express his political and social concerns. The artist figures are separated from the narrators (in a move that prefigures a split between the artist and his psychic twin in *Loon Lake*) facilitating more ambiguity and indirection. Furthermore, in *Ragtime* Doctorow actually does "compose" history, as he has often said novelists do. The use of history in this novel is unlike anything Doctorow has done previous to this novel, and perhaps something no novelist has yet replicated. Rather than imaginatively render a historical event, as *The Book of Daniel* does, *Ragtime* mingles actual historical events (such as the strike in Lawrenceville, Massachusetts) with historical characters in fictional situations (Freud and Jung in the Tunnel of Love), and invented characters. La Capra's distinction between documentary and worklike aspects of texts thus collapses in this novel. This collapse, as well as Doctorow's imaginative use of history, undoubtedly reflects his skepticism about the dividing lines between history and fiction as expressed in "False Documents" and his distrust of claims of fact.

Ragtime's style of fictionalizing history is described by Linda Hutcheon as "historiographic metafiction," work that is both metafictional and historical in its echoes of past texts and contexts. Such work situates readers within historical discourse without surrendering its authority as fiction, and thus satisfies a desire for grounding while querying the very basis for that grounding. Like *The Book of Daniel*, *Ragtime* does establish some tentative truths, and thus may be seen as another work of midfiction. *Ragtime* is, in fact, a highly playful midfiction book. The novel's short, sometimes humorous, and highly accessible prose might be called "mock historical" writing that mimics the prose of history texts. Consider, for example, the following passage: "Everyone wore white in the summer. Tennis racquets were hefty and the racquet faces elliptical. There was a lot of sexual fainting. There were no Negroes. There were no immigrants. On Sunday afternoon, after dinner, Father and Mother went upstairs and closed the bedroom door."

The apparent simplicity here is deceptive, for the excerpt raises questions about the typicality of the life being described, the relationship between individual families and larger society, and society's blindness to racial problems. Moreover, while the novel begins with the vision of white middle-class America (no Negroes, no immigrants) it quickly revises itself to state that there apparently were Negroes and immigrants. In a sense, *Ragtime* is a revisionist historical novel including the stories of women, immigrants, Labor, and others excluded from standard histories until very recently. Because the novel so often subtly prompts readers to reread their own sense of history, it is useful to keep in mind the quotation from Scott Joplin at the beginning of the novel, "Do not play this piece fast. It is never right to play Ragtime fast." The apparent ease of reading *Ragtime* coupled with the complex themes and social commentary that are subtly introduced are likely what account for the commercial and critical success of the novel. Yet the epigraph on ragtime music is worth keeping in mind when pondering the meaning of this novel. The book is indeed a "good read," a quick one, yet the message lingers.

In *Ragtime* Doctorow uses an array of literary devices and genres in addition to postmodern techniques to comment not only on the era itself but the realization of the American Dream in this era. The blend of historical and fictional characters along with the experimental prose allows Doctorow to make a detached, but nonetheless powerful critique of American society and the possibility of true progress in an era of rapid and apparent advances. Doctorow's adaptation of the midfiction subset of postmodernism in *Ragtime* radically disrupts the surface elements of history, chronology, and believability, but it does so while clearly suggesting that there are definite, observable incidents of injustice.

Throughout the novel two distinct image clusters recur, images though seemingly in opposition to one another, actually complement one another. The first is the Boy's fascination with stories from Ovid's *Metamorphoses* and with the possibility that anything could become something else. The second are the images of repetition suggested in Ford's assembly line, Morgan's fascination with reincarnation, and the baseball game that intrigues the narrator because the same action recurs. Together these two kinds of images suggest the historical process: the progress (or illusion of it) that demands constant adaptation and the tendency of historical patterns to repeat, most markedly along issues of inequity. The images of repetition also suggest what Newman has called the "wave motif" in American literature and history: because of continual immigration waves over time the motif is repetitive rather than linear and chronological. The novel's patterns of repetition and metamorphosis converge in the figure of one of *Ragtime*'s most compelling figures, Coalhouse Walker, Jr. He wants to progress, but the force of American racism ultimately destroys him.

The fates of Coalhouse Walker and other characters in this novel—some highly plausible, some requiring suspension of disbelief—are rendered through adaptation of the romance genre. While scholars of the American romance, most notably Richard Chase, once saw the genre as one that evaded direct engagement with sociopolitical issues, new Americanists have seen a political enterprise in the American romance. In her study of this genre Emily Miller Budick argues that the tradition's emphatic rejection of mimetic modes of representation coupled with its equally strong insistence on specified settings in place and time gives the novel a double consciousness. Her analysis of romance writers is particularly applicable to Doctorow, for she claims, "From the late eighteenth century to the contemporary period a remarkable lineage of American writers produces a fiction that acknowledges the force of skepticism and yet allows writing to commit itself to history and society." Similarly, Wilding argues that in romance fiction the confrontation of the hopes of romance with the realities of realism arises from the nature of political fiction, of which the romance is a subgenre. Essentially, what Budick and other revisionist scholars of the American romance see in the form is its ability to grapple with seeming polarities. As this chapter will reveal, oppositions abound in *Ragtime*. Romance hopes are realized in the lives of Tateh and Mother; the actualities of realism are represented in figures that disappear, such as Evelyn Nesbit and Mameh, as well as in those that are oppressed for their political positions, such as Emma Goldman and Coalhouse Walker. Readers' stance toward the "romance" characters might be compared to their stance toward the American Dream: they remember and focus on the characters who have achieved an unlikely happiness rather than the more typical ones who do not.

The juxtaposition of unlikely characters and events in *Ragtime* represents a mosaic in which the lives of different kinds of Americans are placed next to one another. Evoking the image of the mosaic implicitly undercuts the idea of America as a melting pot, complicating ideas of assimilation. Although the lives of characters from diverse backgrounds intersect, they meld unevenly. Evelyn Nesbit disappears from Tateh's life; Ford and Morgan have no sustained interaction; Emma Goldman has little influence outside her radical sphere. Yet when some characters interact with others from different backgrounds, lives are permanently changed: most notably when Sara and Mother interact, and Tateh and Mother meet. Hence, *Ragtime* represents the complex, unpredictable nature of interaction in a multicultural society.

The novel's pastiche quality and the many varied personages within it also thwart impulses to totalize history and raise questions about the depictions of periods in other historical texts. The complexity of characters' motives thwarts simple analysis; for example, we are uncertain whether to admire Tateh for his adaptation or scorn him for betraying his ideals; we condemn Walker's terrorism but admire his uncompromising self-respect. To the extent that any character's actions are predictable, they are expected only if we understand determinism, with Raymond Williams, as not only the setting of limits but also the exertion of pressures, pressures I would argue often specific to given individuals and situations. The accidental nature of many events, such as Mother finding the baby, makes it highly unlikely they would recur, so they could not be predicted. In contrast, Coalhouse Walker's

response to society's refusal to treat him justly—although it is extreme—
might be predicted, given his character and the racial climate of the times.
Hence, although *Ragtime* depicts many contingencies and certainly acknowledges that some events may be beyond human control, the novel as a work
of midfiction affirms some degree of causality.

The sometimes fantastic contingencies in the novel are part of the
romance tradition. In addition to adapting conventions of this genre, *Ragtime*
utilizes, and indeed disrupts, the genre of proletarian fiction, a genre that has
been overlooked until recently. In her study of 1930s fiction, Barbara Foley
defines the proletarian social novel (a kind of proletarian fiction) as one with
multiple protagonists from various social classes as well as using realistic
modes of representation. The novel employs juxtaposition and interaction to
illustrate significant patterns and forces in the class struggle. Typically, a
work focuses on a strike or some similar key event, and readers are prompted
to identify with protagonists who have chosen the correct sides. While some
features of this genre—realistic representation, singular focus on class
struggle—are not applicable to *Ragtime*, there are nonetheless striking similarities in the function of multiple protagonists (undercutting a bourgeois
focus on individual identity), in the juxtaposition of characters, and in the
sympathy *Ragtime* evokes for minority characters. The proletarian social
novel can thus be seen as another genre that Doctorow skillfully revises in
Ragtime, in the process revising the genre itself.

Like many traditional novels, and in the spirit of much recent political debate, *Ragtime* foregrounds individual families. These families represent different ethnic groups and socioeconomic classes: the WASP Mother
and Father's family, the Jewish immigrant Tateh and Mameh's, the African-
American Coalhouse Walker and his girlfriend, Sara. One way to situate
the individual families is to examine their members' responses to the
rapidly-changing society—in the novel's terms their ability to metamorphosize. This focus has its basis in the romance tradition, for as one scholar
notes, the action of historical romances (such as James Fenimore Cooper's)
often "turns on the failure of a character or a class to understand that attitudes and behavior recently appropriate are tenable no longer." These
words describe Father, a successful, relatively affluent businessman curiously unable to adapt to his changing society, especially its increasingly
multicultural character. The beginning of his decline is suggested in what
should have been the pinnacle of his success, his journey with Admiral
Peary to the North Pole. The white explorers are contemptuous of the
natives: Peary says the Eskimos are children and must be treated as such, and
narrator reporting Father's sentiments says, "There was no question that the
Eskimos were primitives. They were affectionate, gentle, emotional, trust-

worthy, and full of pranks." These condescending perceptions, coupled with Father's revulsion at his Eskimo lover's open sexuality, indicate he, like the characters in *Heart of Darkness*, sees the natives as Other and is disoriented by his encounter with them. Yet his sense of superiority as a white male cannot compensate for his body being unsuited for the harsh Arctic climate; the tendency of his extremities to freeze suggests his intrinsic inflexibility, his inability to adapt to new circumstances. Sensing that he is losing his privileged position, Father is threatened by minorities who may surpass him. Although he recognizes the soundness of Peary choosing the African-American Henson (an actual explorer on the mission) as a companion to the North Pole, he resents Henson's presumption he would be the choice, very likely resenting self-confidence in an African-American.

As an explorer and successful businessman, Father represents the limitations of American visions of Manifest Destiny as suggested by Turner and similar frontier theorists. Through him, *Ragtime* scrutinizes the mythology of self-discovery, suggested in works such as Tennyson's "Ulysses," that accompanies narratives of adventure or exploration. Rather than providing Father with an opportunity for discovery and achievement, each exploration further alienates him from himself and his home. Upon his return from the Arctic voyage, he does not even know how to behave in a domestic setting: "The family stood around and watched him on his knees. There was nothing he had to tell them." This novel's examination of a man's decline is also part of the romance tradition, for many American historical romances focus on patriarchs and recount not only the circumstances which alienated them from their society, but also their eventual decline and fall. Working in this tradition, *Ragtime* depicts three patriarchs, revealing not only who can adopt appropriate attitudes and behavior, but also who is allowed to change.

Father's condescending attitude toward nonwhites in the Arctic predicts his attitude toward Coalhouse Walker. Although Father tries to negotiate with authorities on Walker's behalf, Father clearly dislikes him, undoubtedly because the musician is not subservient, and indeed will fight for his rights. That Walker's terrorist gang is alien to Father may at first not be surprising, but on reflection one realizes that at the time of his death Father was smuggling armaments on the *Lusitania*, engaging in the illegal transport of weapons for what he believed to be a just cause, which is not so different from Walker's actually using weapons for his cause. As Daniel would say, Father cannot see the "connection"; as Emma Goldman would say, he cannot see the "correspondence" between his life choices and those from other racial groups. The description of his death makes the resemblance between Father and the other characters, a resemblance forgotten by him, clearer: "Poor Father, I see his final exploration. He arrives at the new place, his hair risen in astonishment, his mouth and eyes dumb. His toe scuffs a soft storm of sand, he kneels and his arms spread in pantomimic celebration, the immigrant, as in every moment of his life, arriving eternally on the shore of his Self." As Linda Mindish lost her own past, Father lost the connection to the struggles of his own immigrant ancestors and their ability to change as needed. He is, as Christopher Morris suggests, a perpetual beginner. But unlike other characters, Father cannot choose a new beginning appropriate for the time. Rather, his "beginning" is continual repetition of previous actions in new guises, futile attempts to reassert his old status. Ironically, his temperament will not allow him to progress.

In contrast to Father, Mother's ability to cope with change is suggested by her unofficially adopting an African-American baby, and marrying Tateh. Moreover, unlike Father, she is courteous to Coalhouse Walker and sympathetic to him both as he courts Sara and seeks recompense for his car. Her open-mindedness is likely the result of the changes she underwent during Father's absence, taking more responsibility for the household and becoming more aware of her own sexuality, a subtle transformation that on a personal level reflects "momentous change coming over the United States." Part of this change is, of course, in the status of women that would close the First Wave of twentieth-century American feminism with the passage of the Nineteenth Amendment to the Constitution granting women the right to vote. As Mother develops, she longs for a "life of genius" beyond what the predictable Father could give her. Her desire might be viewed as typifying the "American Dream" reinterpreted by some contemporary scholars as not only or even primarily upward mobility, but rather the chance to live in freedom and reach one's individual potential. Mother does not, as more radical women might, attempt to live independently, but she is receptive to social changes that give her access to a more rewarding life. In fact, she is first willing to become involved with someone whom she believes is displaced nobility, and nonetheless willing to marry him when she learns he is a self-made member of the *nouveau riche*. (She is perhaps also fortunate in that her first husband happens to die, freeing her to remake her life in a second marriage.)

Mother represents but one possible response of a woman to the changing times. Evelyn Nesbit's role as a sex goddess whose face appears in every paper sensationalizing the Harry K. Thaw trial represents women as repositories of male dreams, a role women have always had but which was intensified by photography's ability to capture and reproduce images of desire. Mameh is significant in that, like Nesbit, she disappears after Tateh abandons her for giving in to her employer's sexual demands, illustrating the vulnerability of working women. Sara, who tries to intercede in Coalhouse's struggle, is, in her naive attempt to approach politicians, even more vulnerable than her future husband. Emma Goldman, the life-long anarchist and advocate for women's rights, is finally exiled from the country, "disappeared" like Mameh and Nesbit. Taken together, the female characters represent the relatively narrow range of options available to women and the high price of transgressing boundaries. In depicting the way political change affects various women, Doctorow is again suggesting that, to use the cliché, the political is personal, and that the personal ramifications left out of history texts provide another example of how history is constructed.

The interrelationships of these various characters' lives are described by Emma Goldman speaking to Evelyn Nesbit as correspondences, "our lives correspond, our spirits touch one another like notes in harmony, and in the total human fate we are sisters." Goldman's words suggest the interrelationship of all characters in this novel with a metaphor appropriate to music that the title itself suggests. The literary precursor for Goldman's sentiment, however, is John Donne's "For Whom the Bell Tolls" suggesting people's interdependence. Correspondences in *Ragtime* also signal the book's affinities with some proletarian novels in which there is a strategic juxtaposition from lives of characters who may or may not know one another, leaving readers to hypothesize why they belong in the same novel. In essence, readers are forced to make the same connection the speaker of the Donne poem does, but also to ponder the dynamics of this connection in the world of inequity the novel depicts.

Some of the inequity in this novel results from the social conditions in urban areas during this time. As Paul Levine notes, *Ragtime* depicts the United States's movement from a smalltown society to a metropolitan one, and much more than *The Book of Daniel*, represents the diversity of this landscape. One of the energizing prospects of these rapidly growing urban environments was a release from small-town enclosures and the possibility of spontaneously, accidentally interacting with very different people.

But while there is potential in rapid industrialization and urbanization, there is also considerable suffering. Many historians have found increasing inequality in America as the nation became more urban. Roy Lubove argues that urban slum problems had their roots in the same ethos of greed that shaped western land development: the counterpoint of the speculator in western lands, represented in *Welcome to Hard Times*, was the urban jerry-builder, eager to expand opportunities and move on. Tenements resulted from rapid growth and poor planning. To some extent, they were also the by-products of acculturation to urban life, a nation's inability to cope with the rapid change from a rural to an urban environment. The poor and dangerous conditions Tateh endures—poverty so stark his wife succumbs to her employer's sexual advances and streets so dangerous Tateh works with his daughter tied to him so she will not be kidnapped—are the results of industrialization, as is the poverty depicted in Charles Dickens's novels. In their insensitivity to human needs, the cities are similar to the town Hard Times in Doctorow's first novel. Furthermore, during the period between the Civil War and World War I, the urban rich in New York moved uptown while the poor stayed downtown in the slums, a development that intensified class stratification. Yet the rich were geographically not that far away from the poor. Such proximity explains the impoverished who in *Ragtime* peer into the banquets of the wealthy, separated by a glass window they know they will not penetrate. Because of the visibility of the slums and the glaring distinctions between owners and workers, cities embarrassingly exposed the falsity of a classless society in America, revealing divisions by race and nationality as well.

Cities also have been the points of arrival for new immigrants, and between 1890 and 1910 over one million immigrants settled in the United States. Immigrants who came to this nation in search of a better life were often shocked at their exploitation and pitiful living conditions. As some scholars point out, in 1893 when Turner offered his thesis on the frontier, millions of European immigrants were living in poverty. His thesis was thus problematized: why such appalling social conditions in this apparently progressive nation. Of course, immigrants were supposed to be able to rise from poverty, or at least see their children achieve better lives. Indeed, Tateh himself achieves the American Dream. But his and many other "metamorphoses" in the novel are at least partially attributable to privilege associated with a character's gender, race, and ethnicity.

Tateh is particularly interesting for the kinds of people he represents: an artist trying to make a living from his sketches, an entrepreneur, and, importantly, an impoverished Jewish activist. The account of Tateh's participation in labor struggles vividly illustrates the class struggle, noted by urban scholars such as Lubove and O'Connell but erased in the text-book accounts of American history, and strengthens *Ragtime*'s resemblance to the proletarian novel. But while in a proletarian novel, especially a proletarian *bildungsroman*, strike involvement might be a turning point in which a character would become more committed to radical action, here it is the point at which Tateh abandons his labor affiliation, even though the strike was successful. When the strike ends, Tateh realizes the essentially conservative goals of American Labor, "The I.W.W. has won . . . But what has it won? A few more pennies in wages? Will it now own the mills? No." Since he now perceives the Labor movement as tied to the status quo, and has often been at odds with labor leaders who wanted "inspirational art," it is not surprising that Tateh decides to "point his life along the flow of American energy," to become an entrepreneur. One might read the seeds of Tateh's decision in his leaving New York City, "the city that has ruined his life," hoping for a more comfortable life on the urban outskirts, as did many who fled the cities after World War II. His decision is further suggested in his fears for his child's future, "Every once in a while he would look at his child, and seeing the sure destruction of her incredible beauty in his continuing victimization, he would clutch her to him and tears would fill his eyes." His desire to provide his daughter with a respectable bourgeois life is further reflected in his revulsion for Emma Goldman's views, as well as in his abrupt rejection of his sexually exploited wife. His radical sympathies do not extend to women's rights, and from his perspective his radical cohorts might have negative influences on his daughter. Consequently, he metamorphosizes or recomposes himself and his art.

Tateh's decision to sell his silhouettes to the Franklin Novelty Company has a few important components. First, it raises the question of how a socialist cause might deal with individual talent. Factory workers are interchangeable in their work; an artist presumably is not and thus must be involved in a different kind of struggle for justice. Also, commodification of art becomes an issue. In a capitalist nation, some commodification is necessary and Tateh commodifies the kind of art that he can effectively market because it is right for the time. Sketches on the street attract little attention. Silhouettes, on the other hand, are appropriate for the age that is discovering how to create the illusion of moving images and that itself might be represented as a rapidly changing image. As Sternlicht said he would blow the American government apart with images, Tateh transforms his future by manipulating them, eventually making motion pictures. Although he is a self-made man in the Gatsby mold, he senses he must remake his identity to be accepted in some segments of society. Hence, he becomes Baron Ashkenazy (the surname, a tease or clue since it indicates one of European Jewish origin), a displaced noble rather than formerly penniless Jewish immigrant.

Ironically then the former socialist activist epitomizes the problem for radicals that Emma Goldman saw embodied in Evelyn Nesbit as an object of desire: "I am often asked the question How the masses permit themselves to be exploited by the few. The answer is By being persuaded to identify with them. Carrying his newspaper with your picture the laborer goes home to his wife, an exhausted workhorse with the veins standing out in her legs, and he dreams not of justice but of being rich." Tateh's upward mobility gives validity to the dream.

Despite his transformation into an affluent entrepreneur, it is unclear whether Tateh has completely abandoned his radical sympathies. He adopts Sara's baby and plans the Little Rascals series in which race and class tensions are erased, and visions of brotherhood are delivered in a palatable form to Americans. Whether his liberal deeds are a pragmatic adaptation of radical sympathies or a sell out is as difficult a question as whether Tateh adapts or sells out his art. Doctorow himself has stated that he sees Tateh as an example of how a man can succeed in the very system he is criticizing, and yet retain a sense of himself as a radical by giving to political causes, and so forth. The liberal as opposed to radical stance toward social change is consistent with Doctorow's stance of skeptical commitment. Since he is passionately committed to social justice, yet ambivalent about the efficacy of sweeping social movements, his position toward change is cautious.

While Tateh is successful in transforming himself into Baron Ashkenazy—a personage more acceptable to wealthy Americans than a Jewish immigrant—Coalhouse Walker is destroyed partially because he does transform himself. Upon first meeting him Father assesses, "Coalhouse didn't seem to know he was a Negro . . . Walker didn't act or talk like a colored man. He seemed to be able to transform the customary deference practiced by his race so that they reflected his own dignity rather than the recipient's." Furthermore, aside from the fact that he comes from St. Louis, we know little of Walker's past: he seems Gatsbyesque in that he comes from the Midwest with a firm sense of himself. The source of his dignity is thus very different from Booker T. Washington's, the esteemed African-American leader who tries to persuade Walker to surrender, for Washington preached "the Negro's advancement with the help of his white neighbor" to provide vocational training and the resulting opportunity for hard work. (Interestingly, Walker tells Washington that they are both "servants of [our] color" demanding respect.) For Walker, dignity rests upon his identity as a musician, his desire to be with Sara and his child, and his sense of justice. Like Tateh, he is an artist and a family man, but unlike Tateh he cannot change his appearance and name to change his social standing. His refusal to play the part of a servile, timid black man causes whites either irritation (Father) or outright hostility (Willy Conklin). In the personage of Coalhouse Walker, Doctorow thus suggests the depth of discrimination against African-Americans—they cannot even try to assimilate into the white middle class (not that doing so is necessarily desirable) because their skin color marks them as different, and many whites will not tolerate deviation from race-assigned roles.

Walker's self-made status is represented in a number of ways—through his fine clothing, his self-assured manner, and his calm assessment of situations. This previously law-abiding man becomes a terrorist only after the law proves unresponsive to him and after his fiancée is accidentally killed by authorities. When Walker resorts to violence, the violence itself is carefully planned, thereby undercutting stereotypes of black men as impulsive and uncontrollable.

Given his rationality, it is both interesting and puzzling that Walker goes to such lengths to get his Model T restored. A band of African-American men (and Younger Brother) do support his cause, but the reaction of an African-American lawyer is probably typical of many African-Americans who have seen far greater miscarriages of injustice than what Walker endured: "I want justice for our people so bad I can taste it. But if you think I would go to Westchester County to plead on a colored man's behalf that someone deposited a bucket of slops in his car, you are very much mistaken." Walker's attitude toward his car can be understood only by considering the importance Americans assign material goods to signify identity as well as status. While Doctorow is likely unaware of it, the persecution Walker suffered because of his car has a historical basis. In the first volume of his autobiography Chester Himes recalls how his African-American family offended white neighbors in rural Mississippi by, shortly after World War I, being the first family to own a car. The townspeople were so incensed that they drove Himes's father from his job and eventually forced the family to leave the state. In addition to suggesting relative affluence, the automobile represents an affinity with progress, allying African-Americans such as the Himes family and Coalhouse Walker with figures such as Mother and Tateh rather than Father. According to Neumeyer, Walker's attachment to the car is also consistent with the repeated themes of manufacturing and production in the novel and the implication that those who manufacture are crucial to progress. Furthermore, in the United States especially, the car has become a symbol of mobility and freedom, and geographic mobility itself has often been associated with upward mobility. Immigrants coming to the United States to escape poverty (rather than to escape political persecution) best exemplify this association. Hence, an African-American who owned a car in the early 1900s was signaling his desire to better his socioeconomic status.

Nonetheless, the question still arises as to why someone as individual as Coalhouse Walker would choose to express his identity through a commodity such as an automobile rather than through his music. Marshall Bruce Gentry in "*Ragtime* as Auto Biography" posits that references to Henry Ford and his assembly line suggest associations between the interchangability of parts on Ford's assembly line and the interchangability of people who purchase cars. One might argue that Walker acts because his dignity is affronted; the item itself is not crucial. Yet Walker has made a very deliberate purchase at a time when Model Ts were not common; it seems more likely that Walker is using the car to express his individuality as people in capitalist countries especially often use material possessions such as clothing or cars to distinguish themselves. Thus through his demeanor, possessions, and the values they imply, Walker signifies his comfort with progress and his desire to gain the trappings of bourgeois society. Walker is resisting his assigned status as an African-American male, but he is resisting in ways that possibly reinscribe existing inequities (although perhaps along class rather than race lines). It is then not surprising that, as he probably realized, he is co-opted as Gerald Graff defines the term: his avenues of resistance are themselves limited by those in power.

To understand Walker's actions and the significance of his car in the novel, we also might consider a comparison Malcolm X made between cars and racism. According to him, racism is similar to a Cadillac: every year General Motors changes the contours of this car, but a Cadillac is a Cadillac despite these modifications. Likewise, racism might take on different guises, but it is racism nonetheless. *Ragtime* indeed represents racism in various guises: from the working class hatred of Willy Conklin, to the opportunistic ruthlessness of the District Attorney Whitman, to Father's smug condescension.

That Walker responds to racism with terrorist acts is jarring not only because his actions are violent, but also as critics have noted, because they are anachronistic, characteristic of the period when the novel was written rather than the one in which it is set. They might be viewed as a warning for the age reading the novel that if races are not treated equally and fairly eventually there will be violence. It is also possible to read this warning in the light of the American romance genre, which often transcends time. Such a reading is reinforced by other occurrences of time sequence being thwarted in *Ragtime*, most notably when the boy urges Houdini to "warn the duke" about the assassination years ahead. Hence, the jeremiad tendencies evident in *Welcome to Hard Times* and *The Book of Daniel* have been adapted in this novel in a subplot that functions like a parable. According to Alan Wilde, midfiction often resembles parable, the advantage of parable being that it challenges the passivity of reader responses and ultimately raises questions about the moral effects of literature on us. Particularly because the Coalhouse Walker story is the most developed subplot in the novel, it prompts readers to consider the relationship between surface and deeper meaning, between the fictional story and the reality of racism in America that make it plausible (perhaps more plausible than Mother's or Tateh's fates).

Ultimately, Walker's terrorism may be best understood by considering the source of this subplot, Heinrich von Kleist's story, "Michael Kohlhaas" (1808) (which was itself based on a chronicle, again suggesting interplay between fact and fiction). In this tale situated in the sixteenth century, Michael Kohlhaas refuses to pay an unjust toll to cross a junker's road. His prize horses are confiscated and mistreated, and the man demands justice. Finally, after his wife is killed in an attempt to intercede, Kohlhaas becomes an outlaw, setting castles and even parts of cities afire. Finally, his horses are restored and he is summarily executed. David Emblidge argues the extended allusion to "Michael Kohlhaas" suggests that injustice in twentieth-century America is comparable to that in sixteenth-century Europe. However, the failures of American justice are already suggested in Harry K. Thaw's trial and Mameh's sexual exploitation. Doctorow's choice of the Kleist tale does not itself represent or even significantly extend the theme of injustice. Walter L. Knorr believes that by drawing so heavily on a somewhat obscure foreign tale Doctorow creates an anxiety of critical reception in readers that balances his own anxiety of influence. While Knorr's point is valid, what is more important is that in alluding to the Kleist tale Doctorow establishes a literary dialogue around issues of injustice, prompting readers to question if there are other literary works dealing with these themes that they have failed to notice. This nod in the direction of literary forefathers; along with the adaptation of romance, proletarian, and postmodern genres; is an earmark that Doctorow is creating an aesthetically fine political novel. Finally, "Michael Kohlhaas" is a story of class injustice and persecution; alluding to it revives questions not only about the racial struggle Walker is fighting, but also about the class injustice suffered by Tateh and Evelyn Nesbit (who is from the working class).

Indeed, the Coalhouse Walker subplot raises questions as to who actually holds power and influence in the democratic United States. Instead of seizing an elected official's home, Walker takes J. P. Morgan's library. According to the narrator, Morgan is "at the top of the business pyramid." To Walker, he is understandably the most powerful man in the United States. Indeed, Morgan bailed out the United States government with a loan during the panic of 1907. He, more than any government agency or official, profoundly affected the nation's welfare. The scope of his actions, coupled with his belief in reincarnation and conviction that he must be descended from great rulers, indicate both his power and elitism. Alan M. Winkler describes Morgan as a man of supreme confidence; a man who, in response to a question about what his yacht costs, replied if one had to ask one couldn't afford it. Such self-assuredness and conspicuous consumption are traits shared by Coalhouse Walker. In seizing Morgan's library, Walker is challenging the epitome of white power as an equal. Moreover, that Walker is satisfied to hold Morgan's property rather than the man himself hostage again indicates the importance of material possessions. (His seizing the building is applauded by Emma Goldman, who sees it as a first step toward toppling the status quo.) Morgan's own advice to law enforcement officials, while ruthless and pragmatic, also acknowledges the importance of recognizing property rights: "GIVE HIM HIS AUTOMOBILE AND HANG HIM."

Morgan's advice suggests the full force of the law delivering the kind of justice that Michael Kohlhaas ultimately received (his horses restored and a swift execution). Yet Coalhouse Walker becomes a terrorist because the law is unwilling to protect him (as it failed to protect Kohlhaas). His treatment may be contrasted with that of Harry K. Thaw—a man who committed premeditated murder and who physically abused Evelyn Nesbit, yet who, while awaiting trial in prison, is given conjugal privileges with Evelyn Nesbit. Coalhouse Walker is shot down before even being formally charged. As Daniel would say, "law protects privilege," but perhaps at a cost to society as a whole. Michael Kohlhaas's words to Martin Luther might as easily be applied to Coalhouse Walker, "I call that man an outcast who is denied the protection of the law! . . . Whoever withholds it from me drives me out into the wilderness among savages." Significantly, Walker is often referred to as a savage by the press and by law enforcement officials.

Walker ultimately is destroyed because he is an African-American man trying to assimilate into American society. The representation of different fates for Tateh and Coalhouse Walker suggests, especially after *The Book of Daniel*, an examination of the different position of Jews and African-Americans in the United States. Furthermore, while Walker certainly receives the harshest treatment in the novel, some other characters also fare badly: Younger Brother is killed in the Mexican revolution, Evelyn Nesbit disappears into obscurity, Emma Goldman is deported, Father sinks on board the *Lusitania*. Taken together, the fates of the characters who endure as compared with those who do not suggest first that the ability to adapt to change is crucial. As I have already stated, differences in this ability explain the differences between Father and Tateh. Furthermore, the enduring landscape of *Ragtime* is like the enduring landscape of American political debates: it is composed of families with middle-class values. Those on the periphery—anarchists, radicals, sensational beauty figures—eventually disappear from the novel. And finally, in the figures of J. P. Morgan, Henry Ford, and Harry K. Thaw, the power of money to buy influence and justice is depicted. Harry K. Thaw marches in the Armistice Day Parade long after Coalhouse Walker has been shot down.

In a number of ways then, *Ragtime* exemplifies how, according to the views of the new Americanists, the romance accommodates political views and social critique, especially with the incorporation of postmodern elements. It has been argued that there is a tendency for literary critics [and I would add for many others as well] to see American politics as operating on a consensus model free of major conflicts. Coalhouse Walker's terrorism, Tateh's union activities, and Emma Goldman's radicalism all show that there is serious disagreement in a society that seems committed to the same goals and values.

Ragtime's ending envisioning the Little Rascals series has been justifiably criticized as sentimental. However, this ending might better be read as any one of the three endings of *The Book of Daniel* is: as one possible, incomplete closing. The fates of all the characters in the novel must be considered for *Ragtime* to suggest how progress and social change might be accommodated, as well as to suggest the serious limitations, especially along race lines, as to who is allowed to progress.

While Morris is certainly correct in stating that the ambiguity of the narration as well as the continual reversals and changes in the plot complicate a simple reading of history, I argue, as I did in discussing *The Book of Daniel*, that *Ragtime* consistently raises questions about the nature of power and inequity, and prompts readers to consider them. Coalhouse Walker's apparent desire to assimilate as well as his terrorism will likely be continually debated by readers, as will Tateh's metamorphosis into Baron Ashkenazy. In considering the fates of the various characters, perhaps especially the "disappeared," readers may ponder not only their history but their complicity in current political and social problems. Houdini, lamenting that unlike the manufacturers and leaders of his time he cannot produce a "real world" act, has been seen as an artist figure, but *Ragtime* does not lament the illusory quality of fiction. Rather, in the romance tradition it uses illusion to raise questions about what is considered reality.

In her work on the political aspects of postmodernism Linda Hutcheon sees intertextuality in novels such as *Ragtime* as drawing attention to the impossibility of constructing rigid boundaries between art and the world, and the impossibility of knowing either. As she and other critics, especially Barbara Foley, have noted, *Ragtime* has affinities with Dos Passos' *U.S.A.*; yet Dos Passos seems to believe that historical reality is knowable, while Doctorow emphasizes that history and identity are continually composed and recomposed. Doctorow emphasizes the artificial nature of such composition while simultaneously rendering the connection between life and art.

In *Ragtime* Doctorow playfully explores the continuing promise of the American Dream. In an era of rapid change and urbanization, the dream is more available to those who can metamorphosize themselves, both by transforming their talents into something the era appreciates and by transforming themselves into acceptable personages. Tateh is able to make the latter transformation; Coalhouse Walker is not permitted to aspire to this dream. His and Sara's deaths reflect the many, often unrecorded lynchings and similar murders of African-Americans who aspired to upward mobility. *Ragtime* is Doctorow's most playful, amusing novel. It is most marked by the ironic distance that characterizes postmodernism. Yet in this novel Doctorow consistently suggests the problems associated with progress—namely that the progress of a few often coexists with the misery of many, that technological progress (Ford's assembly line), and the rewards of progress, are not available to all. The distinction between fact and fiction, between worklike and documentary texts is thoroughly jumbled. Even so, readers are able to make important distinctions between the fates of those allowed to progress and those who are disappeared or annihilated. The novel's panoramic scope particularly implies that it is impossible to remain outside the web; everyone is complicit in the fates of all the characters. Readers will thus very subtly realize their own position in American society and thus come to reflect on the nature of their complicity. *Ragtime* is then a highly effective piece of midfiction. While it may appear to be all surface (as some critics charged), it actually critiques the very surface it represents, beginning, for example, with the mock-factual statement, "There were no Negroes," and then focusing on an African-American family. The novel gives a powerful, yet distanced representation of injustice in America, thus exemplifying Doctorow's preference for indirection in fiction.

In *Ragtime* the achievement of the American Dream, which Father had attained and Walker so strongly desired, is embodied in Tateh. Although his decision to abandon or at least modify his socialist ideology is somewhat problematic, there is nothing sinister in his upward mobility. Yet the callousness of the wealthy at the balls and of J. P. Morgan in particular suggests a much darker side of the American Dream—one that will be thoroughly examined in Doctorow's next novel.

Chronology

1931   Edgar Lawrence Doctorow is born in New York City on January 6 to David R. and Rose Lenin Doctorow.

1952   Graduates with honors and receives a degree in philosophy from Kenyon College, Gambier, Ohio.

1952–53   Does graduate work in drama at Columbia University.

1953–55   Serves in U.S. Army.

1954   Marries Helen Seltser on August 20, and eventually they have three children together.

1955–59   Works as a reservations clerk at LaGuardia Airport. Then, as a senior editor, reads scripts for CBS Television and Columbia Picture Industries, New York City.

1959–64   Editor and then senior editor at New American Library in New York City.

1960   Publishes *Welcome to Hard Times*.

1964–69   Editor in chief at Dial Press; vice president from 1968–69. In 1969, quits to write full time.

1966   Publishes *Big as Life*.

1969–70   Writer-in-residence at the University of California, Irvine.

1971   Publishes *The Book of Daniel*, which is nominated for the National Book Award.

1971–78   Teaches at Sarah Lawrence College, Bronxville, New York.

1975   Publishes *Ragtime*.

1978   *Drinks Before Dinner* is produced off-Broadway at the Public Theatre.

1979   *Drinks Before Dinner* is published.

1980   Publishes *Loon Lake*.

1984   Publishes *Lives of the Poets: Six Stories and a Novella*.

1985   Publishes *World's Fair*.

1986   Awarded the American Book Award for *World's Fair*.

1989   Publishes *Billy Bathgate*. With Eric Fischl, publishes *Scenes and Sequences*.

1993   Publishes *Poets and Presidents*, a collection of essays. Announces his collaboration with two partners to create Booknet, a 24-hour, books-only cable TV service.

1994   Publishes *The Waterworks*.

2000   Publishes *City of God*.

Contributors

HAROLD BLOOM is Sterling Professor of the Humanities at Yale University and Henry W. and Albert A. Berg Professor of English at the New York University Graduate School. He is the author of over 20 books, including *Shelley's Mythmaking* (1959), *The Visionary Company* (1961), *Blake's Apocalypse* (1963), *Yeats* (1970), *A Map of Misreading* (1975), *Kabbalah and Criticism* (1975), *Agon: Toward a Theory of Revisionism* (1982), *The American Religion* (1992), *The Western Canon* (1994), and *Omens of Millennium: The Gnosis of Angels, Dreams, and Resurrection* (1996). *The Anxiety of Influence* (1973) sets forth Professor Bloom's provocative theory of the literary relationships between the great writers and their predecessors. His most recent books include *Shakespeare: The Invention of the Human*, a 1998 National Book Award finalist, and *How to Read and Why*, which was published in 2000. In 1999, Professor Bloom received the prestigious American Academy of Arts and Letters Gold Medal for Criticism.

CHARLES BERRYMAN has taught American literature at the University of Southern California. He has written *Decade of Novels—Fiction of the 1970s: Form & Challenge*.

BARBARA L. ESTRIN is a specialist in Renaissance as well as in contemporary literature. She has writen *Laura: Uncovering Gender & Genre in Wyatt, Donne, & Marvell.*

DOUGLAS FOWLER is Professor of English at Florida State University. His books cover Nabokov, S. J. Perelman and Ira Levin.

MARSHALL BRUCE GENTRY teaches English at the University of Indianapolis. He is the author of *Flannery O'Connor's Religion of the Grotesque* and *Conversations with Raymond Carver.*

PAUL LEVINE has taught at the University of Copenhagen in Denmark.

CHRISTOPHER D. MORRIS has interviewed E. L. Doctorow. Aside from his book on this author, he has published books on social theorists, tudor anthems and southern living.

BERNDT OSTENDORF has taught American Studies at Amerika Institut München. He writes on music and ethnicity in America.

JOHN G. PARKS teaches English at Miami University.

CUSHING STROUT has written about the work of Henry James, Edith Wharton, Nathaniel Hawthorne and others.

MICHELLE M. TOKARCZYK is Associate Professor of English at Goucher College. In addition to work published on contemporary and literary cultural studies, she has written *E. L. Doctorow: An Annotated Bibliography* and co-edited a book on women working in higher education.

JOHN WILLIAMS has written a book on Mary Shelley as well as many others on a wide range of topics.

Bibliography

Bevilacqua, Winifred Farrant. "Narration and History in E. L. Doctorow." *Studies in Scandinavia* 22 (1990): 94–106.

Bloom, Harold, ed. *E. L. Doctorow*. Philadelphia: Chelsea House, 2002.

Brienza, Susan. "Doctorow's *Ragtime*: Narratives as Silhouettes and Syncopations." *Dutch Quarterly Review of Anglo-American Letters* 11 (1981): 97–103.

Campbell, Josie. "Coalhouse Walker and the Model T Ford: Legerdemain in *Ragtime*." *Journal of Popular Culture* 13 (Fall 1979): 302–9.

Claridge, Henry. "Writing on the Margins: E. L. Doctorow and American History." *The New American Writing: Essays in American Literature Since 1970*. Graham Clarke, ed. New York: St. Martin's Press, 1990, 9–28.

Cooper, Barbara. "The Artist as Historian in the Novels of E. L. Doctorow." *The Emporia State Research Studies* 29 (Fall 1980): 5–44.

Cooper, Stephen. "Cutting Both Ways: E. L. Doctorow's Critique of the Left." *South Atlantic Review* 58 (1993): 111–25.

Ditsky, Joan. "The German Source of Ragtime." *Ontario Review* (Spring–Summer 1976): 84–86.

Doctorow, E. L. "The Art of Fiction." Interview with George Plimpton. *Paris Review* 28 (1986): 23–47.

Emblidge, David. "Marching Backwards into the Future: Progress as Illusion in Doctorow's Novels." *Southwest Review* 62 (Autumn 1977): 397–409.

Evans, Thomas G. "Impersonal Dilemmas: The Collision of the Modernist and Popular Tradition in Two Political Novels, *The Grapes of Wrath* and *Ragtime*." *South Atlantic Review* 52 (January 1987): 71–85.

Foley, Barbara. "From *U.S.A.* to *Ragtime*: Notes on the Forms of Historical Consciousness in Modern Fcition," *American Literature* 50 (March 1978): 85–105.

Friedl, Herwig, and Dieter Schulz, eds. *E. L. Doctorow: A Democracy of Perception: A Symposium with and on E. L. Doctorow*. Essen: Blaue Eule, 1988.

Garrison, David. "Ovid's Metamorphoses in E. L. Doctorow's *Ragtime*." *Classical and Modern Literature* 17, no. 2 (Winter 1997): 103–15.

Gentry, Marshall Bruce. "Ventriloquists' Conversations: The Struggle for Gender Dialogue in E. L. Doctorow and Philip Roth." *Contemporary Literature* 34, no. 3 (Fall 1993): 512–535.

Griffin, Bryan F. "Whoring After the New Thing: E. L. Doctorow and the Anxiety of Critical Reception." *American Spectator* 14 (1981): 7–14.

Gross, David S. "Tales of Obscene Power: Money, Culture, and the Historical Fictions of E. L. Doctorow." *Genre* 13, no. 1 (Spring 1980): 71–92.

Harpham, Geoffrey Galt. "E. L. Doctorow and the Technology of Narrative." *PMLA* 100, no. 1 (January 1985: 81–95.

Harter, Carol and James R. Thompson. *E. L. Doctorow*. Boston: Twayne, 1990.

Iannone, Carol. "E L. Doctorow's 'Jewish' Radicalism." *Commentary* 81 (March 1986): 53–56.

Jones, Phyllis. "*Ragtime:* Feminist, Socialist and Black Perspectives on the Self–Made Man." *Journal of American Culture* 2 (1979): 17–28.

Knorr, Walter K. "Doctorow and Kleist: 'Kohlhaas in *Ragtime.*'" *Modern Fiction Studies* 22 (Summer 1976): 224–27.

Matheson, William. "Doctorow's *Ragtime.*" *Explicator* 42 (Winter 1984): 21–22.

Moraru, Christian. "The Reincarnated Plot: E. L. Doctorow's *Ragtime*, Heinrich von Kleist's *Michael Kohlhaas*, and the Spectacle of Modernity." *Comparatist* 21 (May 1997): 92–116.

Morris, Christopher, ed. *Conversations with E. L. Doctorow*. Jackson: University Press of Mississippi, 1999.

Neumeyer, Peter F. "E. L. Doctorow, Kleist, and the Ascendancy of Things." *CEA Critic* 39 (May 1977): 17–21.

Osland, Dianne. "Trusting the Teller: Metaphor in Fiction, and the Case of *Ragtime.*" *Narrative* 5, no. 3 (October 1997): 252–73.

Parks, John G. "The Politics of Polyphony: The Fiction of E. L. Doctorow." *Twentieth-Century Literature* 37 (1991): 454–63.

Piehl, Kathy. "E. L. Doctorow and Random House: The *Ragtime* Rhythm of Cash." *Journal of Popular Culture* 13 (Winter 1979): 404–11.

Quart, Leonard and Barbara. "*Ragtime* Without a Melody." *Literature/Film Quarterly* 10 (1982): 71–74.

Raban, Jonathan. "Easy Virtue: On Doctorow's Ragtime." *Encounter* 46 (1976): 71–74.

Rapf, Joanna E. "Volatile Forms: The Transgressive Energy of *Ragtime* as Novel and Film." *Literature/Film Quarterly* 26, no. 1 (1998): 16–22.

Solataroff, Ted. "Of Melville, Poe, and Doctorow." *Nation* 6 (June 1994): 784–90.

Steinberg, Cobbett. "History and the Novel: Doctorow's *Ragtime.*" *Denver Quarterly* 10, no. 4 (Winter 1976): 126.

Sutherland, John. "The Selling of *Ragtime:* A Novel for Our Times?" *The New Review* 4 (1977): 3–11.

Thomas, David Wayne. "Godel's Theorem and Postmodern Theory." *PMLA* 116 (1995): 248–61.

Thompson, James R. "The Artist as 'Criminal of Perception': E. L. Doctorow and the Politics of Imagination." *Hungarian Journal of English and American Studies* 1 (1996): 147–55.

———. "Categories of Human Form: Some Notes on E. L. Doctorow and Historical Consciousness in American Fiction Since 1960." *Caliban: Le Roman Historique* 28 (1991): 17–24.

Tokarczyk, Michelle M. *E. L. Doctorow: An Annotated Bibliography.* New York: Garland Publishing Co., 1988.

Trenner, Richard, ed. *E. L. Doctorow: Essays and Conversations.* Princeton: Ontario Review Press, 1983.

Vieira, Nelson H. "Politics and the Mode of Fiction." *The Ontario Review* 16 (Spring–Summer 1982): 5–16.

Wright, Derek. "Ragtime Revisited: History and Fiction in Doctorow's Novel." *IFR* 20, no. 1 (1993): 14–16.

Zins, Danel L. "E. L. Doctorow: The Novelist as Historian." *The Hollins Critic* 16 (1979b): 1–14.

Acknowledgments

"Recomposing Time: *Humboldt's Gift* and *Ragtime*," by Barbara L. Estrin. From *Denver Quarterly* 17, no. 1 (Spring 1982): 16–31. © 1982 by the University of Denver. Reprinted by permission.

"*Ragtime* in Retrospect," by Charles Berryman. From *The South Atlantic Quarterly* 81, no. 1 (Winter 1982): 30–42. © 1982 by Duke University Press. Reprinted by permission.

"Fiction and History," by Paul Levine. From *E. L. Doctorow*. © 1985 by Paul Levine. Reprinted by permission.

"*Ragtime* as Auto Biography," by Marshall Bruce Gentry. From *Kansas Quarterly* 21, no. 4 (Fall 1989): 105–112. © 1990 by the *Kansas Quarterly*. Reprinted by permission.

"Twain, Doctorow, and the Anachronistic Adventures of the Arms Mechanic and the Jazz Pianist," by Cushing Strout. From *Making American Tradition: Visions and Revisions from Ben Franklin to Alice Walker*. © 1990 by Cushing Strout. Reprinted by permission.

"Illusions of Demystification in *Ragtime*," by Christopher D. Morris. From *Models of Misrepresentation: On the Fiction of E. L. Doctorow*. © 1991 by the University Press of Mississippi. Reprinted by permission.

"The Musical World of Doctorow's *Ragtime*," by Berndt Ostendorf. From *American Quarterly* 43, no. 4 (December 1991): 570–601. © 1991 by the American Studies Association. Reprinted by permission.

"Compositions of Dissatisfaction: *Ragtime*," by John G. Parks. From *E. L. Doctorow*. © 1991 by John G. Parks. Reprinted by permission.

"*Ragtime*," by Douglas Fowler. *From Understanding E. L. Doctorow*. © 1992 by the University of South Carolina. Reprinted by permission.

"*Ragtime* as Historical Novel 1977–85," by John Williams. From *Fiction as False Document: The Reception of E. L. Doctorow in the Postmodern Age*. ©1996 by Camden House. Reprinted by permission.

"The American Dream, Insiders and Outsiders: *Ragtime*," by Michelle M. Tokarczyk. From *E. L. Doctorow's Skeptical Commitment*. © 2000 by Peter Lang Publishing. Reprinted by permission.

Index